CLICK2SAVE
REBOOT

THE DIGITAL MINISTRY BIBLE

KEITH ANDERSON AND ELIZABETH DRESCHER

Copyright © 2018 by Keith Anderson and Elizabeth Drescher

All rights reserved. No part of this book may be reproduced, stored in a retrieval system, or transmitted in any form or by any means, electronic or mechanical, including photocopying, recording, or otherwise, without the written permission of the publisher.

Unless otherwise noted, the Scripture quotations contained herein are from the New Revised Standard Version Bible, copyright © 1989 by the Division of Christian Education of the National Council of Churches of Christ in the U.S.A. Used by permission. All rights reserved.

Church Publishing
19 East 34th Street
New York, NY 10016
www.churchpublishing.org

Cover design by Marc Whitaker, MTWdesign
Layout and typesetting by Beth Oberholtzer

Library of Congress Cataloging-in-Publication Data

Names: Anderson, Keith, 1974– author. | Drescher, Elizabeth. Click 2 save
Title: Click2save : the digital ministry Bible reboot / by Keith Anderson and Elizabeth Drescher.
Other titles: Click 2 save
Description: New York : Church Publishing, 2018. | Rev. ed. of: Click 2 save : the digital ministry Bible / by Elizabeth Drescher and Keith Anderson. 2012. | Includes bibliographical references.
Identifiers: LCCN 2017051076 (print) | LCCN 2017058811 (ebook) | ISBN 9780898690323 (ebook) | ISBN 9780898690316 (pbk.)
Subjects: LCSH: Internet in church work. | Social media. | Church work.
Classification: LCC BR99.74 (ebook) | LCC BR99.74 .D73 2018 (print) | DDC 253.0285/4678—dc23
LC record available at https://lccn.loc.gov/2017051076

Printed in the United States of America

CONTENTS

Foreword by Mary Hess   vii

A Second Edition of Acknowledgments   ix

Introduction to the Second Edition: Digital Reboot   xi

Introduction: Digital Pilgrimage   1

1 Remapping Our Worlds   15
    How Social Media Have Changed the Landscape

2 The Real Presence   37
    Developing a Unique, Authentic Voice for Digital Ministry

3 I Love to Tell the Story   65
    Social Media Platforms

4 Practicing the Arts of Digital Ministry   149

Conclusion: Digital Incarnation   212

Additional Resources for
Digitally Integrated Ministry   218

For Our Networked Families and Faith Communities

FOREWORD

IT FEELS LIKE A LONG TIME has passed since I first picked up *Click 2 Save*—but it's really only been about five years. Five years is an eon, however, amidst the churn and boil of digital technologies. In that time I have used the first edition of this book over and over again in the many settings in which I support learning. In classes on pastoral leadership and pastoral communication it's been a required text. I have found it a friendly helpmate in congregational settings, particularly because of the ways in which it offers different kinds of tasks to try in each medium. I have even found it useful as a brief introduction for people who do not inhabit religious contexts but are looking for a quick and thoughtful introduction to practices of digital communication.

Hundreds of other books and resources have come out in this time, but I keep returning to *Click 2 Save* for its rare combination of pragmatic advice, thoughtful engagement with digital cultures, and wise pedagogical counsel. I am thrilled to encounter this thoroughly revised edition!

I'm a reader—and not just of academic books. Whether it's stories of vampires (Octavia Butler), of time-traveling women (Diana Gabaldon), of Quebecois homicide inspectors (Louise Penny), and so on, I read because I love visiting other worlds, imagining other relationships, tasting and hearing and feeling through other people's stories. Stories draw me beyond myself and invite me to learn. But I'm also a viewer and a listener and a creator of stories. That is one of the primary gifts of digital tech: it offers us multiple, and multisensory, ways to participate in telling and sharing stories.

We are living in a story-driven world at present. Will you allow digital technologies to invite you into new spaces beyond the familiar, or will you stay in walled-in spaces where you can pretend that that is all there is to reality? Keith Anderson and Elizabeth Drescher are giving us, in this short exquisite book, a traveling companion to support adventures beyond the familiar.

There are quite literally thousands of books, and millions of web essays, available right now that seek to tell pastoral leaders what "to do" about digital technologies. There are very few however—and you hold one of the best in your hands right now—that invite readers into a deeply relational, thoroughly incarnational engagement with all that is around us.

This is not a book about "how to do technology in pastoral ministry"—although there is thoughtful, effective, and stimulating advice here on that topic; this is a book about following Christ in the midst of a world permeated by digital tech, and doing so in ways that invite others into the mystery and love of God in our world of many faiths, many cultures, many forms of technology.

Elizabeth and Keith have created a stunning—both for its brevity and pragmatic approach—companion here, and perhaps my favorite part of the book is that it offers analogies and ideas for engaging digital tools in ways that will continue to be useful long after the specific digital tool has faded into oblivion. They can do so because they recognize that we need digitally integrated ministry (their term) rather than another technique or recipe for digital tech.

Their criteria for success in these practices rings true across eons of ministry—digital ministers are generous, humble, curious, willing to experiment, collaborative, and kind (as Keith and Elizabeth detail in chapter 2). Put this book down right away if all you want is a shallow recipe for fixing a website. But pick it up and keep it close by over the next several years if you want a companion you can return to again and again as you seek to explore how God continues to reveal Godself in the midst of our communication practices, if you want to refine and extend your pastoral leadership ever more deeply into the wounds and joys of this world, if you want to continue to explore and to learn as you walk the sacred and privileged paths of pastoral ministry.

Mary E. Hess
Professor of Educational Leadership
Luther Seminary, St. Paul, Minnesota

A SECOND EDITION OF ACKNOWLEDGMENTS

WHATEVER INSIGHTS of Keith's that appear in the second edition of *Click 2 Save: Reboot* were nurtured significantly through conversations he had at events sponsored by the Center for Congregations, Columbia Theological Seminary, Luther Seminary, the Lutheran Theological Seminary at Philadelphia, the Philadelphia Theological Institute, the Southeastern Pennsylvania Synod of the ELCA, Virginia Theological Seminary, and Wartburg Theological Seminary. Some of Keith's work here appeared in early forms in *Bearings*, the magazine of The BTS Center; *Insights Magazine* of the Uniting Church in Australia; and the blog of the Princeton Seminary Institute for Youth Ministry.

Keith wishes to thank his spouse, Jennifer Anderson, for her willingness six years ago to go along with his crazy idea to write a book with someone he'd never met in person before, for her support for this second edition, as well as his other writing and digital projects. Those projects and that time require Jenny to pick up the slack managing their home and four kids, and he is deeply grateful. He would also like to thank his kids—Ellie, Finn, Dulcie, and Tess—who have become very good writers themselves.

Keith extends his grateful appreciation to the people of congregations that he has been honored to serve as pastor: the Lutheran Church of the Redeemer in Woburn, Massachusetts, and Upper Dublin Lutheran Church in Ambler, Pennsylvania.

Heartfelt thanks are also due to his digitally integrated network of friends, collaborators, and co-conspirators, many of whom appear in the pages below. He would also like to thank those who may not appear but who have provided much personal and professional inspiration and encouragement: Mark and Sarah Huber, Lisa Kimball, Martin Malzahn, Thomas Rusert, Arthur Scherer, and Sarah Stoneseifer.

Elizabeth remains grateful to Kelly Simons for her enduring patience through *another* summer of writing and editing. Elizabeth also gives thanks for the relative peace of a detached garage office funded in large measure by The BTS Center, The Philadelphia Theological Institute, Fordham University Department of Religious Studies, The World Catholic Association for Communication, Luther Seminary, and Archbishop Mitty Preparatory School through engagements during which many of the ideas here developed. Elizabeth's contributions to the second edition of *Click 2 Save: Reboot* were also shaped by articles written for *America Magazine, Bearings,* and *HuffPost.*

The support of Elizabeth's colleagues in the Department of Religious Studies at Santa Clara University has also been invaluable during this project. She especially wishes to thank Vicky Gonzalez, David Gray, Karen Peterson-Iyer, David Pleins, Boo Riley, and her student fellows in the Living Religions Collaborative at SCU, Nicole Nasser and Connor Holttum. Digitally integrated companionship and conversation with Heidi Campbell, Matt Fisher, Mary Hess, Tripp Hudgins, Jim Keat, Gary Macy, Ellen Smith, Rachel Wagner, Jamye Wooten, and Angela Zito have proved worthy distraction from and insight into the territory we explore in this edition.

Finally—though certainly not least—both Keith and Elizabeth owe a debt of gratitude to the many people who took time to talk with us at length about their own digitally integrated ministry practices for both the first and second editions of *Click 2 Save*. In the pages ahead, readers will get glimpses of the remarkable ministries of Jennifer Baskerville-Burrows, Nadia Bolz-Weber, Jamie Coats, Adam Copeland, Christopher Coyne, David Crowley, Lisa Deam, Dan Edwards, Laura Everett, Casey Fitzgerald, Kelly Fryer, Anthony Guillen, David Hansen, Jodi Bjornstad Houge, Mark and Sarah Huber, Tripp Hudgins, Mihee Kim-Kort, Alex Montes-Vela, Kim Morrow, Christine Valters Paintner, Bill Petersen, Darleen Pryds, Emily Scott, Geoff Sinabaldo, Beau Surratt, Diana Wheeler, and Jamye Wooten. Still, though we are so glad to have had the opportunity to lift up the innovation, creativity, and compassion of these digitally integrated ministers in the book, we've barely skimmed the surface of the many gifts they bring to the church and the world.

INTRODUCTION TO THE SECOND EDITION
Digital Reboot

> Why a second edition? Digital social media platforms seem to emerge, grow, and die off at the speed of a click. And the challenges of ministry in the Digital Age have likewise changed considerably since we first wrote *Click 2 Save* five years ago. We've worked to address both in this new edition.

JUST AS WE WERE FINISHING *Click 2 Save* in mid-2011, a new social media platform came upon the digital scene—Google+. An answer to what was by then the clear dominance of Facebook by what remains the leading online search and advertising platform, Google+ seemed poised to mount a significant challenge to the upstart social networking site. After all, it had the incredible financial and technical might of one of the new media world's early innovation giants behind it and a user base that rivaled any other platform. To gild the lily a bit, Google quickly lured in new users with the Google+ Hangout feature—an online video calling and livestreaming service that had eluded Facebook and outperformed Skype.

It seemed obvious to us and to our editor that we had to say something about this new social media platform. So we scrambled to add material into chapter 3, which provides details about how to use various platforms, and the glossary, which defines basic digital media terminology about Google+.

A mere five years later, the tech magazine *Mashable* called Google+ a "sad expensive failure."[1]

Such is life in the new media landscape—for developers and users as well as for those of us who write about technologies that change in a historical blink of an eye. In the years since we wrote the first edition of *Click 2 Save*, not only has Google+ pretty much gone the way of AOL and MySpace, so too have other sites we featured. Back then, for instance, we were really into Foursquare, a geolocation app that had gained tremendous popularity by *gamifying*—applying features of game playing like keeping score, competing with others, and winning prizes—digital check-ins at different locations. We encouraged ministry leaders to use Foursquare to "create a lived map of our ministry" in locations beyond the church. The idea was that Foursquare would help to illustrate a richer story of how ministry plays out in real life and provide further opportunities to connect with others. Friendly competition among users to win badges for checking into different locations and amass the most points at particular places (like your home church or a local coffeehouse) to be named "mayor" seemed like a fun way to expand the social range of ministry and engage with others.

But by 2013, Foursquare had lost steam, and in mid-2014 the company reworked the app to focus entirely on search. The new Foursquare application no longer included the check-in and gamification features, which became part of a new social networking product, Swarm. Both are still around, but you'd be hard pressed to find them in active use on many people's smartphones or tablets.

In place of Foursquare, Google+, Vine—a video platform that came and went between the previous and current edition of *C2S*—folks in your community (especially young people) are likely to have taken a spin with Instagram, Periscope, Pinterest, or Snapchat. The more sophisticated among them, inspired by the tremendous success of the investigative journalism podcast "Serial," which launched in 2014, may also have taken up podcasting through Soundcloud, libsyn, or another audio production and hosting site.

By this point in the story, you might assume that we took up this new edition in large measure to update the platforms ministry leaders might want to consider these days. And, yep, we do indeed include some updated material on a number of new platforms, including Instagram, Periscope, Pinterest, and Snapchat. We also discuss podcasting. We had planned to add a special feature on Pokémon Go, which brought an enchanting form of gamification back to churches when people seeking various Pokémon creatures ambled across church lawns and sometimes through their doors for a few months starting in the summer of 2016. But by the time we were finishing this addition, it was no longer so much of "a thing."[2]

Odds are that by the time we finish writing this sentence, and almost certainly by the time you finish reading it, some other new, cool platform or gadget will have emerged. Wait a paragraph or two and it's likely to have gone the way of the Pokémon Go Wartortle.

This dynamic has pressed us to think differently about how we approach new media platforms. Rather than focusing on specific platforms like Facebook, Twitter, or Instagram, we've organized the center of the book—chapter 3—into categories of platforms in which we discuss specific platforms that are in use as we finalize this edition. We've taken the risk of assuming the social networks Facebook and Twitter, which continue to have a primarily relational function—connecting people to each other around personal, professional, political, religious, and other life interests—will be around for a while. So, too, though they have changed considerably, various forms of long- and short-from blogging continue to be significant. Beyond these *legacy platforms*, however, the digital landscape has tended to organize itself around certain media practices—surfing, catching up, sharing, announcing, collaborating, and archiving images, videos, audio, messages, and text.[3] Within each of the categories, we describe practices that are typically facilitated by platforms in the category.

There's lots of overlap in these categories, of course, and practices move from platform to platform. Facebook is a text-based social network as well as an image and video platform. Arguably, its central practice remains catching-up with family, friends, colleagues, church members, and that dude who sat behind you in AP History. But there's also plenty of sharing and, periodically, collaborating that happen within its boundaries. Likewise, Instagram features images, but is driven significantly by words in the form of hashtags and comments. It largely encourages the practice of surfing for social information, but young people in particular use Instagram extensively to catch up with friends. We're mindful of these overlaps, but our hope is that using a broader organizational scheme will allow readers to more quickly recognize and be able to use the features of new platforms as they emerge by comparing and contrasting them to more familiar platforms in a particular category. That way, when the next must-have platform emerges, you'll be able to assess whether it's more like Snapchat in its messaging functionality or Flickr as an archiving platform.

Changing technologies are not the only reason we've revised the first edition. We've changed a lot, too, in the time since *C2S* was first released—all of us. Way back in 2012, we were all pretty much novices with regard to digital social media. Sure, some of us had probably spent too much time geeking out over new platforms and apps, so we had a bit more technical experience with the ins and outs of life across various social networking landscapes. Much of what we had to offer in the first edition fell into the category of nuts-and-bolts (er, bits and bytes?) information on the uses of each platform in ministry. And many of our readers were still reasonably inexperienced about digital media terminologies, so we felt obligated to include a glossary of key terms like "blog" and "meme" that would be pretty familiar to everyone's grandmother by now.

Our experience has been that the questions people in ministry have about digital social media have changed a good deal since we both began thinking and writing about the subject. When Elizabeth published *Tweet If You ♥ Jesus* in 2011, churches were asking about whether they needed to bother themselves with new media at all. Might this not be just a passing fad, many people wondered. They were curious, too, about whether religious practices in digital spaces were "really religion" and whether they connected in faithful and healthy ways to longstanding Christian traditions.

By the time we began working on the first edition of *Click 2 Save*, these questions had largely been set aside. Just a year later, most ministry leaders and many in their congregations had come to the conclusion that they were called to be present wherever the people of God were gathered, and that surely included digital spaces. The question was *how* to be present in meaningful ways that reflected the values of Christian faith and engaged the practices that have been at the center of Christian ministry since the earliest days of the Church.

The "how" questions are still out there. But more and more we've seen that the people we encounter are interested in exploring how various devices, platforms, and apps impact life in religious and local communities; how they are participating in the formation of spiritual and religious identity; and what effect digital communication practices have on relationships and the values that nurture and sustain them. These are all big subjects related to the cultural valences of new media practice that are mostly beyond the scope of either the original or revised edition of this book. We touch on them throughout, but we've also exchanged the glossary we had in the first edition for a selection of resources for further reading on the cultural aspects of new media.

While you will see many changes from the previous edition in the pages ahead, then, we are pleased to report that much of the content related more directly to the culture of the church and the practice of ministry seems to have held up quite well. We come to this assessment not merely from our own rereading of what we wrote in the first edition, but from feedback from readers, especially from seminary and other graduate school professors and students who have used *Click 2 Save* extensively over the past few years. We might well chalk this up to our great pastoral wisdom, but the truer reality is that we both learned a great deal about attending to and mediating divine presence to others through stories, rituals, and practices of hospitality, care, formation, witness, and community cultivation through the many gifted teachers, theologians, and scholars who we met through our own seminary and graduate educations. Our synthesis of these insights remains in the chapters that follow, although we have updated some of the examples to introduce new voices and perspectives.

So we've updated the digital platforms we've discussed. We've included new examples of ministry practice using digital social media. And, as noted above, we've added a resource guide for further exploration. But before we move into the new edition, a couple important changes in language are worth noting as well.

When we originally worked on *Click 2 Save*, we were writing as language for what we were describing was itself evolving. The media and religion scholar Heidi Campbell talks about the ways in which religious practice in online spaces was described in different ways over time as our understanding of the relationship between religion and new digital media technology evolved. "Cyber-religion," Campbell explains, was an early terminology that described "the importing of religion to the new frontier of cyberspace, or the not-so-real world of virtual reality technologies."[4] The early idea was that online spaces provided opportunities to experiment with religious identities and practices, and that cyber-religions were in effect new forms of religion, or at least forms of religion that challenged traditional understandings and practices.

As it happened, however, cyber-religion wasn't always so new. The cathedral you might encounter in the virtual reality landscape Second Life often had much in common with a bricks-and-mortar cathedral in terms of theologies, ecclesiologies, and the structure of ritual practices. Of course, such digital spaces did challenge many theologies, most notably digital theologies of Eucharist, which were hotly debated for many years. And whole new practices emerged that took on spiritual meanings that would not likely have manifested in physical spaces. For instance, rituals involving everyone presenting her or himself as an animal-human hybrid avatar. Still, a lot of cyber-religion replicated religion as it was lived "in real life"—men mostly served in clerical leadership roles, rituals followed familiar forms, language was rarely updated to reflect new social realities.

This pressed scholars and writers about religion and new digital media to distinguish between "religion online"—traditional practices imported to online locales—and "online religion"—"new forms of religiosity and lived religious practices online."[5] But here again, the line between one thing and the other was problematically blurry. Moreover, as smaller, more portable devices allowed us to carry our digital social networks into local spaces where other companions were physically present, the boundary between the "virtual" and the "real" became porous. Several years ago, for instance, Keith and I gave a talk at The BTS Center in Portland, Maine. During the session, we invited people to poll their social media networks for prayer requests for worship later in the gathering. During the Prayers of the People, tweeted and facebooked prayers scrolled across screens in the front of the room. The gathered community held smartphones, laptops, and tablets as we lifted up the prayers gathered through extended social networks. People posted photos as we prayed, and faraway friends and family commented on the event. Were we not all practicing religion *together*? Is this not even more so the case as we increasingly use Facetime, Facebook Live, Skype, Zoom, and other real-time video platforms to connect people across distributed, digitally integrated landscapes?

As we were first writing the book, scholars began to use the term "digital religion" to point to religious practices that emerge from various intersections—the intersection of digital and local landscapes as well as the intersection of traditional and new practices specifically enabled by new digital technologies as these, in turn, intersect with wider concepts of authority, community, communications, and culture. Not entirely consciously, we adapted this thinking in our use of the term "digital ministry," which we defined as "the set of practices that extend spiritual care, formation, prayer, evangelism, and other manifestations of grace into online spaces like Facebook, Twitter, and YouTube, where more and more people gather to nurture, explore, and share their faith today. It can also refer to these practices in both online and offline spaces as they are influenced by the networked, relational character of digital culture in general."

Our definition seemed to work well, making clear, we believed, that we were talking about ministry as it was shaped by practices that were emerging from digital age culture, whether or not these practices played out on- or off-line. For example, the "networked, relational, character of digital culture in general" is a feature of life in face-to-face as well as digital social networking locales.

Still, despite the increasing blending of our online and off-line lives, we found that the terminology more often than we intended was interpreted to mean that ministry in digital spaces was somehow different from ministry on face-to-face settings. "Digital ministry" was a special category of pastoral practice like "interim ministry" or "young adult ministry." The book plainly insists that this is not the case. But to make it clearer that we see ministry that unfolds in physical geographies, ministry that takes place in digital landscapes, as well as ministry at the intersection of both as similarly influenced by the effects of digital communication technologies on our everyday lives, we have generally adopted the term "*digitally integrated ministry*" throughout this edition.

Another change in language also appears throughout the second edition, beginning with the second part of the definition of "digital ministry" quoted previously: "It can also refer to these practices in both online and offline spaces as they are influenced by the networked, relational character of digital culture in general." You'll see in the revised original introduction and in the chapters that follow that we've added the word "*incarnational*" to "networked" and "relational" to describe the character of what we would now call "digitally integrated" or "digital age" culture.

We add this term because as we spoke with church groups around the country and continued to write about digitally integrated religion and ministry together and separately, we found that it was important to make clear that, as Christians, we understand human personhood to be divinely grounded in the physical. This doesn't, we would also insist, mean that relationships that begin and develop in digital spaces aren't "real," or that they are somehow less valuable than face-to-face relationships. As you'll read in the pages ahead, our own collegial relationship and personal friendship began online and deepened over the period of a couple years on Facebook, Twitter, and other social media sites. It was plenty real enough for us to decide to write a book together.

But we believe that the incarnational tradition of Christianity pulls us all toward physical proximity with one another. Incarnation is how God became known to humanity and it is how we are ideally known to one another.

In fact, incarnation is, theology aside, exactly the point of one of the most significant features of twenty-first-century digitally integrated culture: online dating. Say you started Snapchatting with a person three time zones away, and then became Facebook friends, then started having regular Skype conversations. If that person never wants to meet face-to-face even though it's within the realm of physical and economical possibility—it doesn't seem likely that relationship is going to work out. Sure, you might be fine colleagues with someone on the other side of the globe. You might enjoy a meaningful friendship with someone even though you or they don't have the means to travel for a face-to-face meeting. But most of us would want that to happen even if it were impossible in practical terms. Indeed, as we'll discuss in chapter 2, moving toward incarnational engagement was a critical factor in the development of the online dating industry. In more mundane terms, we see the evidence of this incarnational pull revealed on every one of those wonderful occasions when we do meet someone we've known from social media engagements in a face-to-face context. We don't know of anyone who isn't thrilled by such incarnational moments.

We see the incarnational desire—the desire to encounter those who have come to have meaning in our lives in face-to-face settings—as a critical theological component of digitally integrated ministry. It is networked, relational, *and* profoundly incarnational. This incarnational orientation is essential, we believe, perhaps especially when our desire is unlikely to be realized—when it isn't possible to meet those we encounter online in person. Here, remaining ever mindful of the physical reality of the human person whose words, photos, videos, and livestreams we see on our screen, is an ethical and spiritual anchor in a digitally integrated culture that we have all seen lean toward the dehumanizing through online bullying, hectoring, trolling, and stalking. Where ministry leaders have great power to affect tremendous good in the digitally integrated world, you'll see in the chapters ahead, is in modeling practices that insist on the embodied humanity of everyone we encounter: online, off-line, or in the ever-expanding networked, relational, and incarnational in-between.

At the end of the day, we're quite grateful to have had the opportunity to revisit a project that not only introduced our voices and ideas to a wide range of communities and individuals, but also, to a great extent, to each other. That story—the story of how a religious studies professor and a Lutheran pastor on opposite sides of the country used social media to write a book on social media and ministry—is shared in the original, slightly revised, introduction. We trust it still adequately sets the scene for the exploration that follows into still-evolving fields of digitally integrated ministry.

INTRODUCTION
Digital Pilgrimage

What's this chapter about? How a Lutheran pastor and an Episcopal professor connected through social media and what that has to do with this book, with a bit on the chapters ahead.

OUR DIGITAL SOCIAL MEDIA CONNECTION developed several years ago, just after Elizabeth published an article in the online magazine *Religion Dispatches*. The article was about the encouragement of Pope Benedict XVI for Roman Catholic priests to enter the rapidly developing digital religious landscape by blogging on faith and spirituality whenever they could. While the article lauded the pope for his concern that the church be actively represented among the many voices in the religious blogosphere, it also pointed out that the pontiff had missed the social media mark to a considerable degree because he had assumed that digital social media functioned in the same top-down, one-to-many way as mass broadcast media. The inexperience with digital practice illustrated in the pope's letter was hardly unique to the Roman Catholic Church. Mainline churches of all stripes were more or less bumbling into the digital domain, despite what turns out to be native gifts for relational communication that are ideally suited to life in the Digital Age. (Elizabeth eventually explored mainline engagement with new media in much greater depth in *Tweet If You ♥ Jesus: Practicing Church in the Digital Reformation*.)

But the article on the pope's entree into the digital domain did more than anchor the subsequent book. It also brought us together as colleagues in what we now think of as "digitally integrated ministry"—colleagues whom it is all but impossible to imagine might have connected before the age of digital social media. In the weeks after the article came out, Keith emailed Elizabeth to share some insights from his work on the role of social media in his own church in the form of a presentation he'd recently given to a group of Lutheran clergy in his synod in which he had included a couple of quotes from her article.

Keith's presentation, "From Gutenberg to Zuckerberg: How Social Media Is Changing the Church," moved beyond the commonly offered religious repackaging of marketing advice for profit-making businesses to locate social media participation in the theologies and spiritual practices that shaped and continue to animate the Lutheran Church. And, not for nothing, it had a way cool picture of Charlton Heston holding an iPhone version of the Ten Commandments that Elizabeth was able to poach for an upcoming talk on the Bible and social media.

> **What Is Digitally Integrated Ministry?**
>
> Digitally integrated ministry is the set of practices that extend spiritual care, formation, prayer, evangelism, and other manifestations of grace into online spaces like Facebook, Twitter, and YouTube, where more and more people gather to nurture, explore, and share their faith today.
>
> It can also refer to these practices in both online and off-line spaces as they are influenced by the networked, relational, and incarnational character of digital age culture in general.

It was, then, from three thousand miles and a denomination away that a Lutheran pastor and blogger became a colleague and friend to an Episcopalian(ish) religious studies professor and religion journalist. A couple years later, we became collaborators on *Click 2 Save: The Digital Ministry Bible*, sharing the fruit of an extended conversation about the role of new media not only in our own denominations, but across the church as it attempts to remain engaged in a rapidly changing world. Together, we have become digital pilgrims of a sort, traveling, sometimes together, sometimes apart, through the byways of the rapidly changing digitally integrated landscape and sharing tales of who we meet and what new practices of digitally integrated ministry we find along the way.

We begin with this story not only because it seems a particularly charming, Digital Age way for two writers to come together on a project, but also because it says so much about how relationships are formed, how knowledge is created and shared, and, ultimately, how faith is reinforced and extended in the world today. Over the course of two years, we shared resources and connected one another to colleagues. When Elizabeth put together a relatively impromptu tweeted, global Pentecost prayer service in 2010, Keith and a few members of his congregation at the time, the Lutheran Church of the Redeemer in Woburn, Massachusetts, joined in. So, it's fair to say that we've worshipped together online as well.

All of this unlikely interaction has taken place between a pastor and a religious studies scholar whose face-to-face interaction was, until pretty far along in the writing of the first edition of this book, limited to flickering images on weekly Google+ video "hangouts." Which is to say that without digital social media, this book would absolutely not have been written. More significantly, the church would be a teeny bit smaller, a teeny bit less connected, a teeny bit less catholic. Multiply that by the healthy percentage of mainline Protestants and Catholics among the more than two billion Facebook users,[6] and you get a sense of the impact of social media on the church and on Christian ministry today. It is the reality of our own digitally enabled relationship that is at the root of *Click 2 Save* and of our enthusiasm for the potential that new social media have for enriching and extending the mission of the church. In the chapters ahead, we lay out what we see as a strategic approach to living out that potential.

CHAPTER 1: REMAPPING OUR WORLDS

We certainly wouldn't go as far as to say that effective engagement will *save* a church with rapidly declining membership and increasing cultural marginalization. The truth is that we're pretty confident that "saving the church" is not what ministry is about anyway. But we are confident that much of the hope for maintaining the vitality of our churches and sustaining their good, essential work in the world is related to the ability of leaders in ministry to engage people exactly where they are—reaching out to them rather than expecting them to come to us. And "where they are" increasingly includes social media spaces like Facebook, Twitter, Instagram, and Snapchat.

This means that everything's a bit topsy-turvy these days, with all the world's major newspapers offering religious insight and education; bloggers of all stripes sermonating and otherwise opining on theology, spirituality, and religious life; websites and smartphone apps offering opportunities to pray, meditate, sing, confess, learn about religions, and mount arguments for and against them. Religious formation and spiritual enrichment are now all over the digital map. Chapter 1 begins, then, by exploring how digital media have remapped the world we all share, constructing not only new worldviews that challenge long-held notions of geography and place, but also reorganizing relational possibilities across the planet.

Once we've spent some time mapping the evolving digital planet, we move in chapter 1 to describe the inhabitants of some of its most robust communities—Facebook, Twitter, and Instagram—by way of highlighting the differences between so-called "digital natives" and the people we often see at church on Sunday. It's a huge world with lots and lots of people, so the view is from somewhere above ten thousand feet, but our hope is to orient you to the general terrain so you'll be better prepared to gather resources, make connections, and enter conversations that will help you to develop a social media strategy for your church or religious organization.

Travel across this new landscape of social networking sites is on the rise across generations, demographic groups, and around the globe. Research by the Pew Internet & American Life Project has illustrated this growth in the population in general, but it also points to particular practices of digital engagement that are significant for mainline churches and ministers who wish to connect with believers and seekers alike. Recent Pew research indicates, for instance, that 90 percent of Americans use the internet, a growing portion of which are over the age of sixty-five. Perhaps more significantly, Grammy and Pap-Pap are four times more likely to have a smartphone than they were five years ago.[7] This means that digitally integrated ministry is increasingly an all-ages project, but it also means that understanding different cohorts of social media practitioners is important in that ministry. Chapter 1 helps to differentiate the "natives" and "immigrants" who inhabit online communities and networks and the cultural characteristics and practices that distinguish them.

> Whether or not we choose to bring our ministries actively into the world shaped by social media, citizens of that world always have the opportunity to bring us into it by sharing commentary, images, and other content about us and our churches or organizations.

What chapter 1 should make clear, then, is that, as it has been reshaped by new social media, the world is a very different place than it was even five or ten years ago. Certainly, it's very, very different from the 1950s and '60s worlds with which many mainline churchgoers still identify and which, therefore, continue to have a strong influence on church practice. Back then, in the last great growth period for mainline Christianity in America and globally, people got their religion from the local church and their news from Walter Cronkite, and the two zones for the most part maintained a polite, respectful disengagement. Sure, the local paper probably had a religion section, but that mostly covered service times and socials at neighborhood churches, setting aside any potentially divisive theological debate. The idea was to reinforce religious participation as a civic virtue, not to sow religious disagreement by highlighting substantive differences. And, of course, in the America of that era, mainline Protestant Christianity—perhaps with a bit of Catholicism and Judaism on the side—was the normative form of religion in the nation. The boundaries were clear: there was simply "Christianity" and *everything else.*

The map of the world before social media—the world defined by the practices of the Industrial and Broadcast Ages—showed a world defined by distinction, separation, clear boundaries between this land and that, this community and the others, *our* church and *theirs*. As we'll see, the new world shaped by social networking is mapped relationally. It's defined by the flow of ideas across all kinds of boundaries. And it includes diversities of all sorts—ethnic, national, gender, and, certainly, religious—that few would have imagined, let alone encountered in the world before social media. Navigating in this new world calls on a nuanced understanding of the terrain and the customs of the locals. We'll begin to mark the major byways, landmarks, and populations across the socially networked globe in chapter 1.

CHAPTER 2: THE REAL PRESENCE

Once you've got a handle on the differences among people using social media and the range of social media locales in which they interact—especially as these differ from your face-to-face ministry context—developing a clearer sense of how you and your church want to be present in social media contexts is critical. Chapter 2 focuses on how to communicate an authentic representation of self and ministry that humanizes both individuals and communities. After all, before anyone walks through the door of your church or community service site or pub ministry, odds are that they've already taken a look at your website and moseyed over to your Facebook page. They know something of you and your community, and you want that "something" to be real and meaningful—far beyond the "just the facts, ma'am" tone of all too many church websites and Facebook pages.

> We are ministers, not marketers, so our presence in digital spaces must be very clearly defined in terms of authentic ministry—authentic connection with others from whom we have nothing personally or institutionally to gain and to whom we have much to offer.

The good news is that achieving "real presence" in social media spaces is far less theologically fraught for mainline churches than sorting out the mysteries of the Eucharist or the Trinity has been over the centuries. Drawing on Keith's pastoral experience and that of colleagues in ministry, chapter 2 will guide you through the basics of establishing an authentic voice and taking up practices of relational communication that ground an effective strategy for digitally integrated ministry.

CHAPTER 3: I LOVE TO TELL THE STORY

Developing a sense of how best to be authentically present in social media spaces generally is important. Nuancing that presence for a specific social media locale also matters a great deal. The idea here is to focus on the features of a particular platform that can best help you to tell your story and that of your faith community. In *Click 2 Save*, we highlight what we see as the major categories of social media platforms based on numbers of active participants, our best informed guess at durability in the rapidly changing digital landscape, and compatibility with traditional and emerging mainline ministry practice. The categories we discuss in chapter 3 include:

Legacy Platforms
- Facebook
- Twitter
- Blogging (long-form platforms)
- Tumblr (short-form blogging)

Visual Platforms
- Instagram
- Pinterest

Video Platforms
- YouTube

Broadcast Platforms
- Facebook Live
- Periscope
- Podcasts

Messaging
- Snapchat

This chapter will help you to decide which combination of social media platforms will be most effective for you by providing a range of criteria for decision making, such as congregational style and strengths, intended conversation partners (i.e., age groups, location, members, potential members), congregational goals, level of skill, and available time.

One way to think about your approach to various platforms is to consider how you present yourself, your ministry, and your faith community in different local settings. If you're a spiritual director, for instance, you're unlikely to dole out morsels of spiritual wisdom at the local coffeehouse. But you probably are inclined to express a general attentiveness to those you encounter—perhaps a certain warmth toward the latte-slinger behind the counter—that reflects something true about your spiritual values. This is much the sort of presence you'll want to cultivate on platforms like Twitter, while in spaces that allow for more extended exchange, like Facebook or, more still, blogs, you'll tell the story of your faith, your ministry, and your community somewhat differently. Chapter 3 will acquaint you with a number of major platforms in each category, highlighting those features that will best open your story to others and introducing tools and tips to help as you continue to develop your social media strategy.

Please note: Our approach to these platforms is through the lens of digitally integrated ministry practice. Given this, our exploration of social media platforms in chapter 3 is meant to serve as a guide to ministry, not a manual on the technical features of each platform per se. While our discussions of various platforms will refer to key features and characteristics, and we will provide some basic definitions, we assume that readers have visited the social networking sites we discuss, and that they have a basic familiarity with how they work. If you have not done so already, it will be helpful as we move ahead together if you have set up basic Facebook (facebook.com), Twitter (twitter.com), and Instagram profiles (instagram.com). You can add accounts for other platforms as they make sense within your digital ministry strategy. And, because platforms can come and go pretty quickly, you can add or scratch off platforms in each category as your digitally integrated ministry practice develops.

CHAPTER 4: PRACTICING THE ARTS OF DIGITAL MINISTRY

Given a good idea of who's where and what's what in the digital domain, a clearly articulated sense of presence, and equipped with an understanding of how and when to use various social media platforms, the art of networked, relational, incarnational ministry in social media communities begins. We approach the arts of digitally integrated ministry through a mode of digital participation that Elizabeth introduced in *Tweet If You ♥ Jesus*. There, she described life in the Digital Reformation—"a revitalization of the church driven largely by the *ad hoc* spiritualities of ordinary believers influenced by digital social networking"—as organized around four core practices she calls a "LACE":

- *Listening*—Taking time to get to know people in social networks based on what they share in profiles, posts, tweets, and so on, rather than emphasizing the communication of your own message
- *Attending*—Noticing and being present to the experiences and interests of others as they share themselves in digital spaces
- *Connecting*—Reaching out to others in diverse communities in order to deepen and extend the networks that influence your digital spiritual practice
- *Engaging*—Building relationships by sharing content, collaborating, and connecting people to others

This networked, relational, incarnational LACE, Elizabeth argued, is a reemerging mode of engagement that connects life in the ancient and medieval church to life in the church today, offering opportunities to enrich our relationships, our communities, and our churches after long centuries of increasing separation and distancing brought about by mass media and, in particular, broadcast media like radio, television, and movies.[8]

> **Digital Reformation**
>
> A revitalization of the church driven largely by the ad hoc spiritualities of ordinary believers influenced by digital social networking.
>
> —*Tweet If You ♥ Jesus* (2011:4)

As we move in *Click 2 Save* to draw out the implications of the Digital Reformation for hands-on ministry practice, we explore the LACE more specifically through what we see as basic "arts of digital ministry":

- *Faithful listening* as the basis of true engagement with others that grounds all other arts of ministry
- *Offering spiritual care* to others through practices of prayer, comfort, encouragement, and inspiration

- *Offering hospitality* by extending welcome, creating sacred space, respectfully evangelizing, and incorporating others into the church
- *Forming disciples* and enriching their spiritual lives through preaching, education, and small group ministries
- *Building community* by engaging others and helping to connect them to one another
- *Sharing public witness* through activism, social justice practices, advocacy on behalf of the marginalized and forgotten, and supporting the vitality of local communities
- *Stewarding divine resources* by leveraging new ways of gathering and connecting with other people and institutions and marshalling new digitally integrated giving and gathering technologies.

CONCLUSION: DIGITAL INCARNATION

When we started this project, we talked a lot about what the word "save" in the title meant to us. It's a tricky word for mainline Christians, who have had—at least since the end of overt colonializing—less evangelically oriented, less proselytizing traditions. We tend, that is, not to announce our faith too loudly lest doing so impinge on the beliefs of others. We don't generally call out the personal sinfulness of others and offer absolution within our churches. We don't make a point to articulate, often even privately, the distinctiveness of our denominational traditions.

Elizabeth tells the story of her grandmother, who, as the family passed the churches of other denominations in her small town on the way to "the true church," would sigh and say, "I don't know why those people even bother to get up early on a Sunday. They're all going to damnation anyway. May as well sleep in." (She said that in the car, of course, not on the sidewalk.) The fact that mainline Christians seldom even think such things anymore, focusing more on our commonality as Christians than theological differences across denominations, is surely all to the good.

But it also seems to be the case that our understandable embarrassment over the demeaning and divisive dismissal of those of other faiths that was tolerable in earlier times has turned into a stultifying silence about who we really are as mainline Christians and how our faith allows us to live with others in the world in remarkable, loving, and healing ways. Pew researchers found that "half of U.S. adults seldom or never discuss religion with non-family members."[9] This "silencing of the lambs" has only been exacerbated by what many see as a co-optation of the word "Christian" itself by more fundamentalist believers, whose often condemning approach to sharing the faith has sowed disdain and outright hostility toward all Christians. As a result, many people who believe in God and in fact participate in Christian communities prefer to identify as agnostic, as "spiritual but not religious," or as having "no religious belief in particular."[10] Indeed, research by Boston University sociologist Nancy Ammerman has shown that people who are active members of institutional religious communities are as likely as the religiously unaffiliated—the so-called Nones—to describe themselves as "more spiritual than religious."[11]

Our perspective is that new social networking platforms enable us to extend the love of God to others in ways that make our mainline Christian traditions more authentically present in the world. This may not "save" other believers and seekers in the sense of converting them to our particular denominations, and it may not "save" our churches in terms of numerical and associated financial stability. But, as you'll see in the conclusion, we think our participation in the new media landscape has a profoundly salvific effect nonetheless, saving God's church from a marginalization and irrelevance that prevents us from doing the work of love, compassion, and justice to which we are all called.

📱

We began this chapter by noting that this book itself began in digital conversation. It might almost go without saying that this conversational mode continued as Keith and Elizabeth worked on the book, the ideas in each chapter being shaped through email, Facebook posts, tweets, documents swapped on Dropbox, and Google+ video chats. However, in order to manage the work and avoid creating a schizophrenic tone, we divided the chapters between us and shared comments after each draft. This process has allowed us to produce a book that is very much a collaborative product, drawing upon something of a single authorial direction in each chapter, but nonetheless expressing a shared vision and voice.

Still, because we each also bring unique perspectives to our shared project, from time to time you'll see call-out boxes with short comments from one or the other of us. Likewise, you'll find notes on terminology that might be new and tips on practices and resources that can make your digital ministry easier. And you'll find profiles of digital ministers we interviewed during the course of writing this book. What can we say? Keith is a digital native, and Elizabeth is pretty fully naturalized. Like more and more of the people you encounter in church and other ministries, we roll through the Digital Reformation with a lot of other voices and information in tow. We hope it'll make for lively reading that supports your developing digital ministry while modeling the modes of communication current in the digital domain.

ENOUGH ABOUT US: ABOUT YOU, GENERALLY IN PARTICULAR

Writers typically write for a more or less imagined composite reader—a "you" made up of a variety of backgrounds, characteristics, and experiences drawn from very different people. This is certainly true for *Click 2 Save*, which we address to the broad category of "leaders in ministry" that includes clergy and laypeople in both formal and informal ministry roles. We take a kind of "priesthood of all believers" understanding of readers of this book, assuming that each of us in the Church is called to witness to and welcome others into the faith regardless of our title or role. In that sense, we're all leaders in ministry, our everyday lives enacting the relationship with God in Jesus Christ that is at the center of our faith. So, in the end, we see *Click 2 Save* as a book for disciples in general.

Click 2 Save also speaks to the very particular experiences, stories, and questions we both have encountered in our respective pastoral and educational ministries. It is drawn from conversations not just with the people we interviewed for the book, many of whom will be profiled in the pages ahead, but from ongoing conversations with colleagues, church members, and a rich blend of friends whom we regularly encounter in face-to-face and social media settings. Their questions about social media participation as it might help to address the challenges facing their various communities are very particular, very much located in the realities of sustaining small or large church communities; growing or declining service, community, and social justice programs; and tending established and emerging spiritual friendship networks.

One of the things we've learned as we've studied social media practice in religious contexts, talked with a wide range of practitioners, and mucked around in Facebook, Twitter, YouTube, and so on ourselves is that there is no one-size-fits-all approach that will address the particular needs of each community or individual. But, of course, the beauty of new media is that it is endlessly adaptable, and this is exactly what we invite you to do with this book. In effect, we invite you to write *Click 2 Save* with us, using the information we share in light of your particular needs to develop a social media strategy for your specific ministry. At the end of each chapter you'll find space for this customizing of the ideas and approaches we share. We hope, too, that you'll visit the *Click 2 Save* Facebook page or Twitter feed to share your experience as you adapt and apply the ideas in the chapters ahead in your particular context.

As you get ready to develop a social media strategy for your church or religious organization, we will invite you to step back a bit and consider what motivates your social media participation and what you hope to accomplish by deepening your practice. Throughout the book we've provided space for strategic reflection on the material covered in each chapter. If you're working with a group on social media strategy for your community—a practice we certainly encourage—you may want to copy the strategy pages for participants.

PIRATE THIS BOOK

Back in the day, political activist Abbie Hoffman wrote an ironic best seller called *Steal This Book*, which aimed to promote the overthrow of the government by encouraging a number of ethically questionable and wholly illegal activities. That's hardly our agenda in *Click 2 Save*, but we do want you to make this book your own, to use it as a launch for conversations with friends, colleagues, parishioners, and others involved in the revitalization of mainline churches as they serve God in the world. We've come to almost all of the ideas we share in the book by way of such conversations, and we're very much looking forward to hearing your voice and seeing your community as we continue to develop our own digital ministries.

To get started, please take some time on your own or with friends and colleagues to reflect on the strategic questions below.

DIGITAL MINISTRY STRATEGY

Why do you think digital ministry is important for you and your church or other religious organization?

What are your personal and/or organizational goals for digital ministry?

How much time do you have for digital ministry?

Who will support you and/or join you in digital ministry?

What other resources are available for your digital ministry?

NOTES

1. Seth Fiegerman, "Inside the Failure of Google+, a Very Expensive Attempt to Unseat Facebook" *Mashable,* August 2, 2015, http://mashable.com/2015/08/02/google-plus-history/#oPbYt.G74sqX.

2. Elizabeth did, however, offer commentary on the short-lived phenomenon. See, "Can Pokémon Go Really Help Bring People to the Pews," *America* (October 16, 2016). Available online at https://www.americamagazine.org/issue/virtual-faith.

3. John Postill and Sarah Pink, "Social Media Ethnography: The Digital Researcher in a Messy Web," *Media International Australia* (2012):6–7.

4. Heidi Campbell, "Introduction: The Rise of the Study of Digital Religion," in *Digital Religion: Understanding Religious Practice in New Media Worlds*, ed. Heidi Campbell (New York and London: Routledge, 2013), 2.

5. Ibid., 3.

6. John Constine, "Facebook Now Has 2 Billion Monthly Users . . . and Responsibility," *Tech Crunch*, June 27, 2017, https://techcrunch.com/2017/06/27/facebook-2-billion-users/.

7. Monica Anderson and Andrew Perrin, "Tech Adoption Climbs among Older Adults," Pew Research Center, May 17, 2017, http://www.pewinternet.org/2017/05/17/tech-adoption-climbs-among-older-adults/.

8. Elizabeth Drescher, *Tweet If You ♥ Jesus: Practicing Church in the Digital Reformation* (Harrisburg, PA: Morehouse, 2011), 17–21.

9. Alan Cooperman, "Many Americans Don't Argue about Religion—or Even Talk about It," Pew Research Center, April 15, 2016, http://www.pewresearch.org/fact-tank/2016/04/15/many-americans-dont-argue-about-religion-or-even-talk-about-it/.

10. David Kinnaman and Gabe Lyons, *Unchristian: What a New Generation Thinks About Christianity . . . and Why It Matters* (Grand Rapids, MI: Baker Books, 2007).

11. Nancy Ammerman, *Sacred Stories, Spiritual Tribes: Finding Religion in Everyday Life* (New York: Oxford University Press, 2016), 23–26.

1

REMAPPING OUR WORLDS
How Social Media Have Transformed the Landscape

Social media have remapped the world, pushing beyond all sorts of boundaries—geographic, demographic, and conceptual alike. In this chapter, we look at the new global, social world and the people who inhabit it as background to the upcoming discussion of participation in specific social media platforms from a faith and ministry perspective.

REMAPPING THE WORLD

Even if you happened to be off on a remote, Wi-Fi disabled island vacation in the summer of 2017, by the time you sailed back to reality you would perhaps have caught the news that Facebook had grown to more than two billion monthly users—up dramatically from 750-million-plus users that wowed us when we were writing the first edition.[1] In terms of active users, Facebook eclipses all other social networking communities, with double the number of users of the next most popular platform, Instagram.[2] The continuous growth in Facebook membership and the way in which it has begun to change our view of the world brings to mind the shift in mapmaking in the sixteenth century, after wider global travel and mechanistic, rather than artisan, mapmaking altered the reigning perception of the world.

In the ancient and medieval worlds, a map was less a representation of geopolitical reality than it was an expression of the cultural terrain from the perspective of the mapmaker and his patrons. For example, the famous Hereford *Mappa Mundi* (or "map of the world") situates Jerusalem in the center, the Garden of Eden at the top (which is east on the map), and a variety of other biblical locales—Noah's ark, the Red Sea, Babylon—along with England, Scotland, and Ireland all out of geographical proportion to Asia.[3] And, of course, medieval mapmakers made sure to indicate the dangerous waters leading to unknown territories where "thar be dragons!"— signaled by detailed illustrations of dragons, sea monsters, and other mythical creatures who stood for those locales we know are somewhere around the bend but whose inhabitants we do not know or understand.

A medieval *mappa mundi*, then, marked out not national boundaries or natural terrains, but rather spiritual and psychosocial ones—worldviews, we would call them today. They told stories about how people imagined the world and themselves in it in relationship to the Divine creator. Medievalist Lisa Deam, author of *A World Transformed: Exploring the Spirituality of Medieval Maps* (2015), shared with us: "What I get from medieval maps like the Hereford *mappa mundi* and others is the idea of being grounded morally and spiritually, having a center to anchor us even as the rest of the world is changing."

While we've come to make maps with greater geographical accuracy, we fool ourselves still if we believe that our modern maps reflect any uncomplicated, uncontroversial reality. This is because the nations and the borders we now recognize through the boundaries drawn on modern maps are political *ideas* rather than geographical *facts*, the results of negotiated histories and relationships. Ask the people of Tibet where China *really* is (or vice versa), and you'll come into a swirl of contested history, tradition, and politics. As the saying goes, what you see really does depend on where you stand. Likewise, of course, the lines of longitude and latitude found on some maps don't exist in any physical form. They merely mark a system of vertical and horizontal coordinates used to identify the precise location of any area on the earth for the purposes of navigation and geographical identification.

Though it may be the case that it is far easier to navigate across the globe with a modern, geopolitical map, it is no less the case that such maps also chart a modern worldview, which assumes the idea of separate nation-states and global navigation along gridlines that make the globe into manageable quadrants. Indeed, most modern maps make the assumption that few of us will travel by foot or otherwise on the ground, generally eliminating the challenges of mountains, lakes, and rivers as other than properties of this nation or that state. Modern maps also recenter the spiritual terrain that grounded much of premodern experience. Thus, Lisa Deam contrasts the God-centered medieval mapping practice to contemporary geopolitical mapping and social media practice. "Maps today, and I think social media as well," she says, "encourage us to see ourselves as the center—almost literally as something like a GPS unit where the world is always changing in accordance to where we stand. So, we see it changing around us and we're our own reference points."

But Deam is quick to point out that the shift from medieval, God-centered, narrative maps to modern geopolitical maps is not of course all bad—including in spiritual terms:

> Maps today have shown us how to break down more boundaries, to think more globally, and engage more globally. That is something new in human history, and that's a good thing. . . . It shows us that God is everywhere, not just in our own carefully bounded units—our own churches, our own denominations, our own cherished beliefs, but that God is truly a global god, who created *the whole world*.

This is no less true in maps of the evolving digital world, where social networking sites have allowed people to cross all sorts of boundaries, setting aside traditional and/or political notions of nation, ethnicity, class, ideology, and so on—including religion. Hence China's tight control of social networking participation that could introduce ideas into the culture that might challenge or override the official narrative. While China holds a remarkable advantage in terms of global capital and geographically located population, a new mapping of the world that highlights the population of just the Facebook social networking community tells a very different story. The black areas on the map below are where Facebook is the dominant digital social network. Notably, with the exception of Greenland, where Twitter and icebergs reign, the areas not covered by Facebook are the territories of more repressive regimes in which the networked, relational sharing and cocreating of new knowledge is seen by government leaders as a threat. The remarkable fact is that if the population of people who participate on Facebook across the globe were a nation, that country would be the most populous—ahead of China and India, and having more than five times the population of the United States. What's more, if territory where Facebook dominates were ceded to this new digital nation, it would have as much land mass as North and South America combined, with Africa thrown in for good measure, making it the largest national territory in the world.[4]

Of course, Facebook doesn't exist geopolitically (yet), but a map of the world drawn on the basis of social media participation surely opens a whole new worldview—one in which modern constructions of national identity that are often grounded in religious identity are thrown into flux. This blurring of boundaries that for generations we believed were fixed spills out of the online world into physical reality, where people increasingly question cultural constructions of things like gender, race, sexual identity, class, social status, and vocation. We live in a world that is now characterized by the confluence of ideas, collaboration among those separated by time and distance, and the convergence of written, visual, and auditory media across a less and less ideologically and geopolitically partitioned global landscape.

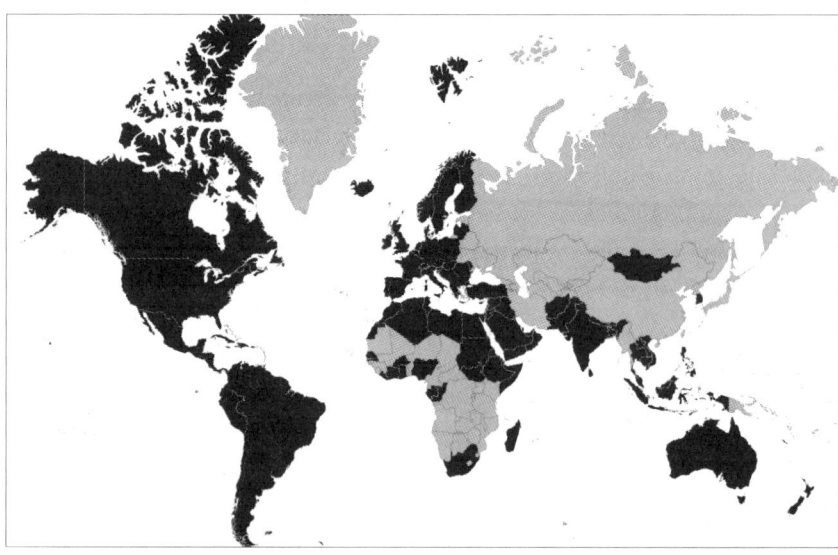

Map of the Facebook World[5]

COSMOPOLITAN CHRISTIANITY

The world that is revealed by this new, digitally integrated social reality is less globalist—having to do with expanding economic, financial, technological, and political relationships of exchange across borders—and more cosmopolitan. Cosmopolitanism, which has come in for much criticism by rightwing nationalists in the current political environment, is not a matter of giving up distinctive elements of regional, national, ethnic, religious, or cultural identity otherwise. Indeed, the valuing of such distinctiveness is at the center of a cosmopolitan outlook. The cosmopolitan sees all humans as part of diverse but interconnected commons within which our distinctive differences add value to the whole.

In contrast to this, globalization is largely about the sale and consumption of material and cultural products further afield. One can be robustly global—traveling to far-flung places for vacations, enjoying Indian food in London or Balinese dance in Los Angeles—and also be profoundly parochial in the sense of the interpersonal relationships and associated ethical commitments one maintains. The globalist often seeks to extract material and cultural goods from international locales in order to enrich his own homeland. Or, he aims to transform another country into a version of his own, overwriting local customs, languages, values, and other cultural practices with new markets in which his products will be attractive. This is the colonializing impulse that lingers in modern globalization, including its religious expressions. Cosmopolitanism, however, is about relationships. It is a practice centered on curiosity about and concern for other people—people who are often very different. It is a matter of considering what must be done to form meaningful, respectful, compassionate relationships with others. Cosmopolitanism's mode of exchange is narrative: it thrives on the sharing of stories that illuminate the lived experience of others and enrich our capacity to understand, appreciate, and, ultimately, to love.

The good news for Christians is that cosmopolitanism is totally in our wheelhouse. When Paul tells the nascent Christian community in Galatia, "There is no longer Jew or Greek, there is no longer slave or free, there is no longer male and female," he is expressing the framework of this cosmopolitan outlook for Christians. We can be in relationship with Gentiles, Paul tells the Galatians, who do not practice Jewish dietary customs or undergo circumcision. We do not require, or even desire, that others give up their distinctive cultural practices and characteristics to become part of "ours" because there is no "ours" and "theirs" in Christ.

What this means at a minimum is that, despite our local, sometimes parochial, orientations, we always conduct our ministries in a digitally integrated, cosmopolitan context that extends far beyond the expanse of the Christian colonializing impulse of the eighteenth and nineteenth centuries—certainly well beyond the doors of our increasingly empty churches, beyond the territories marked out by our various denominations, and beyond even the boundaries of Christianity itself. What's more, the political and economic power that funded Christian colonialism has shifted in the new digitally integrated world order, giving *everyone* with access to a computer, a laptop, or a lowly smartphone the opportunity to enter, reshape, and even dominate conversations about faith in everyday life. Thus, whether or not we choose to bring our ministries actively into the world reshaped by social media, citizens of that world always have the opportunity to draw us into it by sharing commentary, images, and other content about us and our churches or organizations.

CROWDSOURCING CHRISTIANITY

Now, this could mean that we engage social media defensively—finding ways to ferret out negative perceptions of our leaders, denominations, churches, and other organizations. Indeed, a cottage industry of sorts has grown up around this kind of "reputation management," serving mainly corporations, politicians, and celebrities by searching for and attempting to erase negative comments, reviews, images, and the like. But this isn't the only way, nor, we would argue, the best way, to engage the digitally expanded world. We see digitally connected cosmopolitan networks as profound opportunities to reverse Christian parochialism and colonialism by enabling us to more fully enter into conversation, relationship, and common action that doesn't override the gifts of one culture with those of another, but which gathers the best of all of us into the Christian project of kingdom-making.

In a sense, this makes every church a global relief agency, every congregant an active agent of God's love and compassion in the wider world. This work is no longer the narrow purview of church-sponsored NGOs, who collect money from churches to distribute around the globe on behalf of believers. It is a collective, collaborative, cosmopolitan project to which we are all called. In the digital world, this gathering of globally distributed participants in loosely organized communities is called "crowdsourcing," a practice that ignores the traditional boundaries of geography, status, gender, race, class, and so on to draw on the practical wisdom of everyone with an interest in helping to solve a problem, disseminate ideas, or collaborate on projects related to shared interests. Crowdsourcing—or what is referred to as *crowdfunding* when it has to do specifically with financial projects—is used to support the microfinancing of small businesses around the globe whose owners would never qualify for traditional financing (as through the microlending sites Kiva and MicroPlace). Other crowdfunding sites like CrowdRise, GoFundMe, Indiegogo, and Kickstarter cultivate direct giving that does not require repayment.

As the director of the Center for Stewardship Leaders at Luther Seminary, Adam J. Copeland has explained, "Typical stewardship campaigns focus only on congregation members as givers, but the internet allows for anyone and everyone to give. Part of the appeal of crowdfunding for congregations lies in its potential to expand pools of potential givers. *Potentially*, at least."[6] Copeland offers examples of monks at the New Camaldoli Hermitage in Big Sur, California, whose increasingly sophisticated social media presence has enabled them to crowdfund projects to address the effects of fires, flooding, and mudslides on the roads and building at their breathtaking retreat center. A less urgent, but no less important, crowdfunding campaign by the Community Church of Christ in San Jose, California, raised more than $2,000 on GoFundMe to support the development of a community garden. Copeland points out that crowdfunding does more than allow churches to raise money. It can also help to test ideas for future projects by seeing how close they come to meeting stated goals. Maybe the idea for a labyrinth in your churchyard seems like it would be a great way to connect spiritually with the surrounding community. An Indiegogo campaign that surpasses your target for funding the building of the labyrinth is a great affirmation of that instinct. But if you miss the mark financially, that's good data, too. The value goes well beyond meeting financial needs. It puts communities in relationships with people with common interests who might not otherwise encounter one another.

But crowdsourcing is more often not so focused and goal-directed. When you participate in social media networks like Facebook, Instagram, Twitter, and the like as someone who is open and articulate about her or his faith, you are, in effect, crowdsourcing Christianity, crowdsourcing the church. You are extending the love of Christ both within and beyond the boundaries of your local community and, more than that, inviting others to share their faith and their lives with you and your community. If you're like most people on social media platforms, everyone in your network is not exactly the same in terms of faith perspective and other interests and affiliations. Your presence as a member of a Christian community offers various expressions of witness, hospitality, and advocacy that does more than the best sermon might hope to accomplish because it unfolds in the context of relationships that already have some meaning, some shared context. Whether or not social media ministry translates into more "pledging units," you are vastly expanding the reach of the faith in the world. Take Diana Wheeler, a deacon in Episcopal Diocese of California, who ministers extensively in the LGBTQ community in San Francisco. Every Thursday, she posts a prayer appeal on her Facebook feed, inviting a diverse crowd of witnesses to join together in practices of prayerful praise, lament, compassion, and hope. Even people who are not a part of the specific communities to whom she ministers will see her posts and the moving responses to them. She allows a complex collage of networks to witness Christian ministry at its most engaged and compassionate. (Mother Diane's ministry is discussed further in chapter 4.)

RELIGION RULES FACEBOOK

That's just the tip of the iceberg. The average American Facebook user spends about fifty minutes a day checking in on her Facebook news feed, updating her status, and "liking" or commenting on friends' statuses, posting on Instagram (which was acquired by Facebook in 2012), and exchanging notes on the Facebook Messenger app.[7] According to a 2017 study, in the United States, "the average person will spend more than five years of their lives (sic) on social media." And although earlier data that we drew upon in the first edition of *Click 2 Save* showed strong growth in users over age 50, adults under age 50 use Facebook at much higher rates and for much more time on any given day. Instagram is used nearly three times as much by adults between the ages of 18 and 29 as it is by those over age 50.[8] So, if you're curious about what the mysterious cohort of Millennials and the kids of Generation Z—also called "linksters" because they were born into a fully wired world[9]—Instagram and Facebook remain important landscapes for exploration and encounter. And if you think spinning around Instagram is a Kardashian-infused waste of your time, ask yourself this: When was the last time you had the opportunity to garner even a blip of a 23-year-old's attention?

But there's much more! Facebook pages and Instagram feeds focusing on religion and spirituality continue to command not just robust networks of followers but, much more importantly, higher levels of user engagement. Joyce Meyer Ministries, which we marked as among the top of the digital ministry heap in terms of engagement in the first edition, remains in the top ten sites on Facebook. In the top twenty were pages for: "Jesus Christ–Public Figure," "Dios Es Bueno!," "Lord Ganesha," "ILoveAllaah.com," and the Reading, England, version of "The Bible."[10] All of these came in ahead of soccer clubs in Barcelona, Madrid, and Manchester, as well as Justin Bieber, who was rumored to be moving into his own mode of Christian ministry as we were finalizing the second edition.[11] Importantly, the "most engaging" ratings are not based just on the number of members a Facebook page has—Bieber and Lady Gaga are well ahead in terms of raw numbers. Rather, the ranking takes into account the number of interactions on the page, including posts, comments on posts, and likes. What has pulled religion-oriented pages to the top is not, then, that people of faith are interested only in displaying their faith, but that they also want to talk about it with others.

This engagement factor highlights a key aspect of digital ministry that we noted in the introduction and that bears repeating here: ministry in the Digital Reformation—not only in digital locales but also in local spaces in which interaction is increasingly shaped by digital practice—is networked and relational rather than broadcast and numerical. It's about how you connect in meaningful, personal ways with people across diverse networks, not about *how many* people hear your message. It is here that, we feel strongly, approaches to ministry online based on commercial marketing strategies are bound to fail miserably in the long run. People don't want to buy what you're selling. They want to know who you are. And the way people get to know one another in the digitally integrated world is through practices of engagement: checking in, commenting, liking, sharing, and posting for specific individuals within their network.

Before we move on to learn more about who all these religiously engaged social media participants are, take a moment to consider this: what would it mean to your church or other faith organization to have an active cohort of people who, even for five minutes a day, were interested in gathering to pray, comment on scripture, discuss the needs of the world in light of their faith? If those folks were willing to gather outside your doors, would you be willing, as a ministry leader, to take time to encourage them and help to enrich their time together? Well, these folks might not be outside your office door, but they are certainly right outside your digital door, on Facebook, Instagram, Twitter, and more. Indeed, the Pew Forum reports that a full 79 percent of Americans adults who use the internet are members of Facebook—a 20 percent increase since 2012, when we published the first edition of *Click 2 Save*.[12] Another third are on Instagram—double the number in 2012—with that percentage closing in on 60 percent among the under-30 crowd. Twitter, too, has grown, albeit not as rapidly as other platforms, to claim the attention of a quarter of internet users—closer to 40 percent among young adults.

WHO INHABITS THE DIGITAL WORLD?

Some 90 percent of people in the United States and Canada have access to the internet. Globally, 50 percent of the population has internet access, with 37 percent participating in one or more social media platform. In the United States, social media participation is double that.[13] Who are all these social media users?

Because social networking has diversified and differentiated substantially over the past five years, a portrait of a "typical social media user" is tricky to come by. We know that in the United States, more than 80 percent of the population has at least one social media profile. That's up from a diminutive 56 percent in 2012, when we published the first edition of *Click 2 Save*. The 2.5 billion people worldwide who have internet access make up 35 percent of the global population. While the majority of internet users are in East and South Asia—China in the lead, with India a close second—Africa is also in the top three in terms of internet use worldwide, though this ranking hasn't yet translated into social media use at rates seen by the top five social networking countries: China, India, the United States, Indonesia, and Brazil. Despite this global diversity, English is the most common language in the social media world.[14] Importantly, more than half of the world's population now has a smartphone, with two-thirds having a mobile phone over all. This means that information is being shared through smaller and smaller devices, which creates new challenges in terms of shaping words and—especially—images that invite engagement. Indeed, mobile devices now surpass laptops and desktops as platforms for digital information access, sharing, and social connectivity.[15] Some 80 percent of Facebook users access the platform via smartphones throughout the day, though nearly 40 percent also access via laptops or desktop computers.

Globally, social networking participation still skews more toward men, but in the United States, women outpace men slightly in their social media use, according to Pew researchers. Likewise, though social networking continues to have a greater attraction to those with some college education, the trend is leveling as people at all education levels have increased internet access, often through mobile devices, and social media use. Racial differences online have narrowed as well, with 75 percent of Hispanics in the United States now making up the most active of social media users.[16] All of this shows that it's pretty much impossible to identify a "typical" or "average" social media user in the United States or globally. Platform by platform, however, there are some important social networking differences among those with internet access, which we illustrate below.[17]

TYPICAL US FACEBOOK PARTICIPANTS

83% Women
75% Men

In addition to being more present on Facebook, women tend to spend more time each day and to post more often.

88% Age 18-29
84% Age 30-49
72% Age 50-64
62% Age 65+

Though the under-50 crowd dominates on Facebook, those over age 50 continue to have a strong presence. Facebook is the most popular network for adults over age 50.

48% of 18-29 year-olds check Facebook when they wake up.

77% High School or Less
82% Some College
79% College or More

The educational divide that tended to characterize Facebook, which began at a university, has faded.

338 friends make up the network of the average Facebook user.

81% Urban
77% Suburban
81% Rural

Facebook is everywhere, keeping urban hipsters in the know, far flung rural neighbors in contact, and teenaged suburbanites awash in check-ins and selfies.

79% of all U.S. adults who use the internet use Facebook.

Facebook is the online home of the majority of internet users. Indeed, nearly 70 percent of *all* Americans spend significant portions of their time on Facebook.

The population of Facebook users is more than twice that of the next most popular site, Instagram, which was purchased by Facebook as we were finishing the first edition in 2012. As we've noted above, Facebook began as a university project, so its early user base tended to be more educated, slightly more affluent, and predominantly white. But Latina/o and white internet users now prefer Facebook at about 70 percent, with African American users only slightly less at 67 percent.[18]

We've noted below as well that the majority of Facebook users are under age 50, with the largest group being under age 30. Still, both internet use and smartphone use is increasing at a faster pace among those over age 50, so the people who make up the majority of most mainline Protestant and many Catholic congregations are not to be counted out of the conversation. As we will discuss in chapter 3, it's important to recognize that different age cohorts, genders, and people from diverse racial, ethnic, and cultural backgrounds use Facebook in different ways.

TYPICAL US INSTAGRAM PARTICIPANTS

38% Women
26% Men

Though men are not foreigners on Insta, it does tend to have more of a women's vibe.

38% African American
34% Latinx
21% White

Newer platforms like Instagram have opened more space for racial and ethnic diversity in social networking.

#LOVE is the most popular hashtag on Insta.

39% Urban
28% Suburban
31% Rural

Insta captures lots of the kinds of social life that is characteristic of cities, especially among a younger cohort, but it is growing in the burbs, too.

28% of Internet Users

Instagram has grown 300% since 2012, and is now 2nd in popularity only to its parent company, Facebook.

80% of Instagram users live outside the U.S.

Diverse, young people having fun in the city are at the center of Instagram.

Age does seem to make an important difference on the image-based social network Instagram. While a third of online adults in the United States are on Instagram, among the under-age-30 crowd, it's nearly 60 percent. Those over age 50 are only beginning to pick up the Instagram habit. Clearly, "Insta," as younger users often call it, is a Millennial phenomenon. With more than 700 million worldwide users, Insta is much smaller than its outsized parent, but it is rapidly growing, especially as its features are increasingly merged within the Facebook platform. For now, however, the Instagram user is readily distinguishable from users of other social networks by age and diversity as well as gender.

TYPICAL US PINTEREST PARTICIPANTS

45% Women
17% Men

Women make up the majority of Pinterest users, posting social, design, decorating, and inspirational images and memes by the millions.

12% African American
21% Latinx
32% White

After Facebook, Pinterest is the most popular site among white internet users.

Art, Art Supplies & Hobbies is the most popular category on Pinterest.

30% Urban
34% Suburban
25% Rural

Pinterest is a less mobile platform, which seems to make it popular for more settled online image-based sharing.

36% Age 18-29
34% Age 30-49
28% Age 50-64
16% Age 65+

Pinterest has an older demographic, which trend trackers monitor to see what's engaging in terms of food, fashion, travel, weddings, and spirituality among adults over 30.

Over-30 trendsetters in the 'burbs make their mark on Pinterest.

Pinterest was founded in 2010, a few months before Instagram, as a photo-sharing platform, but found the transition to mobile computing more challenging because, as you'll see in the next chapter, it takes up the traditional idea of scrapbooking or creating photo albums as a model. This seemed to make it difficult for designers to adapt to the scrolling, single-image smartphone screen. This slowed the platform's growth as Insta grew beyond it. Still, Pinterest is just behind Instagram in popularity, with 26 percent of internet users visiting regularly. It leans far more toward suburban women participants—the only one of the major sites to capture this American landscape demographic.

TYPICAL US TWITTER PARTICIPANTS

25% Women
24% Men

For much of it's history, Twitter had more of a male lean, but women have balanced out the platform over the past few years.

36% Age 18-29
23% Age 30-49
21% Age 50-64
10% Age 65+

Twitter is a fast-paced network that thrives on mobile devices in the pocket of teens, college kids, and under-30 worker bees.

79% of Twitter users live outside the United States.

29% College+
25% Some College
20% High School or Less

Twitter tends to draw fewer college educated users than other platforms. Within the platform itself Twitter skews toward the college educated.

27% African American
25% Latinx
21% White

Twitter is notable as an important networking and communications network for people of color.

The tweets of religious leaders like Pope Francis and Joyce Meyer out perform Lady Gaga in terms of retweets, likes, and comments by **300%**.

Fast-paced, high volume, event oriented, micro-communications define the Twittersphere.

Twitter is used far less than either Facebook or Instagram. It also trails behind the scrapbooking platform, Pinterest, and the professional networking site, LinkedIn. The political environment of 2016 and 2017 in the United States brought Twitter to great public attention, but much of it has not been positive. It is perhaps not surprising that it is used much more extensively outside the United States, where nearly 80 percent of Twitter participants reside.[19]

In chapter 3, we will provide some further notes on the characteristics of the users of other social media platforms, but this overview of users of the four largest, most influential platforms should help make clear that the people most absent from many mainline communities—those under the age of 50, men, and people of color—are most likely present in social networking communities. And they are far from uninterested in religious or spiritual concerns. To have a fuller, more meaningful map of the worlds in which our mission and ministry unfolds, we have to explore and map this growing territory.

DIGITAL MINISTRY STRATEGY

When we look at the profile of typical Facebook, Instagram, Pinterest, and Twitter users in light of our most immediate communities and those we most hope to engage, important questions are raised about how we map the world from our particular perspectives. From where you sit, what is the center of the universe, toward which the bulk of your interest, energy, and time gravitates? To what extent does that gravitational pull prevent you from engaging the needs of the wider world in your ministry? How would you mark the borders between your world and the worlds outside your door? Where would "thar be dragons"—areas of real or imagined danger that seem off limits in your community—and how do they stand between your ministry and those it would more richly serve?

The worksheets that follow are meant to help you think about what your world looks like from the inside out and, perhaps a bit more, from the outside-in, since we've found that the best social media strategy is one that starts with an assessment of where you are right now. We've also shared a community social media assessment that will help you to better determine the resources and expertise you will be able to bring to your digital ministry and the skills you will want to develop as you move forward. Take some time, then, on your own or in small groups in your community, to think through the worksheets that follow as the basis for a fuller social media strategy.

PART I: MAPPING YOUR WORLD

As we've discussed, a map is both conceptual and spatial. It tells at least as much about how people see the world at any given time as it does about the reality of towns and cities or roads and the rivers they cross. People serving churches and religious organizations carry certain maps of the world in their heads as much as anyone else does, and these maps subtly guide the way we approach and practice our ministries.

For example, Elizabeth led members of a church communications committee through a workshop exploring the challenge of engaging people shaped by digital culture. They began by thinking about the *mappa mundi* within which their church tended to operate.

They noticed that, although their belief and the church's mission put Christian witness at the center of their world, in fact, the challenge of keeping up the building was really, as one group member said, "our Jerusalem." Everything revolved around dealing with the physical property, which hardly allowed them to reach out to those outside the church without a fairly transparent agenda to snag them as pledging members. Moreover, it meant that boundaries between the church and other community organizations were fairly inflexible, as few in the committee had time to take up work that might turn them away from member-seeking and fund-raising. However much they claimed to want to engage young adults and encourage greater diversity in their community, they had mapped their world in such a way as to set such people far beyond their borders, in mysterious, unexplored lands where creatures with which they could not imagine contending might roam.

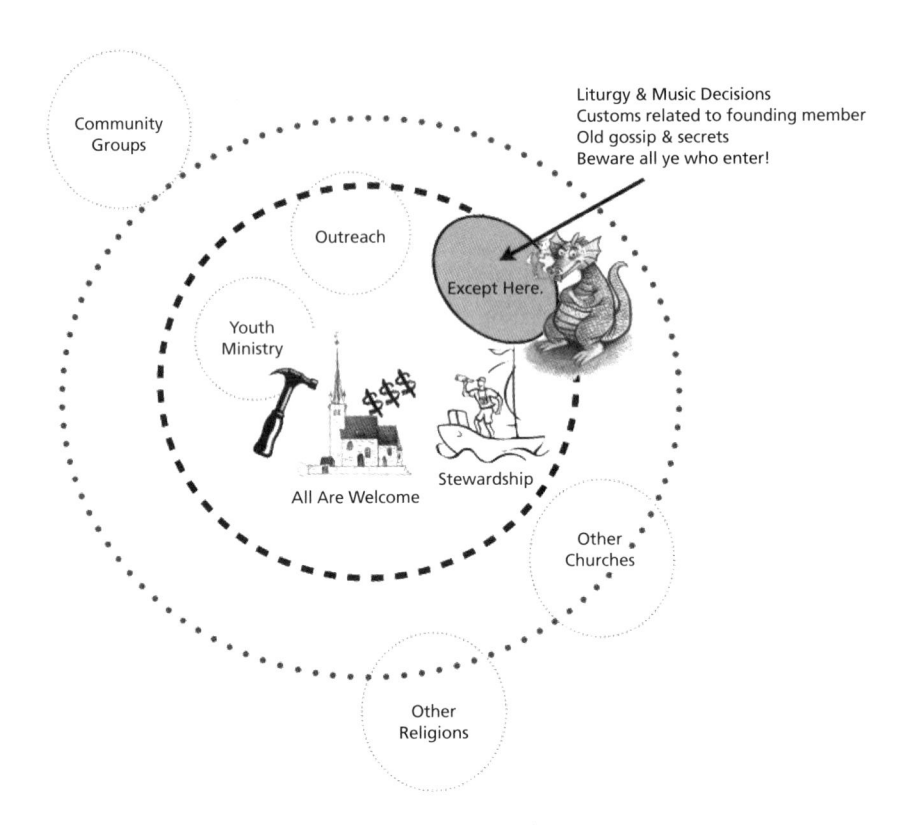

Working together to sketch their map of the world helped them to see their reality more clearly. It also gave them the opportunity to identify places where they might build bridges, crack a window open a bit, or invite new kinds of networked, relational engagement. Of course, this did not just apply to digital ministry, but extended into their local ministry practice as well.

The first step, in both locales, is having a clearer sense of your own *mappa mundi* as it shapes ministry practice. From there, you can move on to consider who lives within your world and with whom you might like to connect and what borders you would need to cross. Use the guidelines below to develop a *mappa mundi* for your community, then go on to develop a fuller profile of yourself and your community members.

PART 1: YOUR MAPPA MUNDI

Using a large sheet of flipchart or butcher paper, draw a map of the world from the perspective of your ministry or those of your faith community. The key below offers some icons that will help you to mark out the territory in which you minister, but be sure to develop your own images to fill out your view of the world.

Step 1

Use the icons here to draw your map.

Solid Border—No one crosses without proper documentation

Porous Border—People can cross, but they still know they're in your territory when they enter

NO TRESPASSING

Where it is just not okay—physically theologically, or otherwise—for the uninitiated to go?

Thar Be Dragons!

Where in your world is it made particularly clear that people are welcome?

Where is it clear that you connect with the world outside?

Step 2

Complete this step after completing the following three worksheets.

How are different individuals and groups located in your world?

PART 2: YOUR SOCIAL MEDIA PROFILE

Before you begin to explore social media platforms that might become sites for digital ministry, takes some time to assess yourself as a social media participant.

Age
☐ 18 to 24   ☐ 25 to 35   ☐ 36 to 45   ☐ 46 to 55
☐ 56 to 65   ☐ Over 65

Education Level
☐ High School   ☐ Some College   ☐ College Degree
☐ Graduate Degree   ☐ Other: _____

Where You Live
☐ Urban   ☐ Suburban   ☐ Rural

Social Media Participation

In which of the following social networking sites do you participate and to what extent?

	A lot	Some	A little	Not at all
☐ Facebook	☐	☐	☐	☐
☐ Instagram	☐	☐	☐	☐
☐ Pinterest	☐	☐	☐	☐
☐ Twitter	☐	☐	☐	☐
☐ YouTube	☐	☐	☐	☐
☐ LinkedIn	☐	☐	☐	☐
☐ Blogs	☐	☐	☐	☐
☐ Podcasts	☐	☐	☐	☐
☐ Snapchat	☐	☐	☐	☐
☐ Other:_____	☐	☐	☐	☐

YOUR TYPICAL CHURCH OR RELIGIOUS ORGANIZATION MEMBER

Now, using your own assessment or results of the Community Social Media Ministry Survey on the next page, develop a social media profile of your typical community member.

Once you've got a reasonable portrait of your community and yourself, place yourselves on your world map in relation to typical Facebook and Twitter users. Where will you need to build bridges to connect more fully with people in your own community and to invite those outside into conversation with you? In the chapters that follow, we'll look at very specific practices that will help you to do this, but it's important to know early on where the opportunities and challenges lie. Looking in from the outside, how would typical social media users see you and your community of faith?

Average Age in Your Community
☐ Under 13   ☐ 14 to 17   ☐ 18 to 24   ☐ 25 to 35
☐ 36 to 45   ☐ 46 to 55   ☐ 56 to 65   ☐ Over 65

Average Education Level in Your Community
☐ High School   ☐ Some College   ☐ College Degree
☐ Graduate Degree   ☐ Other: _____

Where Most People in Your Community Live
☐ Urban   ☐ Suburban   ☐ Rural

Social Media Participation
In which of the following social networking sites do you participate and to what extent?

	A lot	Some	A little	Not at all
☐ Facebook	☐	☐	☐	☐
☐ Instagram	☐	☐	☐	☐
☐ Pinterest	☐	☐	☐	☐
☐ Twitter	☐	☐	☐	☐
☐ YouTube	☐	☐	☐	☐
☐ LinkedIn	☐	☐	☐	☐
☐ Blogs	☐	☐	☐	☐
☐ Podcasts	☐	☐	☐	☐
☐ Snapchat	☐	☐	☐	☐
☐ Other:_____	☐	☐	☐	☐

COMMUNITY SOCIAL MEDIA MINISTRY SURVEY

Social networking sites like Facebook, Instagram, and Twitter have become incredibly popular among almost every age group and demographic cluster. And religion and spirituality are among the hottest topics in social networking communities. As we begin to consider how our ministry might engage this new terrain, we'd like to know about your experience with social media.

Your Age Group
☐ Under 13   ☐ 14 to 17   ☐ 18 to 24   ☐ 25 to 35
☐ 36 to 45   ☐ 46 to 55   ☐ 56 to 65   ☐ Over 65

Your Education Level
☐ High School   ☐ Some College   ☐ College Degree
☐ Graduate Degree   ☐ Other: _____

Where You Live
☐ Urban   ☐ Suburban   ☐ Rural

Social Media Participation

In which of the following social networking sites do you participate and to what extent?

	A lot	Some	A little	Not at all
☐ Facebook	☐	☐	☐	☐
☐ Instagram	☐	☐	☐	☐
☐ Pinterest	☐	☐	☐	☐
☐ Twitter	☐	☐	☐	☐
☐ YouTube	☐	☐	☐	☐
☐ LinkedIn	☐	☐	☐	☐
☐ Blogs	☐	☐	☐	☐
☐ Podcasts	☐	☐	☐	☐
☐ Snapchat	☐	☐	☐	☐
☐ Other:_____	☐	☐	☐	☐

Would you be interested in helping to develop a digital ministry strategy for our church or organization?
☐ Yes   ☐ No   ☐ Tell Me More

Would you be interesting in participating on a digital ministry team?
☐ Yes ☐ No ☐ Tell Me More

Your Name: _____

Email Address: _____

NOTES

1. Josh Constine, "Facebook Now has 2 Billion Users . . . and Responsibility," *Tech Crunch,* June 27, 2017, https://techcrunch.com/2017/06/27/facebook-2-billion-users/.

2. Pew Research Center, "Social Media Fact Sheet," January 12, 2017, http://www.pewinternet.org/fact-sheet/social-media/.

3. Detailed images and descriptions of the Hereford *Mappa Mundi* are available at the Hereford Cathedral website: http://www.herefordcathedral.org/visit-us/mappa-mundi-1.

4. See Kelsey Jones, "The Growth of Social Media v2.0: An Infographic," *Search Engine Journal,* November 15, 2013, https://www.searchenginejournal.com/growth-social-media-2-0-infographic/77055/.

5. Source: Alexa.com (January 2017).

6. Adam J. Copeland, "Crowdfunding Christian Ministry," *Bearings,* June 2, 2017, http://www.thebtscenter.org/crowdfunding-christian-ministry/.

7. James B. Stewart, "Facebook Has 50 Minutes of Your Time Each Day. It Wants More," *The New York Times,* May 5, 2016, https://www.nytimes.com/2016/05/06/business/facebook-bends-the-rules-of-audience-engagement-to-its-advantage.html?mcubz=1.

8. Shannon Greenwood, Andrew Perrin, and Maeve Duggan, "Social Media Update 2016," November 11, 2016, http://www.pewinternet.org/2016/11/11/social-media-update-2016/

9. Meagan Johnson, *Generations Inc.: From Boomers to Linksters—Managing the Friction between Generations at Work* (New York: AMA, 2010).

10. CBS News, "Top 20 Most Engaging Facebook Pages," accessed April 21, 2017, https://www.cbsnews.com/pictures/top-20-most-engaging-facebook-pages/13/.

11. Martha Ross, "Maybe Justin Bieber Quit Tour to Start His Own Church, Reports Say," *San Jose Mercury News,* July 25, 2017, http://www.mercurynews.com/2017/07/25/maybe-justin-bieber-wants-to-start-his-own-church-report-from-down-under-says/.

12. Greenwood, et al, "Social Media Update 2016," and Maeve Duggan and Joanna Brenner, "The Demographics of Social Media Users—2012," Pew Research Center, February 14, 2013, http://www.pewinternet.org/files/old-media/Files/Reports/2013/PIP_SocialMediaUsers.pdf.

13. Simon Kemp, "Digital Snapshot: Internet and Social Media Use in 2017," *Tech in Asia,* February 8, 2017, https://www.techinasia.com/talk/digital-snapshot-internet-social-media-2017.

14. Statista, "Internet Usage Worldwide—Statistics & Facts," The Statistics Portal, https://www.statista.com/topics/1145/internet-usage-worldwide/; Statista, "Number of Social Network Users in Selected Countries in 2017 and 2022 (in Millions)," The Statistics Portal, https://www.statista.com/statistics/278341/number-of-social-network-users-in-selected-countries/.

15. Hootsuite, "Digital in 2017 Global Overview," January 24, 2017, https://www.slideshare.net/wearesocialsg/digital-in-2017-global-overview.

16. Pew Forum, "Social Media Fact Sheet," Pew Research Center, January 12, 2017, http://www.pewinternet.org/fact-sheet/social-media/.

17. Unless otherwise noted, profiles were developed with data from the following sources: Monica Anderson and Andrew Perrin, "Tech Adoption Climbs Among Older Adults," Pew Research Center, May 17, 2017, http://www.pewinternet.org/2017/05/17/tech-adoption-climbs-among-older-adults/; Greenwood, et al, "Social Media Update 2016"; Pew Forum, "Social Media Fact Sheet"; Statista, "Most Popular Pinterest Categories in the United States as of February 2017, by Gender," The Statistics Portal, https://www.statista.com/statistics/251053/most-popular-categories-purchased-on-pinterest/; Amy O'Leary, "Christian Leaders Are Powerhouses on Twitter," *The New York Times.* June 2, 2012.

18. Jens Manuel Krogstad, "Social media preferences vary by race and ethnicity," Pew Research Center, February 3, 2015, http://www.pewresearch.org/fact-tank/2015/02/03/social-media-preferences-vary-by-race-and-ethnicity/.

19. Alex York, "Social Media Demographics to Inform a Better Segmentation Strategy," SproutSocial, March 6, 2017, https://sproutsocial.com/insights/new-social-media-demographics/.

2

THE REAL PRESENCE
Developing a Unique, Authentic Voice for Digital Ministry

Our presence as digital ministers should be compassionate, engaging, inspiring, accessible, and informative. But above all, it must be real. It must be an authentic representation of ourselves as real human beings who are people of faith. The cultivation of a consistently meaningful presence and a distinct voice helps to distinguish us, invite new relationships, and nurture existing ones among the cacophony of conversations and deluge of content in social media communities. In this chapter, we will describe what this "real presence" looks like and share wisdom of ministry leaders and congregations that are bringing a well-defined presence and distinctive voice to bear in their ministry.

BACK WHEN HE WAS JUST BEGINNING parish ministry, Keith received some sage advice that's no less valuable today, especially in the context of digitally integrated ministry:

> I had just been ordained as a pastor and called to my first congregation. The responsibility of that office was weighing heavily on me and I wondered whether I was up for the job. One evening, I shared my worry with my good friend, Knute, who gave me some of the best advice I've ever received about being a pastor, before or since: "Keith, people just want a pastor who's down-to-earth, that they know cares about them."
>
> Of course, I knew that. I had heard and experienced that truth in countless ways throughout my preparation for ministry. However, in my anxiety about being responsible for a parish full of souls, I was overwhelmed with all that I had to do and be in order to fulfill the pastoral

office. Not surprisingly, I had completely overcomplicated the matter. Knute's advice called me back to a simple truth about ministry: hokey as it may sound, we are most effective when we are down-to-earth, real people—when we are ourselves. In the midst of my anxiety, I could hold on to that. I could do that.

Many people feel anxious about embarking on the journey into digital ministry. Doing ministry in the digital media and religious landscape described in the previous chapter feels to many like a new kind of call in a strange new land—one with different patterns of behavior, relationships, etiquette, and modes of communication that require us to refocus our attention and develop new skill sets. It can be both exhilarating and disorienting. For others, social media is as natural as breathing and yet, while they have used it personally, less often have they considered the theological implications for using these platforms in a ministry capacity.

With the variety of digital tools available to us, and with the responsibility of being a minister in a new, rapidly changing digitally integrated space—one in which many of our parishioners, especially young adults, are more advanced than we are—we worry about whether we can manage it all. The number one question we hear from ministry leaders when we travel around the country is, "Where do I find the time to do all this?" In our anxiety—before we even jump in—we debate the proper boundaries about friending and following parishioners, how many profiles we should have, and how much time to spend on it (all of which we will discuss below). Much of the time, we focus on *the terms of engagement* rather than actually *engaging* with members, friends, and our community. However, it is only through engagement and the feedback it provides that we will learn how much time to spend and how to make the most of it.

As we have heard from countless ministry leaders over the past several years, digitally integrated ministry, like much of traditional ministry, is figured out as you are doing it. It is a constant work in progress. The sociologist Zygmunt Bauman refers to this as an effect of "liquid modernity," or "liquid culture," within which, he argues, "flexibility has replaced solidity as the ideal condition to be pursued of things and affairs."[1] As digital platforms rise and fall, as new features are added, and as the landscape for doing ministry at the outset of the twenty-first century moves in new directions, we never really arrive at the one perfect approach to digitally integrated ministry. We are in a continual state of exploring, learning, adapting, and experimenting. Digital ministers do well to cultivate what Buddhists would call a "beginners mind," in which we drop our expectations and preconceptions and approach the world with the fresh, open mind of one who has never done this before.

Thus, Knute's advice is just as salient as when it was first shared. People don't necessarily want or need a pastor that is a social media guru, despite what they may say in the call process, "People just want a pastor who's down-to-earth, that they know cares about them." Inasmuch as social media aids in the ability to extend that care, it can help us to be better ministers. However, while that advice is just as true today as it was when Keith started his ministry career, in some ways, it has also become much harder to follow.

SHIFTING FROM BROADCAST TO SOCIAL MEDIA

Let's step back for a moment. In the five hundred or so years between the inventions of the printing press and the internet, we lived in a broadcast media environment of books, radio, newspapers, and television. These media served as highly effective platforms for sending a single, well-crafted, attention-getting message out to as many people as possible. But broadcast media was controlled by a select handful of organizations and afforded little opportunity for feedback, except, perhaps, for letters to the editor or a call into a talk radio program. This is the world of advertising executive Don Draper in the television show *Mad Men*: a bunch of (largely) white men sitting around a room shaping public opinion. In the church, we have relied on this one-to-many broadcast communication model in our preaching, faith formation, printed newsletters, letters from the pastor, and broadcasting worship services on the radio or local television community access channels. It provided effective avenues for communication and, along with it, no small measure of control over the message, content, and the terms of engagement.

Social media represents a profound shift in this model. Today, each person is his or her own media outlet. Almost anyone can publish a blog, curate a YouTube channel, tell Instagram or Snapchat stories, and host their own podcast. However, unlike a newspaper column or TV show, once you post content online, anyone can comment on, extend, qualify, discuss, and share the content you create. Social media has given platform and voice to millions of people that did not have such access before. This is part of the remarkable promise of social media. However, as we have seen in the 2016 presidential election, there is a downside to all of that openness: facts can become fungible, people can game these technologies, and voices of hate have more of a platform, too. In such a digital environment, it is ever more important to be mindful and vigilant in our use of these technologies for the common good. One voice, one person, and even one small congregation can have an oversized impact through a robust media platform. As Uncle Ben warned Peter Parker (a/k/a Spiderman): "With great power comes great responsibility." The manner in which we use these digital platforms (or not) says just as much about us and our faith communities as the content we share.

These dramatic changes necessarily shape our message, presence, voice, and practice of ministry. However, because the historic broadcast model has been so pervasive, most people first approach social media as simply another form of broadcast media—as one more way to blast our message out there to as many people as possible and get them to join our church or organization. This approach to social media is bound to fall flat. First, this approach emphasizes the needs of the institution rather than the needs of the individual. It's about *our* message, and our poorly veiled desire, or perhaps even desperation, for members and money. However, even social media marketing experts agree, the first rule of social media is to *listen*. Likewise, digital ministry begins with listening (and we would add prayer) with a genuine interest in others rather than ourselves. Secondly, people want and expect to engage with you personally. They don't just want information—we are woefully oversaturated in that department. Rather, people want and expect to have a relationship, and talking about yourself or your church all the time is not the way to accomplish that. After all, nobody wants to hang out at a party with the person that only talks about themselves.

But how do those connections get made in a digital world that is full of so many voices and so much content, and so many people competing for people's *time* and *attention*, those most precious of commodities? It can be incredibly difficult to stand out from the digital pack and be heard, to differentiate between the "signal" you are hoping to send from the "noise" of our crowded digital gathering places.

PERSONAL BRANDING

A common strategy for individuals is to engage in personal branding. "Branding," a marketing term that has been adopted more generally, means having a consistent identity, look, and message, in order to differentiate one's self, product, or organization from others. In a media environment where everyone has a media platform, even if it's just a Facebook profile, everyone, whether they intend it or not, is engaged in some form of personal branding. As Jay Z once sang, "I'm not a businessman. I'm a business, man."[2] Whether we wish it or not, the same is true of us.

For example, the decisions we make each day about what to share and to reveal about ourselves on Facebook and who we share them with is a form of personal branding. We may portray ourselves as urbanists, social justice advocates, artists, family oriented, health enthusiasts, foodies, or engaged in our local community. Post by post, photo by photo, we are painting a portrait of our lives of what we want others to see and they develop impressions of us, a story about us, based on that.

Researcher danah boyd [sic] has referred to this as "identity performance" or "impression management." She writes of teens use of social media, "Their self-representation is constructed through what they explicitly provide, through what their friends share, and as a product of how other people respond to them. . . . Impression management online and off is not just an individual act; it's a social process."[3] The same goes for adults. It's not just what you share, its how people engage with you, and you them, around that content.

Now, there is an element of this that is unavoidable and perhaps even necessary in real life and online. If our goal is to connect with others, individually and as communities of faith, we need to tell a unique story that sets us apart, just as we do in our personal networks.

In the early days of social media, the practice of personal branding was largely shaped by blogging. The best advice on blogging recommended writing relentlessly about a particular area and thus claiming your niche, growing your audience, building name awareness, and becoming recognized as a thought leader in your particular field. Now that social media has gone well beyond blogging, a similar strategy plays itself out across YouTube, SoundCloud, Facebook, Instagram, and more. As Rev. Jim Keat shared with us,

"[Today] you see individuals as digital natives. 'This is a digital landscape that I can play in, and why would I pick just one? I'm not just a blogger, I'm an internet person.'" Increasingly, we see pioneering digital minsters engaging in serial projects, using different media rather than just doing one thing, like blogging, forever.

Branding, when done well, creates new connections and opportunity for meaningful relationship. However, there are countless examples of how personal branding can come off as trying too hard, self-aggrandizement, and even as having a whiff of desperation as people hope to become "church celebrities" (is that an oxymoron?). We all know people who do it. But there is a deeper danger to overdoing personal branding. We run the risk of turning ourselves or our churches into products to be consumed rather than real people or communities with whom to be in relationship.

Frankly, there is an element of being a minister (and a church) that is like being a product to be consumed. As a minister, you share deeply of yourself, your stories, family life, interests, and passions. That sharing helps to inspire, encourage, model, and incarnate faithful living. However, it often feels like people are constantly consuming you. As a church, we hope to create and offer an environment that people want to join and support. And yet, we must resist the temptation to leave it at that—to remain simply a product—and to push for real and meaningful relationship.

TO BE SEEN . . . AND KNOWN

Tom Beaudoin, who has mapped the intersection of faith, consumerism, and branded culture, writes:

> There is an authentic spiritual impulse at the heart of our branding economy. We use brands to do identity work for us, finally, out of desire to be recognized by others, by a power greater than ourselves; and the desire to recognize and know others, to commune with others under a power greater than ourselves. And in this recognizing and being recognized, we experience that greater power that draws us inward and outward.
>
> And so our brand economy discloses a task for spiritual maturity: knowing and being known by ourselves and others, without being governed by entitlement regarding who we are or what we buy.[4]

However, Beaudoin warns, "The brand has become the product."[5] The brand becomes the end itself rather than a step toward relationship. It remains a matter of *seeing* rather than *knowing*. It is a shortcut and poor substitute for identity formation and relationship cultivation.

One of Elizabeth's most memorable examples of the way in which digital social media can participate in practices of seeing that can or cannot lead to knowing comes from a neighbor—let's call him Ray—who was an early developer of a very popular online dating platform. But before he cashed out at the height of the dot-com boom, he had worked in one of the earliest "social" platforms on the internet: online pornography.

Elizabeth got to know Ray and his dog when she took her dog to the local park. As the dogs romped together on the grassy fields, Ray explained that he'd thought at first that a lot of what he'd learned from the porn industry online would directly transfer to the online dating industry, with only minor "dressing up" to shift users attention from casual sexual gratification to companionship and, perhaps, lasting love. But, he and his entrepreneurial team came to learn that the distinction between *seeing* and *knowing* is an important one in human relationships, and this had a tremendous impact on how they came to develop the dating site.

First, Ray explained, online porn sites go to a lot of trouble to amplify images of the people (usually, but not always, women) they were offering to users. Photos and videos were airbrushed and presented in soft hues to hide what might be perceived as imperfections. Images were always carefully staged and participants painstakingly posed to create a certain air of "desirability." The images that were the most polished tended to draw the most users, making more money for the site. So all that effort was worth the investment.

But that backfired on the dating site, where overly staged, posed, and polished images smacked of fakery that suggested the potential match was inauthentic, artificial, narcissistic, or otherwise undesirable. People wanted to see real people in the contexts of their real lives on the dating site—the opposite of the objectifying fantasy images people who frequent online porn sites crave.

Second, in addition to crafting images that branded the sex workers as always sexually willing fantasy objects, profiles and scripts offered stories that were meant to entice but not fully embrace. Ray explained that the goal of the online porn interaction was frequent, brief encounters, not enduring relationships. Indeed, users who became too attached to any one sex worker were a potential problem. Sophisticated algorithms tracked patterns of engagement to reduce the risk of excessive, and potentially dangerous, fixation on any one person. And the language used on the site was meant to keep users wanting more, but not wanting everything.

On the dating site, by contrast, the goal was to invite people into deeper relationship by encouraging real personal revelation in a recognizable style and voice. Dating sites are about envisioning longer-term connections with real people that move—and this is the critical piece—beyond the online setting. So, Ray and his colleagues found that they had to do more to help the dating site users tell their most authentic story, show themselves in a real, warts-and-all light that would reveal their humanness. Over time, then, the company focused more on coaching users on communication skills, understanding their own relationship needs and their strengths and weaknesses, and face-to-face dating skills like making conversation and listening attentively. They had to move, that is, from practicing *seeing* to cultivating *knowing*. That changed the business dramatically, which is why Ray and his pooch are living in some exotic beachfront home rather than visiting Elizabeth's humble neighborhood dog park these days.

The thing is, all of our messaging in the church can have the same sort of objectifying, almost pornographic tone Ray had to leave behind in order to create an online environment that invited the development of *real* relationships with a pull toward incarnation. When we focus too much on what brand we want to construct for our church—coming up with what we think of as a zippy new tagline or a totally boss logo design—we move away from the authenticity and integrity—warts and all—upon which sustained relationships depend.

Jesus himself, who was constantly branded and consumed by others and who could have easily given in to it, continually moved beyond *seeing* to *knowing*. Time and again in his encounters with others his words and actions contrasted what the world saw in each person to understanding something deeper in them. Take, for instance, the Samaritan woman at the well (John 4:1–42). The people of her village saw her as a series of failed relationships. She was branded. Tired of enduring their scorn, she went to the well at midday to draw water and find a few moments of peace. Scandalously, Jesus sat next to her at the well, spoke with her, and told her all about her life in such amazing accuracy that she could say to her neighbors, "Come and see a man who told me everything I have ever done." It was the beginning of her restoration to the community and the inspiration for many to come to faith. As a YouTube video about this encounter between the woman and Jesus says, "To be known is to be loved and to be loved is to be known."[6] It runs in both directions. We need to see others more deeply and be courageous and vulnerable enough to let ourselves be known.

MARKETING WITH SOUL

Keith learned much of what he knows about marketing and branding from his father, who worked in marketing for a small local bank in the 1980s, before the era of big banks, and later for a series of radio stations. Over the years, Keith tagged along for meetings, overheard phone conversations, attended radio remotes, and even popped up in a few TV commercials and radio shows along the way.

Keith learned at an early age that marketing is always about people. It is about developing relationships of trust with your clients and customers. Keith recognized this in the way that his father, who worked in marketing, interacted with clients, customers, and staff at the bank and the radio stations where he worked. Looking back, what seems remarkable and all-too-rare was how he interacted with people outside of work in just the same way. It was real, authentic, human, and it was all part of a whole. The product, the media, and the profits were important to be sure, but not as important as the people, the colleagues, clients, partners, or audience. The personal always transcended the commercial, but they were not mutually exclusive because ultimately our success is tied together, and success is more than the bottom line. Keith learned that you don't just tell your story, you live your story, and that you can, in fact, *do good* and *do well*. However, even this very humane approach to marketing has its limitations.

THE GIFT ECONOMY

One of the digital ministry exemplars we have tracked since our first edition is Jamie Coats, the Director of the Friends of the Society of Saint John the Evangelist (SSJE), an Episcopal monastery in Cambridge, Massachusetts.

Coats' practice of digital ministry is based on his conviction that we live in the "gift economy." He told Keith:

> Although I'm in charge of fundraising and communication, 95 percent of my job is figuring out how to give away the brothers' wisdom. That's what we spend our time figuring out. How do we connect and give people wisdom that feeds them? . . . Most churches get themselves into trouble because in stewardship they're talking about naming a price and really trading for church. Whereas what you need and what the brothers intuitively do, is they help you steward your own life. And later, if we have needs, can you help us? . . . If you understand you truly live in the gift economy and you're truly giving away God's gift for God's love, then it flows back, but if you just ask people to pledge . . . the whole thing collapses at some level.[7]

As Coats told us, digital ministry (and any ministry for that matter) is not a kind of transactional exchange of goods for services. ("Like" our Facebook page and we'll pray for you!) For digital ministers, the meaningful relationships we create and nurture should be ends in themselves, not the means by which we increase our membership or giving units.

This is a subtle but quite powerful distinction that often makes much of the very good advice on using social media for business marketing not always adaptable to church settings. We are ministers, not marketers, so our presence in digital spaces must be very clearly defined in terms of authentic ministry—an authentic connection with others that focuses on the sharing of love, wisdom, and gifts rather than monetary or other transactional exchanges.

People need to know that you care about them and that you are genuinely interested in them—and they need to care about *you* before they will ever care about your *institution,* which some may never do. They must be invested in your mission and ministry, find a common purpose and passion, before they will be invested in the success of your congregation or organization in achieving that mission. Being human, authentic, and caring is the entry point for engagement—knowing and being known.

So, don't just share information about your church. Don't sell your church or yourself. For the love of God (literally), stop trying to make something go viral and instead start promoting others, building connections, making introductions, encouraging others, and sharing your story, experiences, and life of faith. Relationships are nurtured over time through the accumulation of many interactions, not a single viral video. Perhaps most importantly, telling your church's story should always be preceded by sharing something of your own personal story. In social media, the personal is primary. As Elizabeth has argued, "Institutions don't do social. People do social."[8] People want to connect with people. That's the whole point of social media. Effective social media ministry invites and nurtures these personal connections. Dan Zarrella, a social media analyst, summarizes it this way: the best way to approach social media participation is to "stop talking *about* yourself. . . . But start talking *as* yourself and show us how the world looks through your eyes."[9]

PASTORAL AND PUBLIC

Keith has lived this journey over the last ten years, beginning with blogging his sermons in 2008, mainly so his mom could read them, and suddenly finding himself preaching to a larger audience than just those gathered for worship on Sunday morning. That led to more experiments with social media, which, in turn, led to writing the first edition of *Click 2 Save* with Elizabeth in 2012. Today, he writes, speaks, teaches, and consults, while serving full-time as a parish pastor of a thriving congregation. In the process, he has had to balance being a sort of brand and being a real person.

He recognizes the profound temptation for recognition and notoriety, which, as we have seen over the years, has led many digital ministry leaders to "jump the shark." However, he is reminded of Paul's wise counsel in Romans 12:3, "For by the grace given to me I say to everyone among you not to think of yourself more highly than you ought to think, but to think with sober judgment, each according to the measure of faith that God has assigned." Keith attributes his navigation between the physical and digital world, the parish and public ministry, his day job and his side hustles, to Rev. Nadia Bolz-Weber, founding pastor of House for All Sinners and Saints, whom we featured in our first edition and who has gone on to become a *New York*

Times best-selling author. From Nadia, Keith has learned to be fully present in his congregation even as he engages a larger audience online, to be generous with his time, to tell and retell his congregation's stories, and to give his best ideas away. For as much as we are able to do online, it is vital to remain grounded and rooted, whether that is in a congregation, faith community, or through a spiritual discipline or practice.

We would identify six key characteristics of successful digital ministers:

- *Generous*: These leaders are generous with their time, advice, and ideas. They are receptive when people reach out to them online or in person. They listen, encourage, advise, and share their best ideas.
- *Humble*: They don't think too highly of themselves and recognize there is always more to learn because the technologies are always changing. They understand that they are one node in a massive network, but that even a single node can make a difference.
- *Curious*: They know what they don't know and are continually learning about these new and evolving technologies. They are curious about other people, not just in their congregations but in their extended community. They acknowledge, affirm, and go below the surface.
- *Willing to Experiment*: They are willing to try things and see how they go. One of the early mantras of Facebook was "move fast and break things." The idea was that no product is ever perfect. So, push it out, try it, see how users respond, and then make adjustments as you go. These leaders make things, launch them, and learn from them.
- *Collaborative*: They are great collaborators, whether they are involved in digitally facilitated or local projects. They convene people, often from across different disciplines and faith traditions, and are open to ideas that aren't their own. They don't care who gets the credit.
- *Kind*: Perhaps the most important is kindness. There are far too many people online—people of faith not least among them—who traffic in negativity, cynicism, and even hate, who troll others, or who seek their own self-aggrandizement. The internet and our world need a different witness. To quote a Presbyterian minister, who leveraged the broadcast media of television for the sake of the Gospel, Fred Rogers: "There are three ways to ultimate success. The first way is to be kind. The second way is to be kind. The third way is to be kind."[10]

Those who tend to be less effective in digital ministry are often more insular and protective of their digital turf, focused on themselves. They mistake time and activity online for meaningful digital engagement and creative work. For example, we see many ministry leaders investing far too much time and emotional energy in churchy echo chambers like clergy group Facebook pages. While there is certainly some mutual support and crowdsourcing that happens within these groups, on the whole we find a preponderance of complaining and whining and debating over church *adiaphora* rather than engaging the wider world and creating new, meaningful spiritual experiences. If we are only talking amongst ourselves, we fail to engage the wider world beyond our churches and to expand our relational networks.

MINISTRY OF DIGITAL PRESENCE

The advent of new digital media gives us an unprecedented ability to tell our personal and congregational stories—and God's story—and to listen to the stories of others. Every day, many times a day, people are scrolling through news, pictures, and comments. We can appear as a visible reminder of their church community, their faith, and God's grace.

Digital ministers are like chaplains walking the halls of the hospital, or a parish priest walking the streets of the neighborhood, at times offering a smile, a wave, small talk, a prayer, or deeper conversation. Our presence here makes us available to others and points beyond ourselves to the presence of God. This digital ministry presence can unfold in the same way that wearing a clerical collar around town is a way of saying "God is here! There is something worthwhile and, yes, even holy about this place."

It also makes us available and accessible. David Hansen, pastor of Spirit of Joy! Lutheran Church in Houston, is a fourth generation Lutheran pastor. He reflects, "I remember my dad walking around with a beeper and a bag phone in the late '80s so people could reach him. Because, for him, before people can have a personal interaction with you, they have to reach you first. It is all about connection. Ministry is about being part of people's lives." Today, his father, who is semiretired, logs in to Facebook on his iPad.

As Hansen suggests, we can't be just empty profiles. There must be someone at the other end of the line—or the profile. We can't just create an account and expect people to engage with us. We can't automate all our posts or have someone do it for us. Our presence must be demonstrably active and authentically us.

Jodi Bjornstad Hogue, founding pastor of Humble Walk Lutheran Church, a congregation that intentionally gathers in public spaces in the West End neighborhood of St. Paul, Minnesota, describes herself as a "prolific poster" on Facebook. She says, "Since I don't have an office or physical structure, it is the place where I am most present. People know where to find me. It's either by Facebook, email, or text. It's all technology-based and I would have never dreamed that would be my most consistent presence as a pastor. But it really is how it happened and how it continues to happen." People know Pastor Houge is present by virtue of her high level of activity on social media, which today also includes Twitter and Instagram. She uses her digital presence to point to her physical location as she encourages people to drop by the coffee shop for Bible study or the pub for theological conversation.

The more present you are and the more you participate, the more people will engage with you. People generally interact with you according with the level of your activity. If you're not active on social media—if you have few friends or followers and don't post much—people won't even try to contact you for fear you won't see it. They will get in touch with you by email or phone—or, perhaps, not at all. Today, picking up the phone or sending an email is an extra step many people are not willing to take.

THE REAL PRESENCE

The word most often used—and perhaps overused—to describe this kind of real presence in social media is "authenticity." It's been argued that authenticity is a term that is impossible to define. Like "beauty" or "truth," we tend to know it when we see it.

In *The Gifts of Imperfection*, researcher, storyteller, and best-selling author Brené Brown describes authenticity in this helpful way:

> Authenticity is a collection of choices that we have to make every day. It's about the choice to show up and be real. The choice to be honest. The choice to let our true selves be seen. There are people who consciously prac-

tice being authentic, there are people who don't, and there are the rest of us who are authentic on some days and not so authentic on other days.[11]

According to Brown, authenticity is about showing up with our whole selves, warts and all. The work of ministry, both online and in person, continually calls us to "consciously practice being authentic." Life experiences, passions, strengths, and weaknesses are all brought to bear and shape pastoral presence for professional and volunteer ministry leaders alike. Being true to these—and trusting that God is at work in them—is what makes each person's ministry unique and effective. It enables us to empathize with people in their suffering, bring the Word of God home in preaching and teaching, push beyond our own personal comfort zones, pursue new creative endeavors and new learnings, and share faith through the stories of our lived experience, all for the sake of the Gospel and our faith communities. Often when we begin in ministry, we model ourselves on those ministry mentors that have inspired and nurtured us. Eventually, when we come into our own, we discover the power and joy of ministering from our true selves rather than trying to be someone else. The same is true in digital ministry. In this book, you will meet many gifted and thoughtful digital ministry leaders. Their work is inspiring, and you will undoubtedly take their ideas and practices and try them on for yourself. Some of them you will make your own. However, we hope that these will ultimately serve as stepping stones to finding your own unique interests, abilities, passion, presence, and voice, and that one day we can write about you and share your story.

In a noisy digital world, our real presence is essential. By bringing the fullness of our lives to bear through ministry in social media communities, we bear witness to the fullness of life in God. After all, the *really* Real Presence here is God's, and it is through our real and authentic presence in social media that we most clearly and effectively point to God. As we know from face-to-face ministry, this is often how faith is transmitted and God is made manifest: through the stories of the real lives of real people, whether they are in stories from Scripture, the lives of the saints, or the people sitting in our pews. In this way, the work of digital ministry is profoundly incarnational, moving beyond or through the screen to connect with others and God at our most real and human selves.

MAINTAINING BOUNDARIES

The flip side of the unprecedented access that social media gives us to the lives of those to whom we minister is the unprecedented access it gives people to ours. It collapses the barriers we have been taught to raise between our private and public, personal and pastoral lives. Living authentically or "whole heartedly," as Brown has written, also requires us to be vulnerable. This tends to invoke anxiety around social media for many in ministry.

Boundaries are absolutely necessary in ministry for a host of reasons, not least of all to manage power dynamics, safeguard relationships, protect the vulnerable, and avoid emotional and physical burnout. So where do we draw the line in social networking communities?

As in face-to-face ministry, the boundaries will be different for everyone, varying by style, personality, and context. It seems unwise and unhelpful to mandate a particular approach for everyone. For many years, the bright, uncrossable line was not to befriend parishioners personally, because it might compromise our ability to be their minister. As the Reverend Kelly Fryer argues, this may have been more myth than reality, even before the dawn of social media.[12] Fryer explains:

> When I was graduating from seminary, the second most unhelpful piece of advice I received was, "Don't make friends with parishioners." The idea was that you were supposed to keep up a professional distance from the members of your congregation in order to . . . what? I'm not sure. Avoid congregational infighting over who gets to be friends with the pastor? Maybe if we were all in fifth grade.

This already fuzzy concept of not becoming friends with those whom we serve in ministry is further confused because the term "friend" itself has been transformed by Facebook. A "friend" can range from a confidant to a casual acquaintance to someone you've never met in person. To mitigate this aspect of social convergence, some church bodies have advocated for separate ministry and personal accounts, effectively partitioning their online presence. They recommend using ministry profiles for relating to parishioners and their personal profile for friends. However, ministry leaders miss out on the benefits of sharing their faith with friends and their life with their parishioners. As we have seen, the pastoral role is about sharing the Gospel, building community, nurturing relationships, and doing outreach. In many ways, then, social media platforms and the convergence they create are a healthy corrective to the partitioning of our lives. For, just as damage can be done when we blur the pastoral and personal, we can also do damage when we cut ourselves off from different parts of ourselves.

Jodi Houge says of this division between the pastoral and personal, "I just found that to be impossible because it's all interwoven. . . . I recognized right away that because of this call that I have to Word and Sacrament, there is no way to separate 'clergy Jodi' from everything else. And so everything that I put out in social media is still holding a public office. Much of it is just me and my life, but it's always public."

Many of the digital ministers we've met tell us that the practice of setting up two accounts is less about cutting themselves off from parishioners and more about wanting to preserve the fun of social media and freely connect with friends. There is a sense of loss of the freedom that others have to share personally and speak your mind. "Look, once in a while I'm going to want to cuss or to say that your favorite political candidate is an idiot," said a church communicator who maintains two Facebook profiles and separate Twitter feeds (and who asked not to be named). "Yes, I want people in my diocese to see me as a whole person who has a life beyond my ministry in the church, but I don't need for everyone to see me in my bathrobe, or with a lampshade on my head on New Year's Eve, or whatever." The point is well taken. Every piece of content you post is not for everyone. Keith only maintains one profile, however each time he posts something, he has to determine whether to make it completely public so anyone can see it or to limit access by posting just for "friends." He posts to different audience lists on Facebook (more on this in chapter 3) and carefully selects which social media platforms to use in order to help avoid unnecessary dust-ups at church.

We first met Adam Copeland when we were writing the first edition and he was leading the Project F-M in Fargo, North Dakota. He now serves as director for the Center for Stewardship Leaders at Luther Seminary. As Adam reflects on how his various roles and responsibilities have shaped how he uses social media, he says,

> Personally, I wrestle with this question fairly often. It's become increasingly difficult. When I was at the Project F-M the whole idea was that it's a hip

new church plant. Part of our brand identity was that we don't do things normally. No problem. At the seminary now, I feel because of the role that some seminary faculty have as public theologians, I have a difficult time distinguishing between when I post something or make a statement or even blog on my personal blog site, how that is a public voice as me as an individual but always a disciple versus me as an employee of the largest seminary in the ELCA speaking into the broader Christian conversation. This isn't particularly unique, but it has become a more difficult challenge for me to figure out how the different platforms merge. I'm less guarded on Twitter. On Facebook I'm more intentional. I use Facebook professionally a little more to cultivate a more reflective use and thought process. On Twitter I feel like I'm participating in an ongoing conversation.

Of course, this is simply another way in which digital ministry is like face-to-face ministry. Wherever we are, whomever we are with, we represent Christ and the church. We represent the church whether we are on a personal or professional profile, a page or group, whether we have lampshades on our heads or are sipping tea with a circle of kindly church ladies. Using social media in ministry—using social media at all—requires thoughtfulness and discretion.

YOU'RE NOT MY PASTOR

In place of a clichéd "don't be friends with parishioners" rule, a helpful rule of thumb offered by Nadia Bolz-Weber of House for All Sinners and Saints is "don't try to get your emotional needs met by them." Don't try to make your friends, followers, and readers into your personal chaplains and spiritual guides, calling on them to shepherd you through the ups and downs of your life."

Says Bolz-Weber, "My main thing is that I try to never put up any status update that seems emotionally fishing. My parishioners should not feel like they have to take care of me emotionally. I have personal friends for that."

Now, this is not necessarily the same as asking for prayers, admitting that you're having a bad day, sharing a life event, or declaring that you think your sermon sucks. Those things can, in fact, make us human, approachable, and real—and people often respond with great wisdom, compassion, and humor to such posts. But when we post, we have to ask ourselves: "Why am I posting this? What am I looking for? Sympathy? Attention? Intimacy? To fill a deeper need?"

For example, sometime back, Elizabeth was a bit taken aback by a Facebook post from a clergy member who was clearly way too in the thick of it while holding her iPhone in her hand to make particularly clear judgments. "I'm not sure what I like best from my male colleagues," she posted sarcastically, "the condescension or the belittling."

She apparently rallied in a matter of seconds, for the post was deleted almost immediately, and it's likely that few of her flock saw what was probably some measure of legitimate frustration but also a skewering of some of her colleagues that was undoubtedly inappropriate for a public setting like Facebook. Even in the few seconds the comment was up, a number of people did comment on the post, offering a level of "there, there, dear" consolation and "you give 'em what-for!" encouragement that ministers don't usually want to be soliciting from their flock en masse. And one male friend gently suggested that jerks come in all shapes, sizes, and genders.

PUBLIC OR PRIVATE

A more helpful distinction than the *personal and professional* is the *public and the private*. There are some things we are willing to share completely publicly, some we only share with select friends, and some we don't post at all but keep to ourselves. You may wish to post publically about your ministry, but keep your family life more private. You may want to highlight your side projects or creative passions to a broader audience, but keep other things to yourself. That line will be different for everyone. For example, Keith usually doesn't post about meet-ups and conversations with close friends and colleagues on social media, even though in terms of personal branding it would benefit them both. Instead, he tries to savor the moment rather than broadcasting it. This preserves for him some of the intimacy of the experience and makes those all-too-rare face-to-face moments more meaningful. On the flip side, he is more than happy to share about milestones in his family life, which helps to humanize him and creates new points of connection and conversation with friends and followers.

THE DIGITAL WORLD HAS GONE TO THE DOGS (AND CATS)

Ministry leaders often worry about how much personal information to include, especially with regard to their children or partners. Here, take a cue from Nadia Bolz-Weber, Darleen Pryds, and other well-known ministry leaders and thought leaders who, on the one hand, want to establish meaningful relationships in social media settings and who, on the other, want to keep their personal lives relatively private: talk about your dog. This allows you to share content that is personal, but less private than information about your family, your vacations, and the like. Mark and Sarah Huber of Sanctuary Church in Marshfield, Massachusetts, for example, frequently post pictures of their gregarious dog, Graham, who you will find has his own hashtag #instaGraham.

If pets aren't your thing, share about the hobbies you love and that humanize you. For example, Bishop Jennifer Baskerville-Burrows of the Episcopal Diocese of Indianapolis regularly posts about running. Bishop Jim Hazelwood of the New England Synod of the ELCA posts about bicycling, both to share his joy in doing it and to encourage his ministry leaders to stay active and healthy.

Social media is about relationships and you want to offer something for people to relate to rather than just your latest theological epiphany. In a time of rising religious unaffiliation, personal stories rather than church notices are far more likely to invite connections. As Anthony Guillen, missioner of Hispanic/Latino Ministries in The Episcopal Church advises, "Remember that social media is about relationship. We've got to be engaged with people as human beings. A lot of clergy share absolutely nothing about themselves on social media and they're not very engaged because they feel that there's no real return. I tell them, 'Yes, because there's no return on relationship. People need to know something about you first.'" This variety of interests and activities should be complemented with a variety of different types of content or posts, from simple texts, to check-ins, pictures, recorded video, live video, or a combination of all of the above. It's a good idea to mix what you share and how you share it.

In Keith's parish work, he actively friends parishioners and neighbors. He wants to be their pastor in digital space as well as in face-to-face settings.

It is another channel for communication and a way for their pastor to be available. And, especially in light of the worries many have about ethical behavior online, a digital minister can serve as a good example of participation in social media communities with an ethic of kindness and compassion.

Sharing your story and your passions, being present and active in social media, humanizes you. This is a great gift for ministers, parishioners, seekers, and other conversation partners. People learn about what a clergyperson or a lay minister does during the week, but they also learn that a ministry leader is a person with a life beyond church. These other interests also give people some easy connection points, as well as a way into thinking about lived faith that links to your sermon blog and announcements about church events may not offer.

You can often share the same content on your church Facebook page and your profile, but you're very likely to get more "likes" and comments on the profile. The same goes for other social media platforms. That's because people know that you're going to see their reactions and responses personally, and that you will likely respond to them in kind. This just feels better than getting what seems like a generic note from an anonymous administrator.

FINDING YOUR VOICE

There are billions of voices across the digital landscape, and it's natural to wonder what impact a parish pastor, youth minister, diocesan staff member, or lay minister can actually have. The key to distinguishing yourself among the many people within social media is to cultivate your own recognizable voice.

Of course, you already have a voice—you already have something to say or else you wouldn't be in ministry. One of the reasons ministers are well suited to social media is that they regularly create content, specialize in relationships, and usually have a well-honed, distinctive voice. Every week you bring your unique perspective and lens on the Gospel to bear on the world.

Thus, the challenge is not necessarily to create a new voice, but to translate your voice and perspective from your face-to-face ministry into social media.

Generally speaking, a strong social media presence that best articulates a clear and distinctive voice is: consistent, positive (even when critical), diverse in its interests, humorous, focused primarily on others, and responsive. An effective digitally integrated minister shapes her or his voice by using mixed media, not taking her- or himself too seriously, avoiding self-promotion, and highlighting the unique qualities of her or his ministry.

While every voice will necessarily be unique, we have tended to see digitally integrated ministry presence register within five broad vocational categories:

- *Activist* —Provides content on social justice issues, shares their own activity, and asks people to take action
- *Affirming*—Is more active on other people's pages than their own, offering likes and comments
- *Informational*—Provides links to local or national news and other content in areas of particular interest
- *Pastoral*—Offers prayers and blessings, expressions of concern and support for members of a more defined (congregational, denominational, organizational) ministry community
- *Educational*—Shares educational content on topics of interest to themselves and others
- *Social*—Enjoys interacting with many people across platforms, connects social media users to one another, and shares personal content that helps to deepen connections
- *Spiritual*—Shares prayers, spiritual quotes, inspirational images and music, prays for the needs of individuals and the world

Your digital ministry will very likely often fall into multiple categories, but it can be helpful as you're starting out to focus your participation in one primary category. If you're working with a church communication or outreach team, you might want to distribute responsibilities for engagement across the categories above to suit people's natural inclinations and interests. This is important because different social media participants are drawn to different kinds of content and interaction. So, it's important to refocus or extend your personal, digitally integrated ministry into other categories if you see that you are most consistently operating out of only one.

MANAGING YOUR TIME: INTEGRATE DIGITAL AND IRL PRACTICE

Many ministry leaders see social media as an add-on to their already full ministry schedule, one that they simply don't have time for. It's just "one more thing" in an already overbooked schedule.

We're all aware that technology and social media can quickly consume our time. It's no wonder much of the conversation among lay and ordained ministers about social media revolves around how to maintain limits on the amount of time they spend in social media. Indeed, the first message Keith received on his Facebook wall was from one of his parishioners who greeted him, saying, "Welcome to the vortex. Facebook is the biggest time suck ever."

Here's the thing: we don't have time for social media either. Keith has a busy congregation and family. Elizabeth is continually teaching, travelling, speaking, and writing. We have more than enough to keep us busy. And yet, we have chosen to be present in these digital spaces and to write about it for the sake of the Gospel, for the sake of community, and the sake of the church. If our calling as ministry leaders is to share the love of God, create and nurture community, and form faith, then we must be present in this digital space where people are gathering, connecting, and making meaning.

Keith has found that rather than being another add-on to his already busy schedule, social media has become a fully integrated part of his parish work. It has become an essential tool for sermon research and preparation, allowing him to test out ideas before taking them to the pulpit, and to share the sermon afterward to a broader audience via podcast. He finds teaching ideas and shares resources and lesson plans from his Confirmation classes on his blog for others to use.[13] People reach out to him for pastoral care via text, Facebook, and sometimes Twitter. He evangelizes by sharing events and stories with a broader local audience, and builds community through daily engagement with parishioners and neighbors. His theology pub has its own dedicated website and blog[14] and his Instagram feed often serves as a record of his travels. He has created or participated in faith formation projects that have served both his congregation and a broader audience online.

In chapter 4, we'll talk more about digitally integrated practices that, once we become more nimble with social media, organically extend our ministries beyond local communities. As you'll see in the work of activist Jamye Wooten, pastor Jodi Hogue, social justice minister Diana Wheeler, and others tending to the people of God, sharing the Word of God, forming disciples, advocating for justice, and other essential arts of ministry can be deeply enriched by digital media technologies and practices.

DIGITAL SABBATH-TAKING

If you spend a great deal of time online, consider taking time to unplug and provide for a social media sabbath—a designated period of time each week or each month when you step away from all your social media sites. Likewise, you'll do well to set some boundaries on social media on your days off, just as you'd set on how frequently you retrieve phone messages or email. Don't post about or respond to church business on these days, and make a note in your status when you head off on vacation so people know "The Minister Is Not In." You might also change your cover or profile image to denote a change in status or location. If you use the Facebook Messenger feature or other messaging apps, set your status to "off-line."

Shamika Goddard, who, as a Union Theological Seminary student, helped create the position of "Tech Chaplain," which provides pastoral and technical support for the digitally challenged, says:

> Being in social media means you're exposing yourself to the fire hose of information that's out there. It's something you need to know how to step back from to take care of yourself. Being connected doesn't mean you have to be connected all the time. You don't always have to be on. Remember to take breaks. I recently did a digital fast where I stepped away from email and social media for the most part. I put up a vacation responder on my email. I sent out a message on social media that I was on a digital fast. I gave people a heads-up that I would not be available in these ways for a period of time. And it was a great experience to have that time away. Coming back was like jumping into a running stream—it was craziness catching back up with everything—but I would definitely do it again.

RESPONDING TO BAD BEHAVIOR

In the years since the first edition, our culture has become much more aware of bullying online, especially for teens and young adults, though adults and even pastors are not immune from bullying and being bullied. What if one of your friends or followers is behaving badly or bullying? What if someone is posting inappropriate content and/or posting excessively or too personally on your wall?

SET THE GROUND RULES

It can help to set some ground rules in advance. Catholic Jesuit priest, Father James Martin, engages a range of current and oftentimes controversial topics on his Facebook page. He frequently reminds his followers of his rules for engagement, which are some variety of these: "Two post limit. No ad hominem attacks." By setting his expectations in advance, Martin is then able to moderate the conversation according to his initial guidelines.

Remember that ultimately, it is *your* wall, blog, or Twitter stream. You have the right to remove anything you deem inappropriate. You can delete individual posts or block certain users from posting. You can create customized rules on Facebook that prevent specified friends from seeing your posts.

However, we encourage you to try to approach these as opportunities for conversation and modeling appropriate social media behavior. First, should someone behave badly, send the person a direct message explaining your concern. If, however, the bad behavior continues, we recommend responding with "progressive discipline," deleting posts from people who overpost or who post inappropriately.

While we've both had to do it once or twice, we feel that unfriending someone on Facebook or blocking them on Twitter or Instagram should be an absolute last resort for people in ministry. We want to be in relationship even with—maybe sometimes especially with—people who can be challenging or outright difficult. Part of the promise of church in social media communities is that we can stay connected, even when we disagree. We do this face-to-face with difficult people in our congregations all the time.

It may turn out, however, that with some challenging people, a social networking site is not the right context for ministry, not just because it exposes you and your online community to various difficulties, but because it also exposes the offender to everyone's digital gaze. If you ran into a parishioner having a breakdown in the grocery store, odds are you'd do your best to get him or her to a more private space so you could better attend to the matter at hand. So, too, your more intimate online ministry may sometimes move well off-line.

Cases in which we always recommend drawing a firm line by unfriending or blocking someone—and communicating privately that you are doing this—is when there is bullying toward you or any other member of your network, when there is pronounced religious, political, or ideological hostility toward others' views, or when someone seems otherwise unable to adhere to very basic norms of respect for others and discretion in the ideas, photos, videos, and other content they share. In the end, we believe that "keeping it real" and "keeping it kind" in this way is both good pastoral practice and the most effective way to engage people across digital social media locales. It is also the most effective way to not only share but embody the Gospel. In the next chapter we'll describe the digital ministry practices we find most effective for listening, attending, connecting, and engaging.

DIGITAL MINISTRY STRATEGY: REAL PRESENCE

The following questions are designed to help you better articulate your "real presence" in social networking communities. Reflect on them for you personally and, either on your own or with a group, in the context of your ministry community.

1. Using the categories we described for digital ministry presence, note where you see yourself as most comfortable now and what might be a growth area for you. How might you develop in your growth areas? You might want to complete this assessment for both yourself and for your church or organization.

	Comfort Zone?	Growth Area?	How do you engage OR How could you grow in this area?
Activist	☐	☐	
Affirming	☐	☐	
Informational	☐	☐	
Pastoral	☐	☐	
Educational	☐	☐	
Social	☐	☐	
Spiritual	☐	☐	

2. Look through your Facebook friends, the groups you like, and the people you follow on Instagram and Twitter. Who would you identify as your social media role models, both as individuals and organizations? What makes them particularly engaging for you?

Who?   **Why?**

_____   _____

_____   _____

_____   _____

_____   _____

3. What are some personal-but-not-private things you can share to humanize your presence in social networking communities? What forms do these things take (e.g., tags, photos, stories, quotes)?

_____   _____

_____   _____

_____   _____

_____   _____

NOTES

1. Zygmunt Bauman, *Liquid Modernity* (2000; Cambridge: Polity, 2012), 82.

2. Kayne West, "Diamonds from Sierra Leone (Remix) (ft. Jay-Z)," *Late Registration* (Roc-A-Fella/Def Jam, 2005).

3. danah boyd, *It's Complicated: The Social Lives of Networked Teens* (New Haven, CT: Yale University Press, 2014), 49.

4. Tom Beaudoin, *Consuming Faith: Integrating Who We Are with What We Buy* (Lanham, MD: Sheed & Ward, 2003), 106.

5. Ibid, 4.

6. Woman at the Well by lalaland481, June 29, 2007. https://www.youtube.com/watch?v=Q49BbfgJbto.

7. Keith Anderson, *The Digital Cathedral: Networked Ministry in a Wireless World* (New York: Morehouse, 2015), 211.

8. Elizabeth Drescher, "Facebook Doesn't Kill Churches, Churches Kill Churches," *Religion Dispatches*, March 24, 2011, http://www.religiondispatches.org/archive/atheologies/4390/facebook_doesn't_kill_churches,_churches_kill_churches/.

9. Dan Zarrella, "Stop Talking About Yourself, Start Talking As Yourself," *Dan Zarrella*, December 13, 2010, http://danzarrella.com/stop-talking-about-yourself-start-talking-as-yourself, (emphasis added).

10. Fred Rogers, *Life's Journeys According to Mister Rogers: Things to Remember Along the Way* (New York: Hyperion, 2005).

11. Brené Brown, *The Gifts of Imperfection: Let Go of Who You Think You're Supposed to Be and Embrace Who You Are* (Center City, MN: Hazelden, 2010), 49.

12. Kelly Fryer, "Pastors on Facebook: Get Real," *The Renewable Church*, February 10, 2011, http://www.renewablechurch.com/2011/02/pastors-on-facebook-get-real.html.

13. Find resources for your confirmation classes at http://pastorkeithanderson.net/writing/blog.

14. Find God on Tap (Ambler, PA) at http://godontap.net.

3

I LOVE TO TELL THE STORY
Social Media Platforms

Social media, with its facilitation of easy many-to-many communication, has shifted the internet from a warehouse of information to a place for storytelling and connection. Your intentional presence and engaging voice are the basis for sharing a compelling narrative about your life and ministry that unfolds over time in text, pictures, videos, check-ins, posts, snaps, and tweets that invite people into conversation and relationship.

Choosing which social media platforms to use in your ministry will depend on the kind of story you wish to tell, how you wish to tell it, and to whom. Different platforms lend themselves to the different practices we introduced in chapter 1: catching up, sharing, exploring, interacting, and archiving. In this chapter, then, we will explore the major social media platforms that together form the core of an integrated digital ministry practice.

WE WILL BEGIN WITH what we call "legacy platforms"—Facebook, Twitter, LinkedIn, YouTube, and blogs—which we profiled in the first edition. Then we'll move to emerging platforms that didn't even exist back in 2012: Instagram, Pinterest, Periscope, podcasts, and messaging apps like Snapchat.

To illustrate the impact of effective digitally integrated ministry, we share Keith's experience of the way that telling an engaging story well online can bring you into relationship with others, often before you even meet them in person:

> I was the last to speak.
>
> I was attending a ministry workshop led by Christian spirituality scholar Margaret Benefiel on understanding personal and congregational change. We were going around the circle, making the customary introductions—

name, ministry context, a little something about what brought us there. The introductions had begun on the other side of the room. Ministry colleagues, mostly from the United Church of Christ, Methodist, and Catholic traditions, introduced themselves. Finally, when it was my turn, I said, "I'm Keith Anderson and I'm the pastor at the Lutheran Church of the Redeemer in Woburn." Before I could say anything more, someone blurted out, "Are you *that* Keith Anderson?"

I had no idea if I was or not. My mind raced. "Do I know this person?" I wondered. "Wait, am I in trouble?"

I need not have panicked. "Didn't you write some article—something about welcoming people into your church?" my colleague asked. Indeed I had. I was "*that* Keith Anderson."

A couple months earlier, I had posted "Top Ten Things We've Learned About Welcoming Newcomers" on my personal blog. I shared what we'd learned in our efforts over these last five years in our work to become a more welcoming congregation. I posted a link to the post on my Facebook profile. There, it came to the attention of a seminary classmate, who, in turn, recommended it to the Lewis Center for Leadership at Wesley Seminary in Washington, DC. The piece was later included in the Lewis Center's *Leading Ideas* e-newsletter, to which many of the colleagues at this workshop subscribe.

And so, before I uttered a word beyond my name and congregation, there was a story being told about me and my congregation—by people far beyond our geographical location or denominational tradition. It was a story about a pastor and congregation intentionally trying to be a more open and welcoming place.

My colleagues and I chatted briefly about the post, and the conversation continued during the breaks as we talked about our ministries and ways of welcoming newcomers. When the workshop was over and we all returned home, a story that began in social media continued in the same way as we friended one another on Facebook.

More than five years later, this story seems rather quaint, capturing some of the wonderment of the early days of social media when we were simply amazed that we could connect and communicate in new ways. While moments of digitally facilitated serendipity still frequently happen and continue to delight, today we take this kind of networked connectedness for granted, particularly in the relatively small world of the church. We have become more sophisticated in our use of social media, in our self-presentation, and in the messages and signals we send. And yet, the news is filled with high-profile instances when people just lose sight of it, often in spectacular fashion.

Think about this in terms of the demographics we discussed in chapter 1. The network of your potential influence through social media is exponentially larger than the network of people with whom you're connected or you interact directly. You have no idea where the content you share will end up and how it might impact someone's life or your ministry. If *any* message has the potential to connect with that many people, it seems to us that we should try to make *every* message count.

> It bears repeating: if you are participating in social media communities, in any capacity, even casually, you are already telling a story about yourself and your faith community, consciously or not—a story that has the potential at any moment to extend well beyond your own particular local and social media communities.

At least as importantly, if you're not yet participating in social media communities, you are also already telling a story by virtue of your absence of your engagement, and your church's, with the wider world as it is mapped today. Today, before anyone walks through your church doors or meets you in person, they are constructing a story, developing a picture, and forming a preliminary relationship with you and your congregation through what you share (or don't) online. When you are not present in online communities, you're passively telling a story about you and your church's or organization's disinterest in where people spend much of their time and connect to people, organizations, and issues that matter to them. You're saying, "Hey 1.8+ billion people in Facebook Land and every Millennial on social media, we're not really interested in you!" That's probably not the story you intend to tell.

But by being present and active in social media platforms, we can help shape—not control, but shape—our personal and community stories and the relationships they encourage through wise use of social networking platforms and practices. Even the simplest gestures expressing a desire to connect, listen, and be in relationship go a long way.

CHECKING IN ON THE ROAD TO EMMAUS

Just as biblical writers employed different genres—letters, poems, songs, gospels, narrative, and myths—to tell the story of God and God's people, we can use different social media platforms and tools to develop our distinctive stories in engaging and nuanced ways. The types of social media we deploy depends on what kind of story we are trying to tell and to whom.

Stories in social media can be driven by location and movement, as in the Gospels with Jesus's own "check-ins" from Bethlehem to Jerusalem. By checking in, we can share something of our own earthly pilgrimage and show that faith is active and happens in all sorts of places. We can share evocative imagery akin to the psalms in poetic tweets on Twitter and with more literal images of the sort that adorn the stained glass windows in many of our churches through photo sharing on Instagram, Pinterest, Snapchat, and our Facebook profiles and pages. Versions of our epistles can now be blogged or captured on inspirational and thought-provoking videos and shared on YouTube. We can broadcast moments live on Periscope, YouTube, Facebook Live, and Instagram. Today this can all be accomplished with the powerful smartphones we carry around in our pockets.

There are, of course, many other social media platforms at your disposal, including Flickr, WhatsApp, Soundcloud, Medium, and more. All of these services will evolve and will eventually be eclipsed—yes, even Facebook. Indeed, this is a common argument for waiting to engage in social media. People don't want to invest time learning a platform only to see it decline in use or popularity. However, most new technologies will be built on the ones we use now, so the guidance in this book is designed to apply to any social media platform you choose.

For example, over the last few years, many social media platforms have harmonized their nomenclature. Hashtags, which first came into popular use in Twitter, have been incorporated into Facebook and Instagram. Most social media profiles have a similar look inspired by the Facebook Timeline, with a profile picture, short personal description with the option to include a link to your website, and, in some cases, a larger cover photo. Facebook has integrated check-ins and live video, which first appeared on other platforms like the now defunct Foursquare, which we featured in the first edition. Video, once mostly the realm of YouTube, is present on nearly every social media site, and is exploding in popularity. Because of this, time spent on learning one platform usually pays off in getting to know other platforms as well. Whatever social media come next, they will likely draw on similar features. You have to start somewhere. The key is to start.

SEWING UP YOUR STORY

In any story, some basic elements must be present: a plot, characters, dialogue, and, most of the time, movement from place to place, scene to scene. These all serve to create something not simply informative, but something experiential, as when we read a good book and sink into the reality it evokes. Good stories invite the reader to participate, enriching the stories through our imaginations and—in the social storytelling that connects the Digital Age directly to the Middle Ages—in conversations as the story unfolds in the presence of others.

Biblical narratives were frequently compiled from the work of more than one author—a poem or song stitched together with a parable and a bit of a local legend to tell the bigger Truth of God's presence among us. This stitching has left visible seams, frayed edges, and gaps within the biblical text. Rather than undermining the text, this uneven stitching enriches the biblical story, revealing a multitude of meanings, understandings**,** and interpretations and inviting new perspectives into the divine-human narrative. So, too, the patchwork of content and conversation—the overlapping and interwoven voices—in social media spaces can offer great richness and depth. It provides space for stories to emerge from a variety of voices and experiences. Presbyterian minister and biblical storyteller Casey Fitzgerald, who brings biblical storytelling into digital spaces by creating crowdsourced videos of people sharing the lectionary readings (more below), shared with us, "It's important that it isn't just me that people are hearing the story from. They are hearing the story from the mouths of different people. These stories come out of different cultures and backgrounds. That's what social media does. It gives us access to a diversity of voices. It gives us access without having to be in the room. That's significant to me."

In fact, it is really only by stepping back and attending to the full relational, conversational tapestry of social media that we are able to see beyond the common argument that life online is necessarily "shallow" or "impersonal." Take a bit here, a byte there, a pixel or two over yonder, multiplied by relationship upon relationship upon relationship across a vast, global matrix of networks, and considerable aggregated depth and substance has been built. If the story of the first edition of this book was about the serendipitous connections that social media make possible, the story of this second edition is about the deepening of digitally mediated relationships and collaboration over time, just as we have experienced in our own partnership. Elizabeth uses the term "aggregate depth" to describe this gradual, bit-by-bit approach to developing richer relationships one status update, one Instagram picture, Pinterest pin, or one 280-character tweet at a time.[1] At first this incremental approach can seem counterintuitive. Because these digital technologies are so instantaneous, we can often be lured into thinking that the results of our digital ministry will be just as immediate. However, social media is about relationships and relationships are always a long-term investment.

The stories we share—and ask people to enter, shape, and share again—form the overarching narrative of God's redeeming grace. This narrative is woven through each ministry, each congregation, each individual life of faith. Ultimately, it is God's story—the way God is at work in us, in our congregations, our communities, and the world. Despite protests to the contrary, in a distributed, digital way, this makes our social media participation profoundly incarnational. Anytime someone says, "Oh, I saw this article posted on Facebook or Twitter today . . ." in a face-to-face conversation, you're getting a glimpse of the incarnational potential of social media participation. Further, individuals often go out of their way when travelling or attending a conference to meet digital friends and followers in person. It can be as though they are meeting again for the first time.

NOW DEPARTING FROM THE PLATFORM

Note that the term "platform" is used in two different ways when talking in social media. Each type of social media—Facebook, Instagram, blogs, Periscope—is a platform in the sense of being a digital locale in which people can interact around shared interests. Facebook is a place, a location. Thus, you'll hear friends and parishioners say things like, "Oh, I saw you on Instagram yesterday."

The second meaning is more like a political platform: not a specific locale, but rather how you engage across a combination of these sites to connect with others and develop relationships. Your participation on a combination of social media platforms helps you to articulate your ministry philosophy and approach—your own ministry platform—and engage with others.

In social media, an effective ministry platform is developed by integrating a range of social media locales into a consistent, recognizable online presence. Your ministry does not begin and end when you speak from the pulpit. It's also comprised of pastoral care, faith formation, administration, and so on. So, too, your digital ministry is multifaceted. It unfolds across multiple, coordinated social media platforms. Together, they construct your digital ministry platform.

In the era of broadcast media, the most influential ministry platforms tended to be those of large congregations with equally large budgets, judicatory committees, staff functions, seminary professorships, or people who had the opportunity to write for magazines and newspapers. The number of these positions was already limited, and had been commonly reserved for senior ordained clergy. Now, as mainline denominational structures shrink, these traditional opportunities and platforms are becoming more scarce—and less influential. However, today, with just a Facebook profile, an Instagram account, and Twitter feed, conversational influence in the church can be just as great or greater than those in more traditional roles. You can have a disproportionately large influence within the denomination, community, and congregation. (That's how several years ago a parish pastor in Woburn, Massachusetts, could wind up writing this book with a professor in San Jose, California.)

Even small congregations can have a robust presence and influence in the new media landscape. Well before the Rev. Nadia Bolz-Weber (who we profile in more detail in chapter 4) rose to national prominence and church stardom with her best-selling book *Pastrix* in 2013, her congregation, House for All Sinners and Saints (HFASS), exerted an outsized influence within the larger church. Founded in 2008 as a mission start of the Evangelical Lutheran Church in America (ELCA), House for All Sinners and Saints lacked all the traditional media platforms, yet its ministry was and continues to be highly influential. Congregations around the country incorporate some of their signature events such as Beer and Hymns, Blessing of the Bicycles, and Theology Pub in their own ministries. While these practices did not originate with HFASS, they have become identified with the community (at least in the ELCA) precisely because of Bolz-Weber's and the congregation's active social media presence.

Certainly, many other communities have developed and practice innovative and engaging ministries. But according to Bolz-Weber, the influence such ministries has earned HFASS in the wider church has everything to do with how social media has allowed them to be part of a widely distributed narrative of the church and its ministries.

In 2011, when we first interviewed her for this book, Bolz-Weber told us:

> Our church is very well known for being such a small church. Our average worship attendance is seventy people. But we do have a big presence. It's helped us make our case for why the ELCA should keep supporting us. We're like, "You're not just helping pay for a pastor for less than a hundred people. You're helping provide this laboratory where we get to experiment with stuff and publish our results, which has been really useful for people serving other churches that aren't laboratories."

In the intervening years, we have seen grassroots organizations like #occupy and #blacklivesmatter, and church movements like #decolonizelutheranism that have no preexisting institutional structure or support use social media and other digital tools to build an organizational infrastructure, fundraise, and build effective communications platforms.[2]

Before exploring how you and your congregation can develop your own integrated platform for digital ministry, be aware that some of the most important things we do in social media are listening and responding to what people are saying on their platforms. We can and should respond to other's posts by commenting, liking, sharing on Facebook, retweeting and mentioning on Twitter, and leaving blog comments. Indeed, we believe it is possible to have a meaningful presence without investing loads of time managing your own particular platform. Your initial strategy may be to respond to the content and activity of others. Even once you are up and running, it's a good practice to spend more time responding to others than promoting yourself.

In the remainder of the chapter, we will overview the main features of each of the major legacy and emerging social media platforms, and the digital practice that they foster. Each section concludes with a summary of different levels of practice on the platform using traditional religious categories borrowed from monasticism as a way to mark increasing maturity of digital ministry practice: Novice (beginner), Oblate (initiated member), and Superior (expert).

Legacy Platforms

Facebook, Twitter, YouTube, and blogs are what we categorize here as legacy platforms. While they still may be new to some, they are among the biggest, most influential, and enduring social media platforms. Facebook has in many ways become the default social network of choice, receiving wide adoption, driven particularly by the over forty crowd. For younger adults, Facebook functions largely as an open email site. Twitter, while smaller, has helped to shape the cultural zeitgeist, and has become a hub for activism and news. While most other social media platforms incorporate video, YouTube is still *the* place for video sharing. And, though many tech observers have declared the death of blogging, blogs continue to be effective ways to share ideas and shape conversations. Finally, LinkedIn, purchased by Microsoft in 2016, continues to be the social network of choice for professionals. Although the platform is used by many ministry leaders, we've come to the conclusion that it's less useful in digitally integrated ministry practice, so we haven't carried it forward in the second edition.

3.1 Facebook

Origins	Created in 2004 by Mark Zuckerberg
Number of Users	Over 1.8 billion users worldwide,[3] 79 percent of all US internet users are on Facebook, which represents 68 percent of the entire US adult population[4]
Typical User	Facebook usage is high among all demographics. Users are slightly more likely to be women under the age of fifty. See chapter 1.
Key Features	Personal profile, groups, pages, events. Users can check in, post photos, text, videos, live video, and polls. Users can comment on and share content. Messenger app for direct messages.
Benefits of Participation	Almost everyone on social media is on Facebook, so you can reach the largest number of people for your effort. People tend to be most familiar with how to use Facebook.
Limitations	Changing Facebook algorithm effects what and how much people see from their friends, Facebook pages, and news sources. Younger generations are not as active on Facebook.
Practices	Checking in, sharing, interacting

THE BASICS

Facebook enables users to tell a media-rich story to the largest number of people across generations—from teens to grandparents. It is the social networking platform that people tend to use most and understand best.

Facebook is excellent for:

- Sharing a variety of content: pictures, videos, music, links, text
- Sharing links to content from other content sources, such as blogs and YouTube
- Promoting and coordinating events
- Connecting with parishioners, across generational lines
- Leveraging existing contacts—most Facebook friends are already friends (or friends of friends) off-line
- Communicating with and responding to others, either publicly or privately

Digital ministry novices and those with limited time should take Facebook as a starting point. With so many users and the ability to share multiple forms of content, you get the most mileage for your digital time. Facebook is also a great environment for learning the multimedia ropes of the social networking landscape more generally. Through Facebook, you can share not just a personal or community profile and regular status updates, but also pictures, videos, music, longer notes, live video, and geolocation check-ins. The process for adding such content on other social networking sites is largely the same.

Remember, however, that there are millions of people *not* on Facebook or who are also active elsewhere online—often more than they are on Facebook. For example, while teenagers and young adults are likely to have Facebook accounts, they tend to be far less active than their older counterparts. The teens in Keith's church have likened Facebook to email: you have to have it, but it's really not as fun as other ways to connect and communicate. So, once you build competence on Facebook, you'll definitely want to venture further into other platforms.

Within Facebook there are four main venues for telling your story: your personal profile, pages, groups, and events. We'll start with the profile, but many of the practices we discuss here are applicable to Facebook pages, groups, and events as well.

FACEBOOK PROFILE

Your personal profile or timeline is the heart of your Facebook presence. Your profile is your digital identity in the Facebook community, sharing (on your "about" tab) not just your name, birthday, and location, family connections, and professional status, but a full range of perspectives on your life as revealed in photos, videos, favorite quotes, interests, political views, and the often vexed category of "religious views." Your Facebook profile allows people you already know to find you, and invites those with similar interests or friends in common to connect to you and to each other.

The key with any social media profile, as we learned in the previous chapter, is that it should be *consistent* and *authentic*. Just as importantly, it should also be *informative* and *welcoming*. Your profile on any platform should be identifiably you. Fill in as much information about yourself as you feel comfortable sharing, so that people can identify you as a ministry leader in a particular setting. If your profile picture is of your cat and none of your personal information is public, people won't know it's you and won't know or bother to connect. Ultimately, people are more likely to learn about you from your recent posts than from your profile details, so be sure to post with some regularity, and keep your personal information up to date.

The Facebook timeline was just introduced as we went to print on the first edition and we noted then how ministry leaders were using this new format, including the cover photo, to create a welcoming public presence. When we looked at UCC pastor Kim Morrow's profile, we saw a warm and smiling California transplant to Lincoln, Nebraska, whose life extended from ministry to family to vibrant gatherings at an Omaha sushi restaurant. Morrow used videos from her church, of her daughter's inspired back stoop musical performances, photos of the family lounging at home or zipping around the go-cart race track, and links to spiritual and political content to round out the profile of a vibrant, reflective, active ministry leader. A video, which Morrow introduced by posting, "This is what I do on Sundays," shared her offering an awe-inspiring rendition of prayers of the people with a soulful rendition of "Come, Bring Your Burdens to God" offered in the background by the First Plymouth UCC choir. This portrait was so much richer and more dynamic than any church website could be because it was updated much more regularly—several times a week to several times a day. People see who Morrow is as a minister, a mother, a friend, and a community leader because they get an ongoing glimpse of her everyday life. Today, Morrow works for a company that helps organizations to develop greater environmental sustainability and resilience. Her professional Facebook profile and social media presence, and that of her organization, speak to the importance of care for creation and environmental sustainability. Our social media can and should evolve with us, along with us and our work.

FACEBOOK PAGES

Facebook pages function as extensions of a church or organizational webpages—ones which can be more easily updated as often as needed. For most churches, this is the foundation of their social media presence. Most pages are public on Facebook, so anyone can see or like your page, whether they are already a member a not, so it's important to keep in mind that pages have a combination of external but interested and existing internal audiences. People only need to click the "like" button at the top of the page to like and follow you. After that, your updates show up in their news feed. Following a page is easy, but rather passive. You'll want to generate interest and activity through your posts. You may share inspiration quotes, scenes from the life of your congregation, stories of your members, sermon podcasts, faith formation resources, and more. It can be your own content or quality content created by others. Make sure to maintain visual interest by including photos, videos, events, and links along with written updates. Pay attention to what kind of content people respond to most (you might be surprised) and keep that kind of content in regular rotation on your page.

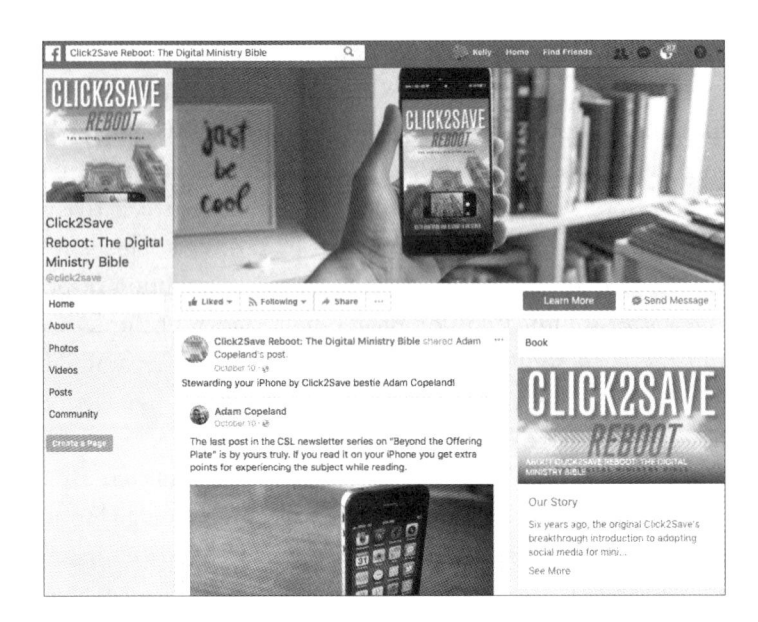

It's a good idea to post something every day to keep the page current. A daily post—even a short quote or a photo from your community archives—will help to keep the page vital and dynamic. Facebook pages allow page administrators to schedule posts into the future, so you could schedule an entire week's worth of posts or more in just one sitting (but it shouldn't feel too automated). A Facebook page can have multiple administrators who have authority to manage, post, and moderate the comments if necessary. It's a good idea to have multiple admins if only for redundancy, and, when possible, to help share the load in managing the page and responding to comments and messages.

If you intend to share the same piece of content on both your ministry page and your personal profile, it's a good idea to post on your ministry page first. From there, share it to your profile. A link to the ministry page will appear along with the content you are sharing. This will point people back to your page and encourage them to follow it.

Keep in mind that your page may provide the only exposure to the Gospel or spirituality people encounter in their work-a-day lives. While social media engagement ideally leads to face-to-face relationships, this doesn't always happen. For some, a Facebook page is a spiritual end in itself. So, it's important to be sure your posts are not all about driving people to your webpage or through the church doors. Providing inspiration, encouragement, or formational insight right there on the page is an important part of your ministry. Indeed, this spiritual element of the Facebook experience is undoubtedly why religious pages are the most popular on Facebook, routinely outranking Justin Bieber and Lady Gaga.[5]

You don't need to post only about your church. Post about the issues and concerns that matter to your faith community. Bishop Dan Edwards of the Episcopal Diocese of Nevada, who oversees his diocese's Facebook page, frequently posts reflections and information on addiction and recovery, which are pressing issues in his territory, in addition to sharing information about the diocese itself.

FACEBOOK PAGE ADS

To promote visibility of your page or content, posts can be "boosted" to be seen more frequently or by more people. Facebook ads are an affordable option for promoting your quality content or special events. Using the aggregated data Facebook collects on its users, you can target a specific audience based on their age, location, and interests—and you set your own budget. Your audience can be as narrow as the people that already like your page, or much broader to their friends, or far beyond. Keith's church creates Facebook ads leading up to Christmas and Easter or when they have a particularly nice piece of content, often a photo or video, they want to promote. Ads will appear more frequently within the main Facebook news feed, and on the right-hand side of the desktop browser window with other ads. A little note will appear next to the post that says "sponsored."

Alex Montes-Vela, priest at St. Mary Magdalene Episcopal Church in Manor, Texas, outside of Austin, uses Facebook ads to invite neighbors to participate in community baptisms. Anthony Guillen lauds this digital ministry:

> A lot of the success around [Alex's] ministry has been in social media. He announces public baptisms at the local park. He says, "Are you interested in being baptized, do you know someone that wants to be baptized, do you have a child or nephew or family member who you think would like

to be baptized? We're having a baptism on such a date in such a place." He then targets that announcement to that community and people are starting to respond and say, "Yes," and they ask questions. He says he has 70 to 80 percent retention from those baptisms. He does it four or five times a year.

Like a modern-day John the Baptist, Montes invites people to the life-changing waters of baptism, not as a voice in the wilderness but through word of mouth on Facebook.

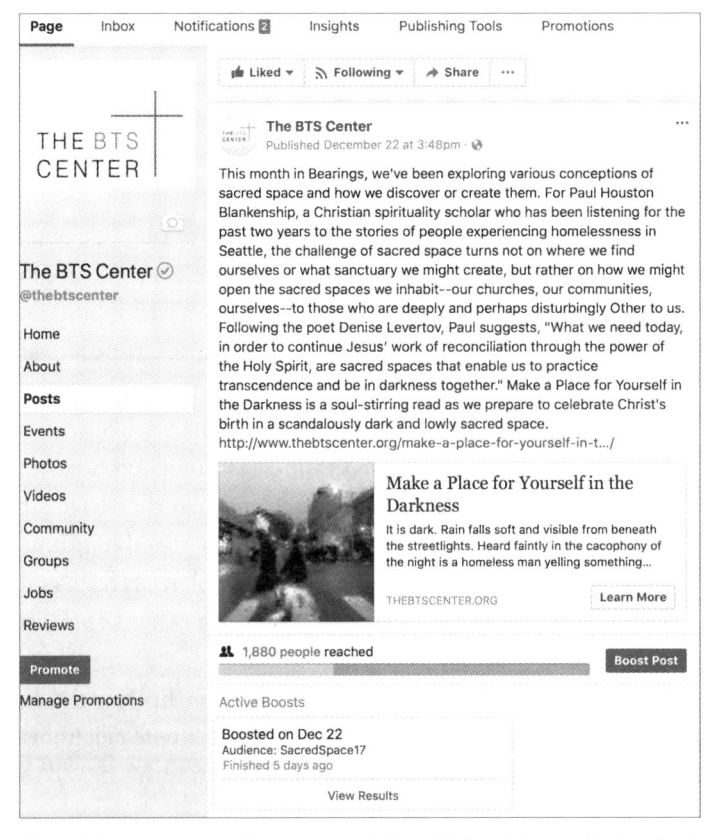

The BTS Center, a twenty-first-century ministry think tank located in Portland, Maine, uses Facebook boosts to extend the reach of its award-winning *Bearings* magazine.

FACEBOOK GROUPS

While Facebook pages are designed to reach a broad, public audience, Facebook groups are designed to connect with a more targeted and generally smaller group of people. Groups tend to be more conversational and egalitarian in nature. They can be "open" so that anyone can join, or "closed," requiring visitors to request permission or be added by the administrator.

In our estimation, it makes sense to create closed groups when the conversation is meant to be more intimate and unguarded. For example, we know of churches that use Facebook to enrich the space between face-to-face covenant groups, spiritual guidance circles, or theology pub cohorts. And, generally, groups for teens should be private.

However, we chafe at the idea of religious groups of a more general nature—Bible study, for instance, or social concerns groups—being closed to "outsiders." Access to such groups can give visitors and inquirers insight into the workings of your community, offer welcome, and form the basis of relationships that may develop further into face-to-face engagement and worship. We are particularly troubled when we come across church pages—the Yellow Pages listing of the internet—that are closed to outsiders. Such practices may salve an anxiety about eroding privacy in the Digital Age, but they send the worst kind of message to those seeking to learn about your church or organization. It just seems, well, unchristian to lock your digital doors in this way.

Facebook groups tend to work best for internal communication. It is common to use Facebook groups for smaller groupings within the congregation. With features like group chat, for example, or the ability to share documents and post events and pictures, they are equally useful for youth groups or church committees. Members of the groups, by default, receive Facebook notifications (which they can turn off, if they wish) when something new is posted. The benefit here is that they won't miss a message on your Facebook group, if they don't happen to be on Facebook that day. Keith's theology pub group, "God on Tap," started with a Facebook page but later determined a group was better because it encouraged more engagement. In addition to updates about their monthly gatherings, the group administrator posts fun links about God and beer.

FACEBOOK EVENTS

Facebook events are an effective way of generating engagement on Facebook and drawing people to your in-person gatherings. You can create events from your profile, group, or page. Give the event a name, description, specify the dates and time of the event, give it an interesting cover photo, and you're on your way. You can then invite people to the event and promote it with a Facebook ad. (Ads are only available through pages, so you will be asked which page you want to use to create the ad.) When people RSVP or express interest, it often appears in their friends' news feeds, organically spreading the word, and building momentum by showing how many people have replied. You can also post within the event itself, allowing the opportunity to share information, promote conversation, and build excitement in participants before, during, and after the event.

FACEBOOK LIVE

One of the newest features is Facebook Live, where pages and profiles can stream live video, which is simultaneously recorded and remains on Facebook for people to view later. Facebook Live and other live video services help to share what is happening in the moment, and facilitate real-time interaction within and across people's and organizations' social networks. Facebook has invested heavily in this new technology. It is such a priority that they have placed it on the main menu bar across the top of its mobile app, along with buttons to post photos and check-ins.

Many churches have turned to Facebook Live rather than more complex streaming services like LiveStream or UStream to broadcast their Sunday services and sermons. Alyssa Bereznak writes, "Though the concept of livestreaming sermons is by no means novel—hundreds of religious institutions across the continent offer some form of online spiritual guidance—Facebook Live offers accessibility to houses of worship that once found the technology too cumbersome or expensive."[6] Lutheran Pastor Geoff Sinabaldo, who regularly broadcasts his sermons on Facebook Live, argues:

> Facebook Live connects your community immediately to the outside world. It is in a sense pure evangelism, proclaiming the gospel in a public space, where anyone, anywhere, immediately (or later on in your feed)

can hear a sermon, see what your congregation is all about, and connect with you as a leader. Critics will say, "Putting the sermon online will just teach people not to go to church in person." I have found the opposite to be true. While attendance has remained steady, those who engage the sermon through Facebook Live have grown to a group often larger than those in the physical space. I figure if these folks are otherwise not engaged by a faith community or would not set foot in the church for whatever reason, why not try to connect with them? Having done it for a while now, I find that my people not only like and comment, they also share the link on their own feeds when they find a message particularly poignant or meaningful to them.

Episcopal priest Anthony Guillen believes live video will only grow in popularity. He says:

> Live video streaming is big. We have a congregation in Maryland that is live video streaming on Facebook Live. They are sending reminders about half an hour before the service that they're going to be live video streaming the service and hundreds of people from Latin America mostly, because the pastor is from El Salvador, but hundreds of people connect and watch. They are getting tremendous response to the live video streaming of the Eucharist. I imagine that that's going to be happening more. I imagine that there is going to be an explosion of Facebook Live users in the very near future.

Facebook Live is especially good for capturing life in the moment without the pressure of having to post a more finished product that would require video editing skill and time. On a recent trip with young adults from his congregation, Keith posted a Facebook live video every morning. While only a few people watched it live, many more watched and commented on the video later, and it remains an archive of the trip experience. Alternatively, you can schedule a specific time for people to tune in to your Live video, just as they would a television show. Keith did this for a conversation he hosted with Bethany Stolle about teens and digital media. He scheduled the conversation for 8:00 p.m. on a Monday night and encouraged people to tune in on his church's Facebook page. Those who watched live shared their questions in the comments below the video, and Keith and Bethany responded in real time. Because Live videos are automatically saved, people who could not watch live were able to go back and watch the recording afterward.

As we noted at the beginning of the chapter, Facebook is by far the most accessible, easiest-to-use social network with the furthest demographic reach. You'll likely want to start your digital ministry there, depending on your context. But if you've already been on Facebook for a while, you can still grow your digital ministry skills. Before moving on to Twitter and the other platforms that follow, assess where you are in Facebook digital ministry expertise:

Novice

- Create a Facebook profile that includes
    - A casual picture of yourself. If you're clergy, this can be in a collar, but make sure it's a relaxed, rather than formal, photo that will make you more relatable. And smile.
    - Some basic information about you, your background, and your interests.
    - Upload some photos that will give people a sense of your everyday life as a minister and a person in general.
- Link to personal and church platforms.
- Like other people's posts, ten times a week.
- Notice people's birthdays and celebrate a bit with them by posting a birthday greeting on their profile.
- Make friend requests to people already in your personal and professional networks.
- Let your church or organization know you're active on Facebook in a newsletter, email list, or other regular communication (even a sermon).

Oblate

- Post at least three times a week.
- Check in.
- Comment on others' posts at least once a day.
- Add more information to your profile like music preferences or favorite quotes.
- Actively share links to online news and magazine articles that you think will be of interest to people in your network.

- Practice offering a "Quote of the Week" or an inspirational photo or video.
- Create a group or page for your organization and invite friends to join.
- Add photos and videos of your community in action (and reflection) to the group or page.

Superior

- Post at least once a day.
- Use weekend slow-read time for in-depth articles and blog links.
- Invite engagement by asking questions and facilitating conversation.
- Post a mix of content: pictures, video, live video, text, check-ins.
- Tag people in your posts.
- Connect your Facebook page(s) to other social media platforms, like Twitter, Pinterest, Instagram, and your blog.
- Experiment with Facebook Live to broadcast church events or engage with people in real-time.

3.2 Twitter

Origins	Created in 2006 by Jack Dorsey, Evan Williams, Biz Stone, and Noah Glass
Number of Users	310 million users worldwide,[7] 65 million in the United States,[8] 23 percent of all US online adults, 20 percent of the entire US population,[9] 33 percent of teens use Twitter[10]
Typical User	More likely to be male, African-American or Latino, under 50[11]
Key Features	Short-form tweets of 280 characters or less, not including links or media content; hashtags, retweets, mentions, direct messages (no character limit)
Benefits of Participation	Entry into a global conversation, discover new connections beyond existing friends or community, access to breaking news, amplifies voices
Limitations	Small user base, most people in congregations likely not on Twitter, can be hard to learn
Practices	Checking in, sharing, exploring, interacting

THE BASICS

When it was first launched in 2006, Twitter described itself as a micro-blogging platform, with every post or "tweet" limited, until very recently, to 140 characters, including the spaces between words. As we were editing this edition in the fall of 2017, Twitter doubled the character limit to 280. Over a decade later, Twitter, while home to far fewer users than Facebook, has become enormously influential in our public life, as we have seen in social justice movements like #blacklivesmatter and in our national politics where presidential tweets drive the daily news cycle. Today, as Gary Vaynerchuk writes, "Twitter is the cocktail party of the internet," host to millions of conversations about every topic imaginable, constantly configured and reconfigured, all in real time.[12] As we have seen firsthand, a single tweet can have a large impact, and the aggregation of those tweets over time tells a more extended story about you, your interests, ministry, character, and networks of relationships. Indeed, the personal, institutional, and social narrative that is unfolding on Twitter is seen as so significant that the Library of Congress intends to archive tweets for future study by scholars and other cultural commentators.[13] Given the diverse participation by people of faith on Twitter, scholars will have an enormous body of data on current religious beliefs, spiritual practices, and other elements in global religious life.

Twitter is an open platform—that is, anyone can see your tweets, whether or not they follow you—that allows you to:

- Comment on news and events
- Participate in open, public conversations
- Create new contacts
- Find real-time information and breaking news locally and from around the world
- Develop professional connections
- Participate in a broader conversation
- Invite people to your website by linking to webpage and other online profiles
- Coordinate groups for social action
- Connect with people on the go

Whereas Facebook leverages your existing real-life social network, Twitter connects you to people beyond your existing social networks based on shared interests. Of course, you'll want to connect with people you already know. However, you can also find people with similar interests and join in geographically distributed—often global—public conversations. It's relatively easy to find people with common interests by simply typing any word, phrase, or hashtag into the Twitter search bar along the top of the webpage or app.

For the most part, anyone can be followed on Twitter. While some people do "lock" their Twitter profiles so permission is required to follow, as with Facebook friends, this practice is not common on Twitter. That means that you're able to follow almost any church, religious organization, ministry colleague, religious thinker, writer, and so on whose minute-by-minute, day-by-day thinking interests you. And, it's likely that many of these people will follow you back, opening the door to tweeted dialogue. It is for this reason that Pastor David Hansen calls Twitter his "online ministerium."

Like Facebook, Twitter enables users to post using a variety of content. While at first tweets had been limited to text and links (in the early days you needed third-party services just to post a picture), users can now post photos and videos, which can be edited within the Twitter app itself, live video through Periscope (more below), polls, or gifs, and share their location. With Twitter's recent announcement that media attachments no longer count against your 280 character limit, users can now say more in every tweet.

DON'T BE AN EGGHEAD

Over the years, the Twitter profile has come to resemble the Facebook timeline design with a profile photo, cover image, and brief self-description, your location, and a link to a website if you have one. As we advised above, make your profile consistent across platforms and identifiably yours.

On Twitter, people get to know each other less from a profile presentation than from conversations, but you do want to make sure to post an engaging profile picture so you're not an anonymous Twitter "egghead." Wit and succinct substance are virtues on Twitter, so take care even with your self-description. Spend some time looking at other people's profiles to get a sense of the cultural norms in your neck of the Twitter neighborhood. It's also not a bad idea to include hashtags in your personal profile, so that when people search for a particular hashtag, your profile will appear, identifying you as someone connected to that conversation.

Once you've set up your profile and followed some people, join the conversation. What follows here are some of the basics of entering the Twitter conversation. On the whole, it's probably a good idea to take some time listening to the conversation before you jump in. If you're not quite sure what to say, it's a good practice to begin with replying to or retweeting other people's tweets. This gives you meaningful content to share and shows that you are paying attention to others' ideas.

BREVITY IS THE SOUL OF DIGITALLY INTEGRATED MINISTRY WIT

Twitter users have devised a variety of strategies for saying what they want to say in 280 characters or less. Twtspk and Txtspk—abbreviations for Twitterspeak and Textspeak—is the abbreviated lexicon originally drawn from the early days of cellphone texting that helps tweeters to keep tweets within the 280 character limit. For the most part, this involves dropping vowels and using the first letters of common phrases, as in the well-known LOL, "laughing out loud," or IMHO, "in my humble opinion." If you aren't sure what a particular phrase means, there are a huge variety of websites that offer Twtspk dictionaries—just google "Twitter abbreviations."

However, it's important not to go overboard. Everyone doesn't use the same set of abbreviations, and abbreviations for complex thoughts can be particularly confusing. Moreover, the idea of Twitter is to keep it short so conversation can move along among groups of followers. Even if you were able to get the Lord's Prayer down to 280 characters, no one would really want to decode and read it.

In those times when you have an idea that just can't fit in 280 characters, some users spread an idea over several tweets ending their tweets with (1/3), (2/3), (3/3) for, in this case, a three-tweet-worthy idea. For something more extensive, you can create a longer Twitter thread by replying to your own original tweet and just removing your username at the beginning of each new tweet. Some people will share a longer statement by posting a picture of written text with their tweet.

On the whole, however, shorter is better. We know brevity can be a challenge for a great many ministry leaders, but as Adam Copeland observes, "The conciseness that Twitter requires actually leads to creativity." An in-person conversation does not consist of one person talking all the time; neither does a digital one. So keep it punchy and short and focus on the interaction and engagement, and keeping the conversation going.

Kyle Oliver, who from 2012 to 2016 served as a digital missioner for The Episcopal Church, advises ministry leaders to "find what you love to do within these platforms." He says:

> I like Twitter. I like wordplay. I like writing. I like being present on Twitter and that's where I find some juice and some sustenance for my work. Twitter at its best is really playful. I'm a pretty serious person, but playfulness is really important and Twitter is a place where I can be playful. I'm not great at being playful in Bible study, but because I'm a writer, because I like jokes, because I like games, Twitter works for me.

He continues:

> What I value most about Twitter is that it's so much easier to hear from and speak to people that you don't necessarily know and to do that in a playful way and a concise way is what I love about Twitter. Twitter at its best acknowledges the reality that with strangers we may only have a passing correspondence and that's okay. Not every relationship we have, not every interaction we have, has to be super deep and imbued with deep meaning and evangelical potential. Just showing and participating as who we are is huge and for me that place where I can do that the most authentically is Twitter.

RESPONDING TO OTHERS

There are four main ways that you can respond to others on Twitter. Three of them are listed at the bottom of every tweet: likes, replies, retweets. The fourth, mentions, is a standard way of engaging with others.

Likes

Most basically, you can simply show your appreciation by clicking the heart icon at the bottom of the tweet. (Your likes are also catalogued and listed on your profile page so you can go back and revisit tweets you found noteworthy. Some people use this as a way of "bookmarking" tweets so they can return to them later.)

Replies

Replies on Twitter are essentially the same as replying to an email, although your response, like most everything on Twitter, is public. Click the reply arrow and a new blank tweet will appear with the username of the person you are replying to. If other users are mentioned in the tweet, their usernames will appear and be included in your reply as well.

Retweets

Retweeting is a way of sharing a tweet that someone else has written. You might share it because it's useful, fun, or you want to give that person a shout-out. When you tap the retweet icon, you are presented with two choices. First, "retweet" simply shares the original tweet just as it is with your followers. You might use this when you feel something like, "I couldn't have said that better myself." Second, "Quote tweet" allows you to add your own perspective and editorial comment by including a new tweet of your own along with the original tweet. You might use this to create emphasis, laying on an additional idea, or to object to or qualify the original tweet. Retweeting is a good way to share content when you aren't sure what to say or aren't feeling particularly witty.

Mentions

Mentions are simply when you include someone's Twitter username in a tweet. This could happen in the context of a reply, or you can add a username to a tweet when you are referring to that person, want to bring something to their attention, or want to bring them into a conversation. For example, Michael Crosbie, editor-in-chief at *Faith and Form*, the Interfaith Journal of Religion, Art, and Architecture (@faithandform), who runs a great Twitter account highlighting a wide range of religious architecture, will often include mentions to highlight stories of religious architecture and community that might be of interest to particular followers.

NOTIFICATIONS

How do you keep up with all these replies, retweets, mentions, and messages? Twitter will provide notifications for any and all of these activities within the Twitter app and website, and even via email. In your account settings, select "Notifications" and determine what items for which you would like to receive notifications, and how you'd like to receive them.

LISTS

Even though tweets are only 280 characters, if you follow enough people, it can be hard to keep up. One way to organize tweets from various followers is to create lists for different groupings of tweeps. You might have a list for parishioners, community leaders, other ministers, thought leaders, or people that share your interests. You can create, view, and manage your lists through your profile page. Conveniently, you can also follow other people's public lists as well. So, if someone has already created a great list of pub theologians, you can follow right along.

DIRECT MESSAGES

These are private messages sent back and forth directly between two users. It's like email or Facebook messages, and it has no character limit. People often reach out via private message to connect further or communicate information that might not be for public consumption.

HASHTAGS

Hashtags are words or short phases (without spaces between words) that begin with the # symbol. These are ways of organizing or indexing conversations on Twitter and now on other social networks, most notably Instagram (more below). Clicking or tapping on a hashtag will show all the tweets using that hashtag (you can choose to view top tweets or all tweets), and usher you into a real-time conversation or ongoing community of interest. Today, hashtags appear on the broadcast of most TV shows and sporting events.

Viewers and fans engage in conversation on their mobile devices or "second screen" as they watch the game or show.

Sometimes hashtags are used just for fun, and other times for meaningful theological conversation. For instance, Mihee Kim-Kort facilitates conversations on intersectionality using the hashtag #presbyintersect. She also coined the hashtag #realclergybios where she and other clergy described their work in a funny, profound, and heartbreaking fashion. Much of the time, hashtags are rather utilitarian. Towns and neighborhoods like Keith's hometown of Ambler will designate a commonly agreed upon hashtag, here #Ambler, for community related tweets. Consider using a unique hashtag for your church.

PRAYING THE MANHUNT ON TWITTER

Keith remembers the moment he realized what a powerful platform Twitter can be for ministry:

> Many of the community leaders in the previous community I served—from our library, Boys and Girls Clubs, YMCA, to community organizers, activists, and neighbors—are active on Twitter. Through Twitter, I was able to interact with them, share information, become more aware of their work and make them more aware of ours.
>
> This all came to have much more than social meaning in the late summer of 2011, when a police officer was shot while responding to a robbery at a local jewelry store.
>
> Twitter immediately lit up about the incident, with tweets from news outlets, community leaders, and residents. Most people used the hashtag #woburn—the general hashtag used for community information—to tag their posts. For much of the day, Woburn was trending on Twitter. So, I jumped in and started retweeting posts.
>
> One suspect had been apprehended. Three other suspects were on the loose, considered armed and dangerous. It was a manhunt. Local and state police, SWAT teams, helicopters were all on scene. There were road blocks. Door to door searches. Schools and the YMCA were in lockdown. Residents were urged to stay inside with their doors locked.
>
> It was chilling. One person tweeted, "Police searching the woods near my house in west #Woburn. I can see them out the window. This is very scary."

I was retweeting news and information as quickly as it came in.

Then I realized that my role, not only as a resident of Woburn, but as a minster in this community, was to try to offer some measure of solace, support, and to point to God's presence in a horrific and confusing situation. So, I began to tweet prayers:

> We pray for the safety of #Woburn residents and the police. Lord have mercy.
> We pray that his manhunt comes to a just and peaceful conclusion. Lord have mercy. #Woburn
> We pray for those who weep and watch and work this night. Lord have mercy. #Woburn

I know these prayers connected because they were retweeted by members of the Woburn community—ordinary residents and leaders alike. Kathi Johnson, a tweeter from Texas, even appropriated one of the prayers to prayer for the central Texas fires.

> "We pray for those who weep and watch and work this night. Lord have mercy. #Woburn #centraltxfires"

She said later, "It struck me how tenuous both situations are and the prayer seemed right for this, too."

At an earlier community event I joked about being a "Twitter chaplain," but on that day it was no joke. And I was pastor to a community of people in Woburn and beyond that were trying to make sense of the violence and tragedy that had just happened.

LIVE TWEETING

Hashtags can also be used for events in a practice called "live tweeting." Church conference organizers will often designate a unique hashtag for a particular event. All the tweets from the event attendees can be found via the hashtag, allowing each individual to contribute and experience the event from multiple perspectives. When deciding on what hashtag to use for your event or topic, search Twitter first to see if anyone else is using it. Choosing a unique hashtag helps filter out the "noise" of other conversations that might be employing the same hashtag. Most annual events include the year of the conference to distinguish it from previous gatherings. When the event is concluded, capture the conversation using the website Storify to archive all the hashtagged tweets to include with the other records of the event.

#SLATESPEAK

The Slate Project, "church with a clean slate," a mission start church in Baltimore sponsored by the ELCA, The Episcopal Church, and the PCUSA, uses a range of social media, including Twitter, to extend its in-person gatherings and to nurture a digitally integrated congregation that reaches far beyond Baltimore.[14]

Slate Project uses Twitter and hashtags extensively in its ministry. They use the hashtag #breakingbread to accompany their Monday dinner church worship gatherings. On Wednesday mornings, they use #wakeupwordup to share and invite a larger digital audience into their weekly Bible study. Wednesday nights they host #slatereads for a live Twitter chat book discussion.

Finally, on Thursdays at 9 p.m. Eastern time, the Slate Project hosts a Tweetchat—a live-tweeted, digital-only, facilitated gathering—called #slatespeak, which they describe as "a live-chat on Twitter with an edgy, radical, progressive bent on a variety of topics."[15] Rev. Sara Shisler Goff explains:

> We have a tweetchat every Thursday night and the topic usually has to do with our theme for the season. We recommend that everybody read an article or watch a video so we have a common starting point. But we also intentionally include sharing of who we are. We're starting to introduce times for prayer requests at the end, so really caring for each other and then beginning and ending with prayer. So, it really is church happening in real time online with people who actually are all over the world. We have someone who lives in Germany and gets up at 3 a.m. . . . and makes popcorn and joins in faithfully every week.[16]

Almost everyone we know in ministry who uses Twitter has taken a while to warm up to the genre. In part, this is because Twitter is used extensively for advertising and for the often narcissistic ramblings of celebrities and politicians. It gets noisy quickly. And most of us in ministry are, well, a bit committed to the Word in its more verbose forms. As Elizabeth has said of her self-described "lazy blogger" practice, "Three or four paragraphs? I'm just getting warmed up by then!"

But when you take care in selecting a community of Tweeters to follow, and develop lists that organize various conversations, participating on Twitter can be a richly rewarding experience, connecting its users to a worldwide community of believers and seekers who are anxious to be in conversation about many issues facing the church. As we saw in chapter 1, Twitter is particularly popular among African Americans and Latina/o Americans, demographics sorely underrepresented in most mainline churches. That fact alone is reason enough to join in the conversation.

As you get started, or raise the bar on your Twitter preparation, take some time to reflect on your current level of expertise and how you might grow:

Novice

- Include a profile picture, cover photo
- Create a succinct, perhaps witty, description, including hashtag when applicable
- Link your profile to personal or church website
- Find people you know and find others with similar interests using Twitter search
- Retweet at least once a day

Oblate

- Tweet two to four times a day
- Share content from your blog, Instagram, or YouTube
- Engage others in conversation (you don't have to already know them)
- Use a social media dashboard such as Hootsuite or Tweetdeck to track tweet themes of interest to you and your community
- Use hashtags both for humor and to highlight your community and its interests

Superior

- Tweet several times daily
- Integrate other applications, such as Instagram and Facebook, with your Twitter feed
- Participate in Tweetchats and other live tweet events
- Attend a local TweetUp
- Engage in conversations with a variety of followers

3.3 Blogging

LONG-FORM PLATFORMS

Origins	First blog created by Justin Hall in 1994[17]
Number of Users	There are more than 300 million blogs online[18]
Key Features	Long-form writing with ability to incorporate photos and videos, and other media, reader comments, categories and tags for organizing content
Benefits of Participation	Centralized location to share your story and develop your ideas, the written word tends to be a more familiar and more comfortable genre to ministry leaders
Limitations	Sufficient time to write with some regularity, time to maintain a website (even if its hosted elsewhere), because there are so many blogs it can take time to develop a significant readership
Cost	Free, paid upgrades available
Popular Platforms	wordpress.com, blogger.com, medium.com, typepad.com, also self-hosting
Practices	Sharing, archiving

THE BASICS

Once you have a presence on the major social networking sites, it's important to begin generating original content to share with the digital community. The whole idea of sharing your story is to bring your unique perspective on the world, the church, and ministry to a wider community. While profiles can show much of that, and links and content will highlight your interests, you also want to illustrate how you practice ministry, how you bring your faith and training together in service of others. Creating your own content is a vital part of this aspect of digital ministry, and blogging is typically a good first step. Since most ministry training revolves around communicating through the written word, blogs tend to be the most familiar form of storytelling for ministry leaders. The longer written content of blogging is closest (though not the same) social media genre to sermons and traditional newsletter articles or devotional writing. Indeed, many leaders in ministry have started blogging long before they entered other social networking communities.

Frequently, churches and individual ministers use blogs to post sermons, share ideas about or beyond church, and as an online journal or travelogue. Here, stories unfold in each post but also across posts, creating a nuanced, detailed, theologically reasoned arc.

Commentators continually warn that blogging is on its way out, but six years after the first edition of this book, blogging is still going strong.[19] Blogging ranks among the less popular forms of social media engagement. However, while that might be true, there are still millions of people blogging and reading blogs that they share across their digital networks every day. Furthermore, for those who blog well, it remains a highly influential genre.

New media guru Seth Godin offers this advice that inspired Keith to begin blogging and still rings true for him today,

> Blogging is free. It doesn't matter if anybody reads it. What matters is the humility that comes from writing it. What matters is the metacognition of thinking about what you're going to say. How do you explain yourself to your few employees or your cat or whoever is going to look at it? How do you force yourself to describe in three paragraphs why you did something? How do you respond out loud? If you're good at it, some people are going to read it. If you're not good at it and you stick with it, you'll get good at it. . . . Basically you're doing it for yourself to force yourself to be part of the conversation, if it's just that much. And that posture change changes an enormous amount.[20]

Blogs are useful places to experiment, reflect, to work out ideas, and solicit feedback, particularly from those beyond your particular ministry setting. That book you want to write? Start by blogging, capturing moments and ideas, get feedback, and connect the dots.

Blogs are good for:

- Developing and sharing your ideas
- Becoming identified as a "thought leader"
- Becoming a better writer and showcasing your writing
- Starting or influencing conversations in areas of interest
- Serving as a personal webpage
- Accumulating content over time
- Telling a more detailed personal and ministry story
- Mission interpretation and theological reflection
- Making content like sermons, newsletters, and articles easily sharable and searchable
- Documenting a changing church

For individuals, blogs are a powerful way to share ideas and establish yourself as a "thought leader"—someone with particular influence in an area of interest—by creating an online portfolio of your ideas and writing, which is archived, categorized, and searchable. The advantage of having a blog, rather than posting on Facebook in the longer form "notes" feature is that the blog will aggregate and organize your portfolio. It also offers some measure of control over the your content and how it is represented. In social networks, content is fleeting, with much of what is shared having the useful life of a day. Blogs participate in this rapid-change environment, but they are also built for the long haul.

POSTING PRACTICE

Posts are the heart of your blog. You'll no doubt have your own style, but conventional wisdom says that individual posts should be limited to about five hundred to a thousand words, though Keith and Elizabeth often push those limits. Above a thousand words, consider breaking it into multiple posts. Over the last six years we have seen attention spans dramatically shrink. While longer posts may feel more substantial and important, it doesn't matter if no one reads them. Always include at least one image in your post; a "thumbnail" of that image appears when the post is shared on social networks, creating more visual interest and making it more likely that others will click on it. Break up the text through subheadings, and keep paragraphs to two to four short sentences. Take advantage of links. Rather than explaining everything, link to it. This will keep your text focused and lean.

Some people write and post whenever the spirit moves them; however, to build a blog and its readership, a regular schedule for posting is critical. Choose a rhythm that you can commit to, even if only twice a month. In starting out, consistency and quality are more important than volume. Likewise, be consistent in your content. Focus on a few key areas, so readers know what to expect. The occasional off-topic post is fine every now and then, but don't make it a habit.

Pastor Chris Duckworth of New Joy Lutheran Church in Westfield, Indiana, has been blogging at *The Lutheran Zephyr*[21] since 2004 and says, "You've got to be really clear about what the heck you're doing or else you're going to be rambling. And once you set it up, as with anything, you've got to do it. You can't set up a blog and then let your last blog post be nine months ago."

Duckworth also recommends that bloggers periodically reevaluate the focus and purpose of their blogs:

> It's like when you're in high school or college and you've been dating someone or you're more like friends or you're kind of dating and you need to have the Define the Relationship conversation. We call those DTRs. I feel like every now and then I need to have a DTR with my blog. What am I doing with this? Why am I doing this?

Finally, anytime you publish anything online, you are writing for multiple audiences. Write for your primary audiences, whether they are colleagues, members, the community, or friends—but be aware of your secondary audiences. Assume that everyone in your social network will see it. So, for example, even if you're primarily writing for ministry colleagues, you can be sure that plenty of people outside of that circle will have access to your thoughts. Don't say anything in public, even if you mean to be talking only with a specific group of friends, if you wouldn't want everyone known and unknown to you to hear.

BLOG CATEGORIES AND TAGS

Categories and tags help organize your posts. A blog should have a number of main categories. For example, Keith's blog posts are organized under four main categories: social media, spirituality, leadership, and church. These are the main subjects of your blog. Each category can have a larger number of subcategories. Each post can have an unlimited number of tags.

Like categories and subcategories, tags make your content sortable. If someone clicks on a tag, they'll see all the other posts with the same tag. Tags are also important for helping you get discovered on search engines because they appear in the page information, which search engines read and catalog.

ABOUT PAGE

A good "about" page—the page on your blog that introduces you to visitors—is crucial to blogging success. Some say it is the most important page on your blog, and it consistently ranks as one of the most visited pages on any blog. Once people engage your ideas—or often before they do—they want to know a little bit about who you are. So, it's important to prominently link to the "about" page. Be sure to include a picture and information about you and your blog, and describe your areas of interest.

DIRTY SEXY MINISTRY

The Rev. Laurie Brock, rector of the Episcopal Church of St. Michael the Archangel, has hosted a blog called *Dirty Sexy Ministry* on Google's Blogger platform since 2009.[22] The name of the blog was actually suggested by a drag queen during a New Year's Eve party in the French Quarter, which, Brock quips, "is where all good things of Jesus come from." Eight years later, she likes to describe it as "the most disappointing porn site on the internet." The name certainly gets people to pay attention. She says, "One of the most important things in social media is to get people to your site. Nobody's coming if it's not interesting. Nobody wants a blog titled *The Dissection of the Hermeneutic of the Gospel of John.* Nobody's clicking to that site."

For Brock, the practice of blogging is deeply rooted in her ministry practice. It is a platform on which she can share extended thoughts on faith, justice, current events, and more practical ministry considerations. She describes her audience as "people who had their heart broken by the church," which includes people in her church and those well beyond it.

For those considering blogging—and for those that have been at it for some time—Brock offers this insightful question: "How is blogging going to help you establish nurture and maintain a personal connection with your audience?" Most times we start a blog because we feel we have something to say—and that's a perfectly fine way and reason to start—and this is a content-oriented approach. As Brock suggests, we should, sooner rather than later, start to think of our blog as a platform nurturing a relationship to our readers. This orientation toward relationship with your readers helps to focus your content and helps elevate your blog beyond your own personal soapbox into a hub for community, which the very best and most popular blogs, like Rachel Held Evans, do.

When we asked her for her advice for ministry leaders in digital spaces, Brock shared some wisdom about keeping it real as a blogger and ministry leader:

> Trust your brokenness that has been transformed and your vulnerability—that's what the church needs to hear more often. We don't need more "I'm awesome and have my life together" on social media. We need more people on social media, particularly clergy, who are willing to talk about transformation and be vulnerable in that.

PUBLICIZING YOUR POSTS

There are millions upon millions of blogs floating across cyberspace. Mostly, no one ever reads them. This is because the majority of bloggers don't adequately publicize their new content. Some of them are happy with that. Their blogging is more of a digital diary that will flicker on in obscurity until anthropologists in some far-off future come upon it quite by accident. In the context of digital ministry, however, sharing your story is in aid of developing and extending relationships. You want to create opportunities for conversation and connection. And, to do that, you will need to get the word out that you'd love to chat with all those who have eyes to see and ears to hear.

Once a post is written, then, link to it on Facebook and Twitter. On Facebook, share a link to the post (not the home page but the post itself) and provide a small quote or short explanation of what it's about.

On Twitter, share the link with a very brief explanation, including the Twitter handle of anyone you mention in the post or of anyone who might have a particular interest. If it applies, include a hashtag. Keith might add #ambler for his town, #elca for his national denomination, #chsocm for the church and social media tweetchat community. Elizabeth uses #TEC for "The Episcopal Church," often along with #Anglican, so her tweets are signaled to a wider, global community. (Review hashtags and mentions in section 3.2 on Twitter.)

There are also opportunities to engage people more directly in ways that both improve content quality of your blog and enhance its distribution across social networks. For example, occasionally share a draft with other bloggers and get feedback. When they become invested in the post, they will be more likely to share with their networks, which may be better developed. They may even blog a response and keep the conversation going. Send the link specifically via email, on Facebook private message (see section 3.1 above), or via Twitter to individuals you hope will find it of interest or worthy of response.

Mention those individuals you're featuring or whose ideas you're mulling when you share it on Facebook or Twitter. For example, Elizabeth might post on Facebook or Twitter, "Thinking about @prkanderson as 'Twitter Chaplain' for next blog post." Such advance comments are likely to generate conversation or at least cue interest in the forthcoming post—a hook, quote, question to encourage to click (images are important here, too).

BLOG COMMENTS

A blog post may represent your freshest thinking on a topic, but it is only the beginning of the conversation. The comments below the post and on social media are where the conversation really begins. Responding to comments made on the blog itself as well as on Facebook or Twitter will encourage people to engage with you and your ideas. There is no need to respond to every comment, but reply to some—especially the more thoughtful and substantive comments or those of people who are new to your network. When people take the time to comment, they appreciate being acknowledged. Otherwise, you're just like every other broadcast medium where some anonymous person blah, blah, blahs what they think without bothering to pay attention to what anyone else thinks. (Elizabeth calls this "blabcasting.")

On hosting services like Wordpress, the comment systems are built in and can be turned on or off. There are typically a range of options for comment moderation from approving all comments automatically, requiring your approval before they are posted on the site, or blocking certain users. Most of the time comments are constructive and can serve to clarify the ideas in your post. It's a good idea to allow for a range of opinions on your blog—that's how conversations happen—but you do have the right to address people who behave inappropriately.

A good approach to problematic commenters is "progressive discipline." Depending on the tenor of the comment, you might begin by emailing the person and explaining your concerns about the comment, indicating that future such comments will result in the person being blocked from the blog. If it comes to that, have no compunction about blocking anyone who is unwilling to participate in a rational, respectful way. As with such people in the rest of our lives, it's seldom helpful to engage in open argument. And, in a social media setting, remember that your responses are always public.

Surprisingly, remarkable relationships can indeed develop out of the insights and ideas—your self-presentation as a minister—that you share on a blog. This opportunity to connect and engage, to extend the welcome that is the centerpiece of Christian ministry, is why we feel so strongly about focusing our participation in social media communities on developing the kinds of open, inviting content that build relationships and strengthen the wider community of faith. It's not so much about your message per se—it's not so much about you at all—but about the ways in which the words and images you share open the hearts and minds of others to deeper and more engaged, consequential faith.

As you reflect on how blogging currently fits into your personal, professional, or institutional digital ministry strategy, consider where you are on the learning curve and what it will take to move to the next level:

Novice

- Create a blog at a hosted service like wordpress.com, blogger.com, typepad.com, or medium.com
- Create a good "about" page with a picture of yourself

- Post at least once a month
- Read other blogs and comment on one other blog a week
- Define the 3 to 5 topics you will blog about
- Link to your other social media platforms
- Enable people to sign up by email or RSS (most blog services have this built in)

Oblate

- Post four times a month
- Get your own domain name
- Follow a few other similar blogs and occasionally leave a comment

Superior

- Post more than once a week
- Create a self-hosted, customized blog (Wordpress.org is the most popular site that allows extensive customization.)
- Invite guest bloggers to post

3.4 Tumblr

SHORT-FORM BLOGGING

Origins	Founded in 2007 by David Karp, bought by Yahoo! in 2013 for $1.1 billion
Number of Users	More than 280 million Tumblr blogs with over 550 million monthly users;[23] 14 percent of teens use Tumblr; 23 percent of teen girls[24]
Key Features	Easily share images, videos, gifs, short text
Benefits of Participation	Expectations of shorter content; content is more sharable than a traditional blogging platform
Limitations	Tumblr is focused on short-form content. If you want to wax theological for more than 300 words, better to find a more traditional blogging platform
Practices	Sharing, exploring, archiving

THE BASICS

Tumblr is a popular "short-form" blogging platform, which is driven more by images, gifs, memes, and videos than by long-form text. It is more social than most long-form blogs and capitalizes on our short attention spans and the increasing popularity of visual content. Whereas people can also like and comment on Tumblr posts, they can also "reblog" them, essentially sharing them on their own Tumblr. In this way, it is more like a mash-up of a traditional blog and the Facebook news feed. Users can have multiple Tumblrs under one account, so they can easily manage different topics or themes. Tumblr is fun and irreverent, so don't take yourself or you content too seriously.

Tumblr is good for:

- Multimedia content
- Social sharing
- Punchy content
- A running list of things you find fun or interesting

THEMES

A variety of free and paid themes and formats are available. Choose a template that fits your project. Some lend themselves more to written text, while others are more visual and highlight photos or videos.

CONTENT OPTIONS

Each time a new post is created, content options are available:

Text—Text can be long-form like a traditional blog. However, shorter is better when it comes to Tumblr.

Photo—Single or multiple photos can be uploaded and shared. Certain Tumblr themes lend themselves better to displaying photo content

Quote—This option will format your quote into a more artistic look with a larger font for greater visibility

Link—The title of your post will link directly to another website

Chat—You can begin a conversation with your Tumblr followers

Audio—Tumblr will host and play audio files

Video—Tumblr will host and play video files

EVERYDAY I'M PASTORIN'

Check out the Tumblr blog *Ev'ry Day I'm Pastorin'*, which captures the travails and triumphs of ministry all in gifs. Twenty-first-century ministry leaders will want to bookmark it for challenging days that demand a good, hearty laugh.[25] In an interview about the site, the anonymous creator says:

> Gifs seemed to me like memes on steroids—a great visual way of putting emotion into motion. And yes, planning worship with parishioners is sometimes a lot like jumping on an exercise ball on a running treadmill. The inspiration—well, let's keep the mystery and simply say that it involved two United Methodists, a Presbyterian (Wesley and Calvin would be so proud, I'm sure), some Episcopalian and UCC voices, and a very small dog with the name of a Canaanite goddess. That's the way all church nerd blogs are started, right? There also may have been some amount of wine involved.[26]

As with most humor, there is something deeper going on below the surface. In a profound turn, the creator shares:

> So it's mostly catharsis. It's a way of making fun of ourselves, sharing experiences, and occasionally expressing how much we genuinely love our jobs and our people. It's also a way of reaching out and finding community in common experiences. If you're a small church pastor in a Midwestern or deep Southern state, and you're the only one around who doesn't think that President Obama is the antichrist or that queer people are terrible, it can get lonely. This is my way of reaching out and remembering that I'm not alone, and hopefully reminding others that they aren't, either.[27]

If traditional long-form blogging seems intimidating at first, Tumblr can be a good way to get your feet wet. You don't have to produce as much content at first and the sociability of the site will provide you more feedback more quickly so you can hone your blogging craft.

Novice

- Create an account and a single Tumblr blog
- Occasionally share content

Oblate
- Post more frequently
- Reblog content you like and that complements your Tumblr theme

Superior
- Curate multiple Tumblrs with distinct content

Visual Platforms

Visual social media platforms have exploded in popularity in recent years. More people are sharing photos and videos than ever before both on legacy platforms like Facebook and Twitter, as well as entirely new platforms like Instagram and Pinterest, which are designed to highlight visual content. Today, people capture photos and video on their smartphones and edit and upload it to social media platforms in a matter of seconds. We can even broadcast live video, skipping the steps of saving and posting altogether.

Studies show that visual content generates more interest and engagement than text alone. Currently videos attract three times more "likes" than text-only posts and the number of videos appearing on Facebook's newsfeed has increased 3.6 times. Tweets with images earned up to 18 percent more clicks, 89 percent more favorites, and 150 percent more retweets; posts that include images produce 650 percent higher engagement than text only. And it is estimated that by 2018 84 percent of communications will be visual and 79 percent of internet traffic will be video content.[28]

While Facebook usage appears to have plateaued and Twitter and LinkedIn remain stable, Instagram and Pinterest have exploded in popularity, more than doubling their users over the last five years, with Instagram moving from 13 to 28 percent of all online adults and Pinterest 15 to 31 percent.[29] They are particularly popular with younger adults.

These visual storytelling platforms invite us to share our stories, open windows into the life of our communities, and convey sacred moments in images. This can be a challenge for ministry leaders in Reformation traditions that have been text oriented. We are accustomed to telling a good story through the written and spoken word. We are less practiced in the art of visual storytelling. However, those are part of our Christian tradition, particularly in pre-printing press traditions of art and architecture. Elizabeth has called these visual social media "postmodern stained glass,"[30] which provide both windows into the soul, the heart of God, and into the Christian story. Pastor Katy McCallum Sachse observes:

> Visual is big for people. For us as a congregation, and the Lutheran church in general, we're a very verbal, very wordy congregation. So we're not super visual. There are a lot of people who need, and rightfully so, a visual cue. . . . They may not be comfortable going up to somebody and saying, "Hey, let me tell you about my church." But they might show them a photo. It increases the number of ways people can connect.[31]

Instagram and Pinterest invite us to tell visual stories about our lives, the lives of our churches and communities, and to capture sacred and sublime moments in the everyday.

3.5 Instagram

Origins	Launched in 2010, bought by Facebook in 2012 for $1 billion
Number of Users	800+ million monthly users, 500+ million daily users, 250+ million daily active users;[32] 28 percent of all online US adults, 24 percent of the entire population,[33] and 52 percent of all teens 13 to 17 years old use Instagram[34]
Typical User	Women of color between 18 to 29,[35] see chapter 1 for more details
Key Features	Personal profile; post pictures and edit them, choosing from 24 different adjustable "filters" like Twitter; hashtags help users discover similar interests; short videos 60 seconds long
Benefits of Participation	Connecting with much younger, more diverse users in a more elegant platform, visual story-telling, share pictures immediately to other platforms; add locations, tag people, comments
Limitations	You can't refer people to your website because hyperlinks don't work in the comments.
Practices	Sharing, exploring, archiving

THE BASICS

Instagram is an elegant photo and video sharing app especially popular with young adults and teens. Photos and videos (up to 60 seconds long) can be taken from your smartphone camera or selected from your camera roll and then edited by choosing from twenty-three different adjustable "filters." While a caption can and should be included along with lots of hashtags, the focus of Instagram is on the images. A recent major redesign of the app put all the functionalities in grayscale, making it simpler and cleaner, giving the photos even more prominence.[36] Instagram recently also introduced a desktop version at Instagram.com, but it has limited functionality. For the best Instagram experience, use the app.

Instagram is good for:

- Connecting with young adults (under thirty) and teens
- Creating and composing attractive and engaging images using the Instagram filters
- Practicing visual storytelling with photos and videos
- Connecting with people beyond your existing groups of social media friends and followers
- The simplicity of the app creates a less noisy, more peaceful social media environment

PROFILE

Creating and managing your Instagram is much like other social media platforms. Upload a photo for your profile and add a brief personal description, including a website address. Everything posted on Instagram is public, unless you protect your account and require people to request to connect. You can follow others and they can follow you. The pictures of those you follow will appear on your app home screen. Instagram allows users to create and manage different profiles from the app, so it's possible to operate as yourself and then switch to your church's profile (just tap the username on top of your profile page) and post there.

FILTERS

Although other social media platforms and smartphones have added filters to photo editing, Instagram originated it, and we think they are still the best. The filters, which once would have needed a program like Photoshop to achieve, bring life to photos taken on smartphones, illuminating pictures taken in low light, accentuating colors, and offering a few black-and-white filters for dramatic impact. Instagram filters are a matter of personal taste. Click through them to see how they look applied to a particular photo or video, choosing the one that seems most appropriate. Studies show that Clarendon is the most popular filter in the United States and worldwide; others lend themselves to certain subject matter. Valencia is most popular for nature, Kelvin for fashion, Skyline for food, and most skip the filters altogether for selfies.[37]

HASHTAGS

Instagram is driven by two things: beautiful images and hashtags. Hashtags are clickable links that display all the photos marked with that particular hashtag. On Instagram, hashtags are used extensively. It's not uncommon to use five, ten, or more for one photo. [A photo might be #church #lutheran #philly #baptism, #water, #childofgod, #ambler.] These hashtags could be descriptive, location-oriented, ironic, or humorous. We recommend using hashtags that have a wide appeal (not just #lutheran or #episcopal) to make your photos more discoverable to others.

In addition to being a place to share your photos, Instagram is also a discovery tool to view photos of others. Clicking through hashtags on Instagram creates a continually reconfigured photo gallery ripe for exploration. As with Twitter, it's also a good idea to include hashtags in your Instagram profile, like Keith, "#Lutheran pastor at Upper Dublin LC in #Ambler PA, author of The Digital Cathedral #digitalcathedral, coauthor #click2savebook."

Hashtags can create all kinds of serendipitous connections. A couple of winters ago, Keith and his family were driving home from Christmas vacation and were stuck in a lake-effect snowstorm. They pulled off the highway, checked into the hotel, and had some hours to kill. What better way to pass the time than to play with social media? Keith posted a picture of their dog, Charlie, lying on the couch next to Keith's laptop. Keith posted it on Instagram and hashtagged it #dogwithablog after the Disney kids show of the same name. The official Instagram account of the dog of the show commented and reshared it, which garnered thousands of likes and comments, much to the delight of Keith's kids.

ENGAGEMENT

Engagement on Instagram is about appreciating the images and moments others have captured. Click the heart icon to "like" an image and leave a comment. (People generally keep their comments positive and short.) Like Facebook, Instagram allows tagging. Tag others in the photos you post. Photos in which you are tagged will appear under the tag icon on your profile page. You can remove tags if you so choose. There is no public sharing or retweeting like other platforms, but there are apps like "Repost" that repost Instagram images.[38] Engagement on Instagram is driven by posting beautiful images with broad appeal.

INVITE OTHERS TO SHARE A STORY

One way to engage with others on Instagram, besides your presence and participation, is to invite them to post on a theme. Keith introduced the hashtag for his congregation, #myudlc (shorthand for "my Upper Dublin Lutheran Church"), and invited people to make their social media posts with the same hashtag so they are easier to find and curate.

FINDING AND SHARING BEAUTY

Each social media platform lends itself to a unique way of communication and storytelling and to certain spiritual practices. In this sense, Instagram is really about discovering and sharing beauty, whether it's the beauty of a sunset, the joy of friends together, the magic of small things that often go unnoticed. Instagram invites us into the spiritual practice of "noticing," seeing our everyday lives with more care, imagination, and appreciation for creation and divine presence. The filters are lenses through which we see the world.

Keep this in mind when posting as yourself or for your church. Whatever content you share—pictures of the sanctuary, people, activities, mission trips—should be visually interesting and pleasing.

"I FOUND MY FAVORITE BIBLE VERSE ON INSTAGRAM"

As the capstone to their confirmation experience, each confirmand at Keith's church is asked to respond to a series of questions for their "faith statement," including one asking about their favorite Bible verse. One confirmand told Keith that she found her favorite Bible verse on Instagram. She follows the account "instapray," which posts Bible verses and inspirational messages. One day she found the verse from Psalm 46:5: "God is within her, she will not fail." She even shared it with a friend who was going through a difficult time.

PARALLEL BIBLE

Along with his brother, Andrew, Chris Brietenberg has created an app called Parallel Bible, which *Time* magazine has called "Like Instagram, but for the Bible." On the Parallel Bible app, users can post photos and pair them with Bible verses. You can choose a Bible verse you already know or find verses arranged by theme or keyword. For instance, Keith recently posted a picture from a local creek. Searching for verses in the category "rivers," he found this gem from John 7:38: "He who believes in me, as the Scripture has said, from within him will flow rivers of living water." The app provides a way of connecting the Bible to the everyday, bringing the biblical text to life. *Time* writer Elizabeth Dias states, "The app signals a new evangelism, the communal sharing of stories rather than overt proselytization." "Ultimately faith is not individual but communal with God and the people around you," says Chris.[39] Apps like Instagram and Parallel Bible help us to see our world and each other in new ways, with greater appreciation and depth.

Novice

- Create a profile with a good picture of yourself and description that includes hashtags
- Post twice a week using hashtags
- Like and comment on some other pictures

Oblate

- Follow hashtags of interest, like your town (#ambler, #woburn); like and comment
- Post more frequently
- Consider posting along certain themes (nature, travel, local, spiritual)

Superior

- If you choose to create a church account, add a small logo to pictures so you are immediately identifiable
- Create a unique hashtag and encourage your community to use it
- Share other users' pictures with their permission
- Post more than once a day

3.6 Pinterest

Origins	Founded in 2010 by Ben Silberman, Evan Sharp, and Paul Sciarra[40]
Number of Users	Over 100 million users,[41]
Typical User	Overwhelmingly female, white or Hispanic, under 50
Key Features	Visual discovery tool, personal profile, "boards" onto which people "pin" content like links, pictures, videos
Benefits of Participation	Connect with women around creativity and visual content, boards make it easy to organize and categorize different social media content
Limitations	A very niche platform
Practices	Sharing, exploring, archiving

THE BASICS

Another rapidly growing visually driven social media platform, Pinterest, which has both a robust desktop version and app, describes itself as "the world's catalog of ideas." Here, users create "boards" onto which they "pin" content. People use Pinterest to save, organize, and share ideas from wedding plans, to home improvements, arts and crafts, children's activities, ministry ideas, and inspirational content.

Pinterest is good for:
- Connecting with women, who represent 85 percent of the users on Pinterest[42]
- Aggregating content like blog posts, videos, images, event materials
- Capturing, organizing, and sharing ideas and discovering new ideas through its search function
- Organizing and coordinating group projects in which people can share content to a board

PROFILE

The Pinterest profile is much like Instagram's. It includes a picture, brief description, and website and social media links. On Pinterest, you can follow other people and they can follow you, or you can simply follow some boards. Pins from the people or boards you follow will appear on the Pinterest home screen. You can also link your Facebook account to Pinterest, so people can see your pins on Facebook, widening your reach.

BOARDS

Once you've created your profile, you can create "boards." Each board needs a name, description, and category. Boards and the content you pin to them are public, unless you make your board secret so that only you can see it. This can be useful; for instance, Keith uses secret boards for book research. You can also create group boards and invite collaborators to share pins. If you create the group board, you can control who gets invited and remove people and pins if necessary.

PINS

Pins are the pieces of content that you share on boards. They can be pictures, videos, files uploaded from your computer, or links to content discovered around the web. The easiest way to pin something to Pinterest is to install the browser button for your web browser.[43] You can also upload content from your computer or paste a link to a webpage using the + sign in the bottom right of the desktop version or the + at the top of your profile picture on the Pinterest app. Pins highlight the visual content from the links you share, picking up the image from the web page, and using the name of the page or your description as a caption.

ENGAGEMENT

Each pin offers several options for engagement. You can "save" it, meaning you can save it to one of your own boards. You can "like" it by clicking the heart button. You can comment on it. You can send it directly and privately to one of your Pinterest contacts or share on social media Facebook, Twitter, Facebook Messenger, or copy the link. You can also embed the pin on a blog.

PINTEREST GUIDED SEARCH

The Pinterest search bar is a powerful tool for finding ideas and content. Type a search term or terms in the search box to review results. Along with the relevant pins, refined search terms with image backgrounds appear to help you refine your search. A search for the broad term "bible" generates more specific options such as "verses, study, quotes, faith, journaling, art, scriptures, tattoo, book, devotions," and more. Each search and each refinement reconfigures the results.

ORGANIZE CREATIVE MINISTRY IDEAS

Because of the vast amount of information and ideas, ease of discovery, and organization, ministry leaders have found Pinterest remarkably useful for discovering, sharing, and organizing ministry ideas. Sunday school teachers curate boards with ideas for children's Bible activities. Youth ministry leaders curate boards with youth ministry resources. Pastors capture images for preaching and teaching. Music ministers post children's songs and share them with parents.

Like much of the web, there is so much content on Pinterest that simply capturing, curating, and sharing good content, rather than making your own, can be an extremely effective way to be meaningfully present on Pinterest. Your church could maintain boards for faith and parenting young children and/or teens, ideas for faith-based summer projects for families. Church knitting or prayer shawl groups could share patterns and ideas.

BE SALT FOR THE EARTH

In addition to bright ideas, another important element of the Pinterest ecosystem is inspiration. Pinterest is replete with encouraging quotes, Bible verses, and more. One of our favorite Pinterest uses is the Emmy award–winning Salt Project. The Salt Project creates beautiful visual content on their website and organizes them on Pinterest boards under headings of "spirituality, scripture, Jesus, justice, parenting and spirituality, Sunday school ideas, progressive Christian resources, care of creation, Advent/Christmas, Lent/Easter," and more.

SEEING THE CHRISTIAN TRADITION

For an undergraduate class on the Christian tradition, Elizabeth created a Pinterest board called "Seeing the Christian Tradition." Each week, students were required to find images on the web or from their own everyday lives that spoke to them about the theme of that week's class. They posted them to the board and when the class met again, they would discuss them and decide what image best captured the theme.

#ADVENTWORD

Our favorite thing on Pinterest is an Advent calendar created by the Society of Saint John the Evangelist for their #AdventWord project.[44] At the beginning of Advent, all the days were listed with a place holder. For each day of Advent that pin was replaced with a picture from the monastery and a short reflection based on the word of the day, which people were invited to post about using the hashtag #adventword and the word for the day.

AGGREGATING CONTENT

Another way to use Pinterest is as an aggregator for your content. For instance, Keith shares all his blog posts to a board he calls Blog Posts. (How creative!) All the posts are in the same place and can be easily scanned visually.

KEEP IT VISUAL

Remember, the best way to encourage engagement on Pinterest is to share eye-catching, inspirational, and useful content.

Novice

- Create a profile with picture and description
- Install the Pinterest browser button
- Create two boards and "pin" content
- Connect with parishioners already on Pinterest

Oblate

- Search Pinterest and repin content from others onto your boards
- Promote boards with appropriate constituencies
- Actively comment on others' pins

Superior

- Curate multiple boards
- Curate shared boards for group projects or activities

Video Platforms

Since the first edition of *Click 2 Save*, the volume of online video and the number of video sharing platforms have risen dramatically. Today, people post video, both recorded and live, on Facebook, Twitter, Instagram, Periscope, and more. Streaming services such as Netflix, Amazon Prime Video, and HBO Now have revolutionized the way we consume video content. Facebook founder Mark Zuckerberg has said, "We're entering this new golden age of video. . . . I wouldn't be surprised if you fast-forward five years and most of the content that people see on Facebook and are sharing on a day-to-day basis is video."[45] Today, video is cheap and ubiquitous, like an "ever rolling stream" of binge watching. And yet, with over a billion users, YouTube remains the dominant video sharing platform on the web.

3.7 YouTube

Origins	Founded in 2005 by Chad Hurley, Steve Chen, and Jawed Karim, bought by Google for $1.65 billion in 2006
Number of Users	Over 1 billion,[46] hundreds of millions of hours of video viewed daily
Key Features	Easy sharing of video, profiles, channels, online editing tools
Benefits of Participation	Your largest video platform and largest search engines
Limitations	Ads that may appear over your video
Practices	Sharing, exploring, archiving

THE BASICS

Online videos are enormously popular. People are engaging video at increasingly higher rates than other social media. Engagement with video increases with each subsequent generation—the younger the user, the more video. For Millennials (18–33 year olds), watching videos is the most popular online activity behind email, search, and social networking. And because images and music speak beyond language barriers, videos have a huge international attraction.

YouTube is the web's largest video sharing site, where more than twenty-four hours of video are uploaded every minute. It is also one of the web's largest search engines. That means that many of the people who are looking for a church or organization like yours will go to YouTube rather than to Google or Bing. They want to see you in action, hear your voice, not just read your words.

YouTube is good for:

- Reaching a large segment of people beyond and within Facebook and Twitter
- Reaching younger generations, who watch video at higher rates
- Creating an online video catalogue in a high traffic area
- Organizing videos into theme-related playlists
- Speaking personally and directly
- Being creative and playful in our message
- Creating and sharing a video response to someone else's video
- Hosting videos for free without storing them on your website

Video is often overlooked or dismissed among those in ministry because of a perceived lack of equipment, time, and resources to make something of professional quality. However, part of the charm of YouTube (and what makes videos popular) is the amateur production value. It turns out to be endearing, funny, real, and authentic when someone creates an engaging video on nothing more than a smartphone. Have you seen the one where the three-year-old recites a Billy Collins poem? There's nothing not to like about that, the lack of Hollywood production values notwithstanding. The charm and quirkiness of these sorts of video has had a tremendous influence on television and in movies, where directors imitate the amateur, first-person style of YouTube.

All of this is possible, of course, because it is so much easier to shoot and produce video than it was even a few years ago. Any smartphone can record video these days and most of them in high definition with video editing software on board. Most computers now include built-in webcams, and video editing software is often included, and has become much more user friendly. YouTube now even offers its own set of online editing tools (more below).

The Rev. Matthew Moretz, an Episcopal priest and creator of the classic YouTube series *Father Matthew Presents,* told us in the first edition, "If you can learn in seminary how to craft a fifteen-minute archaic rhetorical speech, you can learn how to make video—something that's actually contemporary, something that's actually in the *lingua franca* of the world. This is how people are made who they are—by what they see on video on the ever-omnipresent screen." It's even more true today.

The average American watches five hours of video content a day, increasingly on our mobile devices. Video is a primary way we communicate, and has only grown with the rise of streaming video services, yet it's use is largely lacking in mainline churches.

"It's the way people tell stories. Other institutions are telling our stories. They're telling my little ones what Christianity is," says Moretz. "By the time they get in confirmation class, they already know what Christianity is because *Family Guy* told them. They know who Jesus is because they saw him on *South Park*. There's got to be more."

Video allows users to tell an expansive, emotive story, combining voice, physical expression, and visual interest. In just a few minutes, a host of ideas can be conveyed. Video gives users a much better sense of the person or institution on the screen, allowing you to speak to them at work, at home, and wherever they may be on their smartphone.

ARE YOU READY FOR YOUR CLOSE-UP?

As we've discussed, the amateur quality of most YouTube videos are a central element of their charm. You don't need to be Sofia Coppola to create engaging video for your community and those who may be drawn to it.

For example, Casey Fitzgerald has created a number of crowdsourced biblical storytelling videos. She takes a Bible passage and breaks it up into several different small parts, like a script, distributing those parts to participants. People record themselves telling their part of the story and send it back into Casey, who strings them all together into a video. The result is a funny, charming, and highly engaging video that is great for viewing at church and sharing online.[47] Inspired by Casey's project, Keith's church did a similar project for Christmas and Easter. The videos were a great way to tell the story, highlighting the people in his congregation, and they turned out to be great faith formation projects, with families reading the scripture together and deciding how to represent it.[48]

Videos like this can be shot with even the most basic smartphone cameras and some basic video editing. Everyone can get involved. For instance, you might ask members of your community to shoot short videos at church events like picnics, community service projects, special worship services, and so on. Such collaborative video projects can be a particularly effective way to engage the talents and interests of teens and young adults in your community. These videos can be posted on your Facebook page, but they can also be edited together into short montages of life in your community. This gets you into the video zone without much scripting or editing effort.

From there, work with staff and other members of your community to create more crafted videos to be shared on a YouTube channel for your organization (see below).

KEEP IT SHORT, SKIP THE SERMON

Whatever the technology you use to create a video, keep it short to match our ever-shrinking attention spans. That means focusing on one key point, illustrating it as vividly as you can, and connecting with viewers by showing the depth and warmth of your personality. Which is to say: smile and relax. Rather than starting with the generic "Hi, I'm Pastor Sally, and I'd like to talk with you about Matthew 25 today," begin with a captivating statement or question, then introduce yourself. "Ever wonder what the Bible says about investing?" you might ask in a video on stewardship or economic justice.

The short time frame for videos also means that your scintillating sermon on the Beatitudes is not the best material. This is especially true if you read your sermon. Indeed, avoid reading into the camera. For the feel of a conversation, you'll want to practice what you plan to say in advance, perhaps making some notes on key points on large index cards. As we hope has become a clear theme in this book, your digital ministry will be most meaningful, most apt to engage others and invite relationship, when it is most authentically expressive of who you are as a person. Dryly reading from a prepared statement is not going to do that, but it's also the case that over-rehearsing to the point of appearing to be a shopping channel huckster is not going to win you any fans either.

It's certainly wonderful if you've got lots to share about your church, organization, and the faith in general, but you'll want to serve that up in bit-sized pieces that people can access from home, work, or on the go. Think what you will about short digital-age attention spans and sound-bite culture, but that's the reality of much of life today. A two-minute meditation offered into the midst of an overscheduled day will have far more impact than if we insist on blabcasting a twenty-minute sermon via a video platform.

NINETY SECOND SERMONS

Richard Hong, the minister at First Presbyterian Church in Englewood, New Jersey, hosts a project called *90 Second Sermons*, a weekly video series that reflects on the upcoming lectionary texts.[49] They serve as a preview for the Sunday morning message for the congregation, but they also offer self-contained messages for those who may not walk through the church doors on

Sunday. The message is direct, to the point, and always has an interesting story or twist to hold viewers' attention. They post the videos on Vimeo and iTunes. (If YouTube is the big movie theatre with stadium seating, Vimeo is an art house cinema.) Interested in creating your own series? Hong shares his secret method and tools to build your own 90 second sermon.[50]

THIRTY SECONDS OR LESS

If you want to go even shorter, take inspiration from Jim Keat, associate minister of digital strategy and online engagement at The Riverside Church in the City of New York, and creator of the video and podcast series *Thirty Seconds or Less*,[51] which he describes as "the world's shortest podcast, a flash mob of ideas, hundreds of voices exploring the art of elimination. If you can't say it in thirty seconds, you're probably not ready to say it at all." As the name suggests, the site features short, 30-second(ish) voice recordings from a wide variety of people about a broad range of faith topics, including creativity, technology, ministry practice, social justice, Pride month, the Bible, and much more, including a popular Thirty Second Bible series, which has multiple thirty second recordings about almost every book in the Bible.[52]

Early on in the project, Jim paired each voice recording with a single image and some rights-free music to create the video. Later, he used video clips to create a short but powerful pop of insight and inspiration. While he posted the videos on Facebook and YouTube and embedded them on his website, he also posted the audio on iTunes, so people could listen to the reflections as a podcast. *Thirty Seconds or Less* fits our rapidly shrinking attention spans while providing excellent, thought-provoking content. As preachers sometimes need reminding, you don't have talk a long time to say something profound.

SETTING UP YOUR YOUTUBE ACCOUNT

Like Facebook, Twitter, and other social networking sites, YouTube allows account personalization by adding a photo, personal or organizational information, and background formatting. Videos can actually be uploaded before any of these steps are completed, but it's a good idea to invest the ten to fifteen minutes or so it will take to set up an account before uploading.

CHANNELS

After setting up an account and selecting a user name (which can be different from the email address that became your default user name when you signed in), YouTube will prompt new users to set up a channel. A YouTube channel is like having your own television station to which you can add videos. A channel keeps all of your ministry videos in one place. Once you've established a channel, you will have a unique web address that will look like this: http://www.youtube.com/Click2SaveBook. From the "settings" tab on the channel, you will be able to develop a fully customized environment that shares basic information about you and your community along with all of your videos.

CHANNEL TABS

- *Settings*—Create basic information of your site like tags, name, whether to make your channel public or private
- *Themes and Colors*—Choose from ten different color combinations with the advanced options to customize or create your own. It's a good idea to have your channel match the general look of your website or social media.
- *Modules*—Determine what information is displayed on your channel's pages. This all appears under the videos. It's a good idea to include some of these to help fill out the page and demonstrate activity.
- *Videos and Playlists*—This setting determines what content you highlight and display.
- *Featured Video*—You can also designate a featured video that will automatically play when your YouTube channel loads.

PLAYLISTS

Within your channel, playlists can be created to organize videos, developing themed content streams within the channel. Think about them as Pinterest boards for videos. YouTube creates basic playlists automatically: favorites, liked, history, and watch later.

Playlists can be used to organize your own original videos or other videos already on YouTube that you find interesting and relevant to your audience.

This allows more options for expressing the personality and character of your community by sharing not only videos that you have created, but those which you enjoy and value yourself. On the *Click 2 Save* YouTube channel, for example, we've created playlists for videos related to social media, spiritual practices, religious thinkers we admire, and other thought leaders.

To create a playlist, choose a video that will go in the playlist. Underneath the video is the link "playlist." Click, and a drop-down menu appears. You can either assign the video to an existing playlist or enter the name of a newly created one.

CURATING VERSUS CREATING

Not everyone has the time or aptitude to create a video series like *90 Second Sermons* or *Thirty Seconds or Less*. Although it is ideal to create some original video content, there is a plenty that can be collected and shared: (known as "curating content") TED talks, the Soul Pancake religion channel, Chuck Knows Church, the Salt Project, and countless worship resources are good options, as are paid video services like The Work of the People and Animate, for worship or faith-formation classes.

John Roberto, president of Lifelong Faith Associates and author of several books on faith formation in the twenty-first century, is an advocate for becoming digital curators of content to supplement faith formation experiences. He told us:

> Curating in the digital world is a new skillset for church leaders. Leaders have experience in curating print content—like curriculum, texts, and programs, but the digital world dramatically increases the scope and quantity of the resources to curate. It is important today that every church leader have a plan for curation: identify the trusted "experts"—people who are knowledgeable about resources, identify the trusted publishers and organizations that produce spiritual and religious resources (and get on their mailing list), and subscribe to blogs and newsletters from trusted experts and organizations that can keep you current on resources. Curating is one of the most essential roles and skills for the twenty-first-century church leader.

EDITING VIDEO

YouTube now offers a suite of video editing capabilities available right on the website at no cost. These options are available to enhance your project:

- *Info and Settings*—Update the description and details of the project. The more information and details the better. All that information helps you to get discovered on YouTube and Google search.
- *Enhancements*—Apply visual edits like color saturation, slow motion, time-lapse, and trim the video clip to your desired length
- *Audio*—Select and apply music from more than 150,000 rights-free music tracks
- *Annotation*—Add additional titles, notes, or speech bubbles that overlay the video and provide views with additional information or links to learn more. For example, you may want to put an annotation toward the end of each video with a link to your church's website. The benefit of annotations is that they don't become a permanent part of your video, so you can easily remove or change them later.
- *Cards*—Suggest another video or playlists for additional watching as the current video concludes
- *Subtitles and CC [Closed Caption]*—Upload a script or transcribe the audio to make your videos more accessible.

YOUTUBE LIVE (HANGOUTS)

Although Google±, Google's attempt at a social network, came and went, one feature that has endured is Google Hangouts. Google Hangouts offers simple and free video calling for multiple users. These videos can also be shared live publically to invite people into the conversation. This spun into YouTube Live, in which users can stream their live videos. Some churches use this for live-streaming their worship services. Others use it to engage people that are geographically dispersed in conversation. For example, early users of YouTube Live were Archbishop Desmond Tutu and the Dali Lama for the Inaugural Desmond Tutu Peace Lecture. When they were not able to meet together in person, they talked and live-streamed the conversation.[53]

A NOTE ABOUT NATIVE CONTENT

From its inception, the purpose of YouTube has been to make video sharing simple: users can share on Facebook, Twitter, Pinterest, or embed a video on your website or blog. If you create video content, it is best to have it available on YouTube, since, like Facebook, it's popularity makes content more likely to be found, but we also recommend posting video natively to other websites. Rather than sharing the YouTube link on your Facebook, upload the video directly to Facebook. It is an extra step, but engagement is higher on native video, which means that people are more likely to click on the video and watch it. In addition, you may wish to take a shorter version of your video and post it on Instagram and point back to the longer version on YouTube.

Our experience is that video is far and away the most anxiety-producing aspect of implementing a social media strategy for most ministry leaders, churches, and other organizations. Those of us raised in the Broadcast Age may still consider video as something not unlike reading the Bible was to pre-Reformation believers: something best left to the experts. But affordable, easy-to-use digital cameras and user-friendly editing software has changed all that, allowing almost anyone to become a filmmaker. This ability allows us to share our stories with a larger audience—especially young adults, who are more drawn to video—and to make our stories more dynamic and engaging.

The good news for even the most cinemographically uncertain is that YouTube provides the opportunity, through channels and playlists for hosting theme-related videos rather than sharing original ones, to wade into the water a bit. That puts you at the novice level, from where you can assess your readiness as an individual or organization to move into more customized video-enriched digital ministry practice.

Novice

- Create a YouTube channel
- Complete profile
- Create 2–3 playlist categories
- Favorite videos
- Search for other church related videos to add to your playlist

Oblate

- Post a video you already have
- Leave comments on other people's videos, inviting viewers to your channel
- Subscribe to the video channels of people whose videos you admire

Superior

- Purchase an inexpensive tripod so your videos are steady and you can record yourself more easily
- Create a video series or more than one on the same theme
- Use your videos in religious education, formation, spiritual practice, or other church and organizational settings
- Invite members of your congregation or community into the video creation process

Live Broadcasting Platforms

As we have already seen on Facebook and YouTube, live video is in its ascendency. Another live video service owned and integrated into Twitter is Periscope.

3.8 Periscope

Origins	Created by Kayvon Beykpour and Joe Bernsteinand, launched and bought by Twitter in 2015
Number of Users	More than 10 million users, 2 million daily active users,[54] 200 million broadcasts in its first year[55]
Key Features	Live video streaming, Twitter integration
Benefits of Participation	Broadcast live in the moment, includes Apple TV app
Limitations	Requires Twitter account
Practices	Checking in, sharing, exploring

THE BASICS

Awarded the Apple Store "App of the Year" in 2015 when it launched, Periscope, a live video streaming app, has revolutionized how we watch video, by enabling users to share video from our phones. Whereas we once could only show video after the fact, now we can share video in real time, as it happens.

Periscope and similar live video platforms really arrived in the public consciousness in the summer of 2016 during the sit-in for gun control in the US House of Representatives. When C-SPAN was shut down to prevent broadcasting of the event, C-SPAN rebroadcast the Periscope and Facebook Live feeds on the air.[56] Shortly after, the shooting death of Philando Castile by police was broadcast using Facebook Live video.[57]

People choose between Periscope and Facebook Live for reasons much like those they use to choose between their parent platforms, Twitter and Facebook. Facebook tends to leverage existing social networks of friends and is a more familiar and friendly social media environment. Twitter and Periscope tend to connect people more broadly through shared interests. While you can opt to share Facebook Live video with friends or make it public, Periscope video is, by default, available to the whole Twittersphere. If Twitter is a key part of your congregation's digital ministry strategy, then Periscope will be a natural extension of your Twitter presence.

Periscope features first-person broadcasts from all over the world. Tune in and you may see singer-songwriters playing live from their living room and interacting with viewers, or breaking news shared by, quite literally, the man on the street. A map of live broadcasts allows you to move around the globe, dipping into the sublime and the mundane of life here on Earth.

Periscope is good for:

- Broadcasting live
- Diversifying and expanding your Twitter content
- Viewing first-person perspectives from around the world

PROFILE

The easiest way to create an account and log in—and the way to get the most from Periscope—is by using your Twitter account. So, if you don't have one already, you'll want to create a Twitter account. Linking your accounts in this way will allow you to broadcast live directly to Twitter. If you manage multiple Twitter accounts, you can choose which one to use for broadcast. This process will also import your profile information from Twitter. Like Twitter, you can follow others and be followed.

Once you've logged in, navigate through the app using the four icons at the bottom of the Periscope home screen. These will show whether anyone you follow is currently live, provide a summary of the variety of live video from around the world in list or a map, or allow a search for specific topics. Click around the map and see who is broadcasting in your neighborhood, or around the world. The people icon suggests individuals you may want to follow based on your contacts and current news events.

LIVE STREAMING

To live stream, click the camera icon. You'll be presented with options of whether to share your precise location or not, whether to make your broadcast public or just available to certain followers. You can determine whether people can chat with you as they watch, and finally whether to broadcast the video on Twitter as well. When you are ready, tap "Start Broadcast." As you broadcast, people can comment below the video and tap the screen to make hearts appear and share some love. You can respond to them conversationally by speaking as you show your video. Remember, they are not only seeing what you are seeing, they are watching because they want to engage with you about it, so interaction is key.

By default all videos are saved and stored indefinitely; change settings to auto-delete after twenty-four hours or to save on your phone's camera roll in the Periscope account settings.

WHAT TO BROADCAST

Again, some congregations will opt to use Periscope to live-stream services or sermons to a wider online audience, especially if they already use Twitter. The value of Periscope and any live broadcast platform is in immediacy, to share as an event is happening, and often to share what is newsworthy.

Novice

- Download Periscope and link it with your Twitter account(s)
- Follow some people you know
- View videos from around the world

Oblate

- Occasionally broadcast videos and get the hang of it
- Pay attention to the level of engagement you receive

Superior

- Regularly broadcast live videos
- Live stream worship services

3.9 Podcasts

Origins	With precursors in the 1980s, podcasting became more popular and accessible when Apple added podcasting support to iTunes in 2005, coupled with the widespread adoption of the iPod and other portable music players
Number of Users	67 million Americans listen to podcasts monthly, 42 million listen weekly[58]
Key Features	Audio recordings automatically download to your smartphone or computer
Benefits of Participation	Podcasting is exploding in popularity, but there is not yet a lot of competition. Podcasts are free to upload and offers portable, mobile-friendly content
Limitations	Time-consuming to produce, may require purchase of extra audio equipment
Platforms	iTunes, Podcast app for iPhone, stitcher.com, libsyn.com, soundcloud.com, blubrry.com
Practices	Sharing, archiving

THE BASICS

Podcasts are not exactly new, but they are a booming sector of the social media universe. In 2015 Pew Research reported that "the percentage of Americans who have listened to a podcast in the past month has almost doubled since 2008, from 9% to 17% by January of 2015." Awareness of podcasts has more than doubled since 2006. One-third of Americans have listened to a podcast.[59] In the last few years, those numbers have only increased.

Compared to other legacy platforms, podcasting is a relatively new community of creators and listeners. It still feels like a young and evolving genre without too much noise or oversaturation. Much of the popularity of podcasts comes in the ability to listen to podcasts on the go—at the gym, on a run, while walking, or in newer cars via Bluetooth connection. It is also easier to produce a good quality podcast than it once was with recording and editing tools like Garageband for the Mac and Audacity for PCs.

Podcasts are good for:

- Providing portable content that people can listen to on the go
- Developing an engaging, interactive, and personal connection with listeners
- Promoting events and activities to your listeners
- Talking about faith, spirituality, or current events in a genuine and open way

PODCASTING SERMONS

As we've noted before with blogging, podcasting sermons allows parishioners to listen if they missed worship and others to tune in from afar.

A sophisticated sound system isn't necessary to podcast sermons: capture audio as a voice memo on your iPhone or use a portable recording device (Keith likes Zoom recorders), then upload to a service like buzzsprout.com (another of Keith's favorites), SoundCloud, or Stitcher, which will upload to iTunes so individuals can subscribe and receive updates on their smartphones. Audio players can also be embedded on your website and shared to other social media.

Remember, however, just as with other social media, podcasting as a genre is something different than preaching. As Jim Keat says, "The best things churches can do is create online-first content. Every church can say they have a podcast because they can podcast a sermon, but that's just giving the internet sloppy seconds. That was an experience designed for the people in the room and then, oh, we can toss this to the internet too. There's a huge difference when you sit in a room with a few people and record it for the hundreds of people that aren't in the room. It makes you create it differently." Podcasting is a conversational take on a particular topic or theme. It is more like a radio program designed for the audience rather than eavesdropping in to something that happened Sunday at church. (Think something more like *This American Life* or *Car Talk* on National Public Radio.)

Most podcasts range between twenty and sixty minutes long and can cover every possible topic. Christian podcasts like Rob Bell's *Robcast*, the long-running *Pray as You Go* by British Jesuits, Tripp Fuller's *Homebrewed Christianity*, and even the *Friendly Atheist Podcast* are quite popular in the religion genre. Sometimes podcasts are hosted by one person, others are conversation between two people, or sometimes entire panels. Some podcasts are regular, some seasonal, or episodic. You never know when and where matters of faith will spring up. In one of Keith's favorite sports podcasts, *The Bill Simmons Podcast*, Bill waxes theological about the role of karma in sports—or maybe the pathos of Boston sports fans.[60]

STORY DIVINE

One of the podcasts in heavy rotation on our phones has been Presbyterian minister Casey Fitzgerald's *Story Divine*, which is part of her Faith and Wonder website.[61] Fitzgerald jokingly told us, "I do as little as possible for it to qualify as a podcast," but there's obviously more to it than that. Each week on *Story Divine*, Casey—always accompanied by her dog, King—introduces the lectionary passages for the coming Sunday. She reads the texts, shares her reflections, and invites listeners to consider not only how the texts engage their own stories, but also how they might share the lectionary narratives with others. Casey helps many preachers prepare for Sunday, but it also helps listeners better understand the important role that story plays in creating connection between people within and beyond their congregations. In a world oversaturated with information, we crave stories that connect us to the story of faith, our neighbors, and God.

Fitzgerald recommends that podcasters be predictable about how long their podcasts run. Hers are designed to spark further conversation at home, so she keeps it short. Like all the podcasters we spoke with, Casey emphasized the importance of having high sound quality. She uses a Yeti Blue Microphone that connects via the USB port on her computer. For mobile recording, she recommends Zoom recorders. It takes her between two and five hours to edit each episode, which she does in Final Cut Pro on her Mac. She uses Libsyn, a paid service, to host the audio, which is set up to feed up to iTunes. Unlike some other podcasts, Fitzgerald doesn't use a script, she records her thoughts and then goes back and edits. She says, in terms of putting her podcast together, "For me, it's more like being in the middle of my process than at the end."

THIS EVERYDAY HOLY

This Everyday Holy is a podcast and website about "ordinary living in the lectionary" created by Presbyterian minister and author Mihee Kim-Kort.[62] In her podcast, Mihee connects lectionary readings to our everyday lived experiences. The podcast is peppered with recordings from Mihee's everyday life—conversations in the car with her husband, interactions with her young children around the dinner table, and the general household chaos of life with kids. Interspersed between these everyday moments are Mihee's insightful reflections on the intersection of faith and life, inspired by the lectionary. Mihee also has invited people to share their reflections, as Keith and his spouse, Jenny, did on the lectionary for Advent 4.[63]

Mihee says that "after eight or nine episodes I felt like I was starting to develop a little bit of a rhythm, a little of a routine, around collecting audio, writing a script, recording, and then doing the very meticulous editing." Time investment: "It took forever at the very beginning . . . now for a 20-minute episode it probably takes around 5 hours, maybe a little less."[64]

THE OA FOR LENT

Last Lent, Keith and his friend Martin Malzahn, chaplain at Wagner College in New York, took a crack at podcasting for a project called *The OA for Lent*, in which they reflected on the spiritual themes of the hit Netflix show *The OA*.[65] With Keith in Philly and Martin in New York, they investigated how to record themselves remotely and found a common practice among podcasters, which was to record the audio of their Skype conversation using the inexpensive software Call Recorder, which integrates with Skype and records the conversation in two tracks, making it easier to edit later on. Armed with Skype, Call Recorder, over-the-ear headphones to minimize audio feedback, a Blue Yeti microphone, Soundcloud, and Garageband, these podcasting novices managed to produce nine episodes for the project.

While Keith became more proficient in editing the podcast, which was much simpler compared to a project like *This Everyday Holy*, it still took a significant amount of time. Plan on at least four hours of editing for a single forty-five-minute podcast episode.

FINDING GOD IN THE EVERYDAY

Podcasts like *Story Divine* and *This Everyday Holy*, are great listens and ambitious, in that they seek to be more than just a sermon preparation aid. Ultimately, they help audience members identify the sacred amidst the seemingly mundane rhythms of everyday life, with helpful links in each episode to aid listeners to go deeper and further.

Podcasts like these enable listeners to connect faith with everyday life, not only because of their particular subject matter, but because of how people access the content: listening to something about faith and God in the midst of the everyday places of their lives, on the trail, at the gym, in the car, or at the park. This mash-up of familiar surroundings with content about God helps to create and foster a connection between the everyday and the holy that a sermon or a traditional adult forum struggles to provide.

Novice

- Listen to podcasts (not just religious ones) and share them with others on social media
- Curate a list of recommended podcasts for your congregation or community

Oblate

- Contribute to a podcast, respond to a call for contributors, or pitch an idea, episode, or content
- Engage with podcast hosts by leaving questions if possible, or through other social media platforms

Superior

- Create and host your own podcast

Messaging

Messaging Apps like Facebook Messenger and WhatsApp have grown in popularity in the last few years, but one of the most popular and noteworthy of them all (with both private and public sharing) is Snapchat.

3.10 Snapchat

Origins	Founded in 2011 by Evan Spiegel, Bobby Murphy, and Reggie Brown
Number of Users	More than 166 million daily active users sharing 3 billion snaps a day[66]
Typical User	Typically teens and young adults: 41 percent of teens 13 to 17 use Snapchat[67]
Key Features	Pictures and videos shared for 10 seconds or less, filters, stickers, chat, stories, and memories
Benefits of Participation	Reaching younger generations, platform lends itself to having fun
Limitations	Fleeting, snaps last 10 seconds, stories for 24 hours, memories can be stored indefinitely, the Snapchat interface can be hard to learn if you're over 25
Practices	Checking in, sharing

THE BASICS

Snapchat is a photo and video messaging app that is exceedingly popular with teens and young adults—so popular that as of June 2016, Snapchat had exceeded the daily usage of Twitter, a platform with much more notoriety and a five year head start.[68] Snapchat enables users to send pictures or video, called "snaps," directly to their Snapchat contacts. The photos and video can be embellished with a wide array of filters, stickers, and captions. Once the snaps are sent, they can be viewed for up to ten seconds and then they are deleted. However, there are options for displaying content longer by adding them to your Snapchat "story," which lasts for twenty-four hours, or "memories," which last indefinitely. "Snaps" can also be saved to the camera photo roll and shared on other platforms.

Snapchat marks a significant departure from the other social media platforms we have previously profiled in a number of important ways. Unlike blogs or YouTube channels, content is not permanently stored and accumulated over time by default. Snapchat is not about carefully curating a public profile like Facebook or curating an ever-growing body of content like Pinterest. Snapchat is all about capturing the moment and sharing it with friends. As technology columnist Joanna Stern writes, "Snapchat is for bearing witness—telling stories in raw, often humorous, behind-the-scenes clips or messages."[69] Bearing witness. That's something ministry leaders can get behind.

Youth minister Tyler Smither draws a helpful distinction between Instagram and Snapchat. He writes, "It seems that what is happening here is that Snapchat is an app that allows teenagers to be their authentic self in front of another, and thus our students flock to it. On Instagram, they felt they had to post "good" pictures of themselves, but on Snapchat they could be honest and real with their close friends about who they feel they are, in all of its imperfection. Seen this way, one might even call Snapchat an app of grace."[70] Grace. With rainbow barf.

Snapchat is one of the hottest apps in an emerging class of messaging platforms like Facebook Messenger, WhatsApp, YikYak, and more, through which users connect directly and personally with their friends. This marks a shift for ministry leaders accustomed to posting content publically or even to small groups. Snapchat is a direct message sent to one or many people to which they can respond with their own snaps or a text chat. Pew Research reports that 33 percent of teens (slightly more female, tend to be of color) with cell phones use messaging apps.[71]

Snapchat is good for:

- Connecting with teens and young adults
- Direct communication and interaction. You don't just post something and then hope people see it. You send it to your contacts directly, individually, or to several at a time, and can see when it has been delivered and viewed.
- Having fun. Silliness is part of the Snapchat ethos. Have fun with it. Communicating in the moment

PROFILE AND SNAPCODE

Touch the Ghost at the top center of the home screen or swipe down to access your profile, add friends, view your friends, and see who's added you as a friend. Use the settings (wheel icon at the top right) to adjust privacy settings and activate location-based lenses (special lenses that appear depending on your location like out and about in your town, at a concert, or, hey, even a church—see below).

As part of creating a profile, you'll be asked to create a unique Snapcode for your profile. It functions like a unique QR code for your Snapchat profile. People can save your Snapcode to their phone and use it to add you as a friend. People often share their Snapcodes on other social media to encourage people to add them on Snapchat.

In addition to using the Snapcode, you can add friends by searching for them on Snapchat, adding them by username, from your address book, or finding people nearby.

SNAPS

Taking a picture or video is only the beginning of creating a fun and engaging snap. These are the additional functions at your disposal. Once you've taken your photo or video:

- *Filters*—Swipe to the left to view Instagram-like photo filters, as well as location-inspired graphics, including time, temperature, and how fast you are travelling
- *Lenses*—If you've taken a selfie, tap and hold your finger on your face. A series of "lenses" will make you look like a dog, give you a crown, put your face inside a piece of toast, let you barf rainbows
- *Stickers*—Tap the sticker icon at the top right of the screen to add stickers to your snap
- *Text Caption*—Tap the text icon on the top right to write a caption that runs across the screen and can be dragged higher or lower on the screen
- *Drawing*—Tap the crayon icon at the top right to pick a color and draw with your finger over the photo
- *Save*—Tap the download icon at the bottom left to save your snap to your camera roll before you send it (you can only save snaps before you send)
- *Add to Story*—Tap the story icon at the bottom left to add this snap to your story. It will be saved for twenty-four hours and be publicly available to your followers.

STORIES

From the home screen, swipe to the left (or tap the three circles at the bottom right) to view stories from media outlets and people you follow on Snapchat. Recently updated stories from those you follow will appear in the middle of the screen. Stories are a good option for reaching more people with your chats and telling the story of a mission trip, and even worship.

MEMORIES

From the home screen, swipe up (or tap the circle at the bottom center) to view your memories, a personal collection of snaps and stories that you have saved. This is a private collection of selected snaps and stories that you can show to friends or use to create new stories.

CHAT

Tap the blue circle with the quote bubble at the bottom left (or swipe to the right) to send simple text chat messages to friends.

CREATE YOUR OWN GEOLOCATION FILTERS

You can create your own geolocation filters from your church or hire someone to create one for you.[72] These filters are fun ways to "check-in" at a location and have been called "the new hashtag."[73]

Novice

- Play around on the Snapchat app, create a Snapcode
- Connect with some friends; use the buddy system: get a friend to learn together, or a youth or young adult in your life to help you.
- Chat, send some snaps with friends

Oblate

- Chat, send some snaps with friends
- Create stories
- Become more proficient at sending snaps

Superior

- Snaps make great reminders for upcoming events
- Curate stories of mission trips, a day-in-the-life of your congregation
- Create geo-filters for your congregation or ministry site by going to snapchat.com/on-demand

DIGITAL MINISTRY STRATEGY: BUILD YOUR SOCIAL MEDIA PLATFORM

The following steps are designed to help you build a digital social media platform based on your particular ministry context, the people you hope to reach, and the story you wish to tell. It's most effective if you gather input from your community as you work through the steps below.

1. Prioritize. Given your ministry setting, the network of relationships you hope to develop, and available time, rank the following social media featured in this chapter in order of priority:

Social Media	High	Medium	Low
Facebook	☐	☐	☐
Twitter	☐	☐	☐
Blog	☐	☐	☐
Instagram	☐	☐	☐
Pinterest	☐	☐	☐
YouTube	☐	☐	☐
Live Video	☐	☐	☐
Podcasting	☐	☐	☐
Snapchat	☐	☐	☐

2. Build Your Platform. Your high priority social media communities will make up the core of your digital ministry presence, where you will develop and share the heart of your story. Apply the following questions to each of your top three platforms. As you become more proficient in these, you may want to add other platforms to your digital ministry portfolio. But, complete Step 2—assessment—before you revise your strategy.

Platform A: _____

With whom do you hope to connect?

_____

What story do you wish to tell about your faith, your ministry, your community, or your life more generally?

_____

_____

_____

_____

_____

What techniques and/or examples from the chapter will help you tell that story?

Who might you consider as role models on this platform as you develop your own digital ministry practice?

Platform B: _____

With whom do you hope to connect?

What story do you wish to tell about your faith, your ministry, your community, or your life more generally?

What techniques and/or examples from the chapter will help you tell that story?

Who might you consider as role models on this platform as you develop your own digital ministry practice?

Platform C: _____

With whom do you hope to connect?

What story do you wish to tell about your faith, your ministry, your community, or your life more generally?

What techniques and/or examples from the chapter will help you tell that story?

Who might you consider as role models on this platform as you develop your own digital ministry practice?

3. Assess Engagement and Impact. The mega-church movement, and American culture in general, has impressed upon us the idea that "more is better"—more friends, more followers, platforms, more members. As we've stressed throughout this book, the key measures in digital media are not numerical, but relational. The questions below will help you to assess meaningful ministry engagement in each platform. We suggest that you review this assessment on a quarterly basis and make adjustments to your strategy in consultation with your social media and local communities.

What specific stories illustrate how each platform has helped to engage with members of your local church or faith community?

_____

_____

_____

What specific stories illustrate how each platform has helped to engage with people in your area who are not members of your faith community?

_____

_____

_____

What specific stories illustrate how each platform has helped to engage with people from different social or demographic groups than those usually represented in your community?

_____

_____

_____

What specific stories illustrate how each platform has helped to connect with people outside of your area professional, spiritually, or otherwise?

_____

_____

_____

How much time do you now spend on digital ministry?

_____ Minutes a Day _____ Minutes a Week

Is this too much or too little in light of the engagement and impact you've observed?

_____
_____
_____

How might expanding to other platforms help your ministry? Again, more isn't necessarily better. How will connecting with new social networks help you to extend God's love, fellowship, and compassion to others? How might it take away from other aspects of your ministry?

_____
_____
_____
_____

4. Next Steps. Based on your quarterly assessment, what specific practices will you (and your community) take to deepen your networked, relational, incarnational digital ministry?

- ☐ None. Staying the course and getting more proficient where I/we are seems like the best approach right now.

- ☐ Deeper practice in current platforms. I/we will work on connecting more with people in our current networks in the following ways:

  _____
  _____
  _____

- ☐ Adding new networks. I/we will start developing networks in order to extend our story and connect more widely.

- ☐ Pulling back from networks in order to focus time and attentiveness more fully where I/we seem to be having the most engagement and impact.

NOTES

1. On this, see Elizabeth Drescher, "HWJT (How Would Jesus Tweet?): Reimaging Media as Social," *Explore* (Fall 2011).
2. Learn more about #decolonizelutheranism at http://decolonizelutheranism.org.
3. Facebook, Company Info, accessed January 7, 2016, http://newsroom.fb.com/company-info/.
4. "Social Media Update 2016," Pew Research Center, November 11, 2016, http://www.pewinternet.org/2016/11/11/social-media-update-2016/.
5. Jennifer Preston, "Facebook Page for Jesus, With Highly Active Fans," *New York Times*, September 4, 2011. http://www.nytimes.com/2011/09/05/technology/jesus-daily-on-facebook-nurtures-highly-active-fans.html.
6. Alyssa Bereznak, "The New Tech Evangelists," The Ringer, July 11, 2016, https://theringer.com/the-new-tech-evangelists-d6d222605fbf#.mf7wsbxoy.
7. Statista, "Number of Monthly Active Twitter Users Worldwide from 1st Quarter 2010 to 1st Quarter 2016 (in millions)," The Statistics Portal, accessed November 13, 2017, http://www.statista.com/statistics/282087/number-of-monthly-active-twitter-users/.
8. Statista, "Number of Monthly Active Twitter Users in the United States from 1st Quarter 2010 to 1st Quarter 2016 (in millions)," The Statistics Portal, accessed November 13, 2017, http://www.statista.com/statistics/274564/monthly-active-twitter-users-in-the-united-states/.
9. Maeve Duggan, "Mobile Messaging and Social Media 2015," Pew Research Center, August 19, 2015, http://www.pewinternet.org/2015/08/19/mobile-messaging-and-social-media-2015/.
10. Amanda Lenhart, "Teens Social Media & Technology Overview 2015," Pew Research Center, April 9, 2015, http://www.pewinternet.org/2015/04/09/teens-social-media-technology-2015/.
11. Duggan, "Mobile Messaging and Social Media 2015."
12. Gary Vaynerchuk, *Jab, Jab, Jab, Right Hook: How to Tell Your Story in a Noisy Social World* (New York: Harper Business, 2013), 85.
13. Andrew McGill, "Can Twitter Fit Inside the Library of Congress?" *Atlantic*, August 4, 2016, https://www.theatlantic.com/technology/archive/2016/08/can-twitter-fit-inside-the-library-of-congress/494339/.
14. Learn more at http://www.slateproject.org.
15. More about #slatespeak at http://www.slateproject.org/slatespeak.html.
16. The Slate Project by The Episcopal Church on YouTube (April 24, 2016). Available online at https://www.youtube.com/watch?v=SuJbpxw67aw.
17. Webdesigner Depot Staff, "A Brief History of Blogging," Webdesigner Depot, March 14, 2011, http://www.webdesignerdepot.com/2011/03/a-brief-history-of-blogging/.
18. Julia McCoy, "52 Incredible Blogging Statistics to Inspire You to Blog," Express Writers, April 4, 2017, https://expresswriters.com/blogging-statistics/.
19. Douglas Quenqua, "Blogs Falling in an Empty Forest," *New York Times*, June 5, 2009, http://www.nytimes.com/2009/06/07/fashion/07blogs.html; Elizabeth Drescher,

"New Media and the Reshaping of Religious Practice," *Immanent Frame*, March 16, 2010, http://blogs.ssrc.org/tif/2010/03/16/new-media-and-the-reshaping-of-religious-practice/.

20. Seth Godin & Tom Peters on blogging, YouTube, April 18, 2009, https://www.youtube.com/watch?v=livzJTIWlmY.

21. Read the Lutheran Zephyr at https://lutheranzephyr.com.

22. Read Dirty Sexy Ministry at http://www.dirtysexyministry.com.

23. Craig Smith, "96 Amazing Tumblr Facts (February 2016)," DMR, March 18, 2017, http://expandedramblings.com/index.php/tumblr-user-stats-fact/.

24. Lenhart, "Teens Social Media & Technology Overview 2015."

25. Enjoy Ev'ry Day I'm Pastorin' at http://everydayimpastoring.tumblr.com.

26. Jeremy Smith, "Holy Humor 03: Interview with Ev'ry Day I'm Pastorin,'" Hacking Christianity, February 5, 2013, http://hackingchristianity.net/2013/02/holy-humor-03-interview-with-evry-day-im-pastorin.html.

27. Ibid.

28. Larry Kim, "16 Eye-Popping Statistics You Need to Know About Visual Content Marketing," *Inc.*. November 23, 2015, www.inc.com/larry-kim/visual-content-marketing-16-eye-popping-statistics-you-need-to-know.html.

29. Duggan, "Mobile Messaging and Social Media 2015."

30. Keith Anderson, *The Digital Cathedral: Networked Ministry in a Wireless World* (New York: Morehouse, 2015), 172.

31. Ibid, 183.

32. Instagram Press News at Instagram.com/press, accessed November 13, 2017.

33. Duggan, "Mobile Messaging and Social Media 2015."

34. Lenhart, "Teens Social Media & Technology Overview 2015."

35. Duggan, "Mobile Messaging and Social Media 2015."

36. Instagram, "A New Look for Instagram," Instagram blog, May 2016, http://blog.instagram.com/post/144198429587/160511-a-new-look.

37. Staff Writers, "Study: The Most Popular Instagram Filters From Around the World," Canva, February 10, 2016, https://designschool.canva.com/blog/popular-instagram-filters/.

38. Learn more about the Repost app at http://instarepostapp.com.

39. Elizabeth Dias, "Like Instagram, But For the Bible," *Time*, March 6, 2015, http://time.com/3735239/parallel-bible-app/.

40. Pinterest, "It Starts with a Great Idea," Pinterest Press page, accessed November 13, 2017, https://about.pinterest.com/press.

41. Enid Hwang, "100 Million of the Most Interesting People We Know," Pinterest, September 16, 2016, https://blog.pinterest.com/en/100-million-most-interesting-people-we-know.

42. Craig Smith, **"**By the Numbers: 270 Amazing Pinterest Statistics," DMR, March 2016, http://expandedramblings.com/index.php/pinterest-stats/, accessed January 2, 2017.

43. Pinterest, "All About the Pinterest Browser Button," accessed January 2, 2017, https://help.pinterest.com/en/articles/add-pinterest-browser-button#Web.

44. Learn more about #AdventWord at http://adventword.org.

45. Mat Honan, "Why Facebook and Mark Zuckerberg Went All In on Video," *BuzzFeed,* April 6, 2016, https://www.buzzfeed.com/mathonan/why-facebook-and-mark-zuckerberg-went-all-in-on-live-video.

46. YouTube, "Statistics." Availble at https://www.youtube.com/yt/press/statistics.html.

47. Casey Fitzgerald, The Easter Story. Available online at https://vimeo.com/124118281.

48. UDLC Families Tell the Christmas Story (Luke 2:1–20), https://vimeo.com/196332956, and UDLC Families Tell the Easter Story, https://vimeo.com/213432452.

49. Learn more at http://www.90secondsermon.com.

50. How to Build a 90 Second Sermon, available online at http://www.90secondsermon.com/BuildIt.html.

51. View more at http://thirtysecondsorless.net/.

52. #30SecondBible available online at http://thirtysecondsorless.net/30secondbible/.

53. Google+, Dalai Lama & Desmond Tutu in a Google+ Hangout On Air (October 8, 2011). Available online at https://www.youtube.com/watch?v=1_HqVFEzY2U.

54. Craig Smith, "17 Interesting Periscope Statistics (December 2016)," DMR, December 21, 2016, http://expandedramblings.com/index.php/periscope-statistics/.

55. Team Periscope, "Year One," Periscope blog, March 28, 2016, https://medium.com/@periscope/year-one-81c4c625f5bc#.wey3cmy9t.

56. Casey Newton, "Politicians Have a Powerful New Tool in Periscope, and Democracy Is Better Off for It," *The Verge,* June 23, 2016, http://www.theverge.com/2016/6/23/12011374/congress-sit-in-periscope-c-span-meerkat-election.

57. Cynthia Littleton, "Facebook Live Coverage of Falcon Heights Shooting Stirs Outrage, Protests," *Variety,* July 7, 2016. http://variety.com/2016/biz/news/falcon-heights-facebook-live-police-shooting-philando-castile-1201809862/.

58. Jay Baer, "The 11 Critical Podcast Statistics of 2017," Convine&Concert, March 15, 2017, http://www.convinceandconvert.com/podcast-research/the-11-critical-podcast-statistics-of-2017/.

59. Pew Research, "State of the News Media 2015," Pew Research Center, April 29, 2015, http://www.journalism.org/2015/04/29/podcasting-fact-sheet-2015/.

60. "'The B.S. Podcast': Bill Simmons and Chuck Klosterman on Joe Lacob, Karma, and Chance, The Ringer, April 7, 2016, https://www.facebook.com/notes/the-ringer/the-bs-podcast-bill-simmons-and-chuck-klosterman-on-joe-lacob-karma-and-chance/1697733873826396.

61. Learn more at http://www.storydivine.com/ and http://faithandwonder.com/.

62. Learn more at http://thiseverydayholy.com/.

63. "Episode 19: Advent Themes of Love," *This Everyday Holy,* December 18, 2015, https://thiseverydayholy.com/2015/12/18/episode-19-advent-themes-on-love/.

64. "Live from eFormation 2016," *The Collect Call,* June 8, 2016, http://www.acts8movement.org/the-collect-call-live-from-eformation-2016/.

65. Learn more at http://theoaforlent.com.

66. Craig Smith, "135 Amazing Snapchat Facts and Statistics (September 2017)," *DMR,* October 30, 2017, http://expandedramblings.com/index.php/snapchat-statistics/.

67. Lenhart, "Teens Social Media & Technology Overview 2015."

68. Sarah Frier, "Snapchat Passes Twitter in Daily Usage," *Bloomberg,* June 2, 2016, http://www.bloomberg.com/news/articles/2016-06-02/snapchat-passes-twitter-in-daily-usage.

69. Joanna Stern, "How to Use Snapchat," *Wall Street Journal,* January 12, 2016, http://www.wsj.com/articles/snapchat-101-learn-to-love-the-worlds-most-confusing-social-network-1452628322.

70. Tyler Smither, "Snapchat as an App of Grace," Winona Lake Free Methodist Church, March 18, 2014, http://wlfmc.org/parents-progress-3-27-14/.

71. Lenhart, "Teens Social Media & Technology Overview 2015."

72. More about On Demand Geofilters at https://www.snapchat.com/on-demand.

73. Molly McHugh, "Inside the Newest Snapchat Megatrend," The Ringer, July 5, 2016, https://www.theringer.com/2016/7/5/16047070/geofilters-are-the-newest-snapchat-megatrend.

4

PRACTICING THE ARTS OF DIGITAL MINISTRY

Digital ministry isn't just about the new spaces into which we extend our ministry in the Digital Age. It's also about how we adapt basic practices of ministry to these spaces. In this chapter, we explore the ministry arts of faithful listening, offering hospitality, caring for God's people, forming disciples, building community, making public witness, and stewarding God-given resources as these practices play out in social networking communities and as they're shaped by social digital culture. In the final section of the chapter, we share three profiles of ministry leaders who have effectively adapted these practices in the context of digital ministry.

DIGITAL MINISTRY CALLS US INTO NEW SPACES and invites us to develop new relationships with people from our own communities, with neighbors we may never otherwise have known, and with those who might never step inside our churches or organizations. But the newness of our participation in digital spaces can sometimes obscure the fact that we rely on very basic, indeed, very traditional modes of engaging that have served us well for generations. In the introduction, we revisited these core practices though the LACE model that Elizabeth introduced in *Tweet If You ♥ Jesus*:

- *Listening*—Taking time to get to know people in social networks based on what they share in profiles, posts, tweets, and so on, rather than making communicating your message the priority
- *Attending*—Noticing and being present to the experiences and interests of others as they share themselves in digital spaces

- *Connecting*—Reaching out to others in diverse communities in order to deepen and extend the networks that influence your digital spiritual practice
- *Engaging*—Building relationships by sharing content, collaborating, and connecting people to others

These basic practices allow people of faith to enter digital communities from a networked, relational, incarnational perspective, with the goal of getting to know others in a more sustained way over time and connecting more deeply within and across communities. This contrasts with what amounts to a marketing effort aimed at getting a message to as many people as possible without regard to who they are as particular persons in community. The LACE model is the starting point for meaningful relationship in the digitally integrated world.

But for those who are engaged more specifically in serving and attending God's people wherever they are, participating in digital communities calls on distinctive practices for the vocation of ministry. This vocational distinction has nothing, of course, to do with status or rank. Rather, it has to do with being present very clearly as servants of God's people in digital spaces, much in the way that ordained ministers wear collars in local spaces so that people see and understand their vocational calling. Lay ministers distinguish themselves in other ways—through profile descriptions that include descriptions of their lay ministry, for instance—but as with clergy, they also make themselves available to people for specific kinds of engagement meant to enrich the lives of others and invite them into deeper relationship with God.

For those specifically called to serve God's diverse people in their communities, these practices must incorporate listening, attending, connecting, and engaging in concrete ways. In this chapter, we have included seven specific arts of ministry that bring Christian belief, tradition, and action into conversation with the spiritual dimensions of everyday life as they are encountered in digital and physical spaces. These digital ministry arts are:

- *Faithful Listening*—Attending deeply to others on the basis of their concerns, needs, and interests rather than our own agendas
- *Offering Hospitality*—Creating sacred space and welcoming others into it
- *Caring for God's People*—Sharing prayer, encouragement, inspiration, and wisdom

- *Forming Disciples*—Enriching spiritual lives through education, small group practice, and preaching
- *Building Community*—Connecting within and across local and digital networks and connecting others to those with complementary interests
- *Making Public Witness*—Bearing witness to the love of God in Jesus Christ through words and actions so that others are inspired and invited to experience this love; and advocating for and encouraging action on behalf of those in need
- *Stewarding God-Given Resources*—Ensuring that the work of God's people can be sustained by cultivating, tending, and sharing the abundance of time, treasure, and talents that enable us to be Christ's Church in the world.

We might have included any number of other ministry arts, such as worship, sacramental ministries, formal spiritual direction, or vocational mentoring. And there are those who would argue, not without merit, that preaching could easily be called out as a separate category that combines formation, witness, and proclamation. As we noted in chapter 3, preaching is, as a genre, not always particularly well-suited to digital spaces, and our observation has been that it invites a certain overmessaging among those whose offline ministries involve a good deal of preaching. For this reason, and because of the practical demand that we narrow the list of practices we explore, we limited our discussion of preaching to its role in formation.

We narrowed our list not only because of the limits of space within this book, but also because we are keen to situate digital ministry across the often rigidly conceived boundaries between the laity and the ordained. Among the great gifts of digital social media communities are the opportunities they present to members of what Protestants refer to as "the priesthood of all believers" to explore and share their faith and to develop their own vocations as ministers in the church, formally or as affirmed by the people they serve.

That said, we did expand the list in the second edition with two new categories: faithful listening and stewarding God-given resources. In the first case, we return to the discussion of listening faithfully and attentively to others that Elizabeth began in *Tweet If You* ♥ *Jesus* because we've come to the conclusion that the content saturation we've all experienced through growing social networking participation in the past five years has significantly undermined basic practices of listening that are central to the Christian tradition and human experience in general. Because listening is the basis, really, of all arts of ministry, it seemed timely and worthwhile to give it new consideration.

Likewise, though stewardship may well be the least popular of all of the arts of ministry, it is increasingly important in all of our congregational communities and organizations as well as in the everyday lives of people of faith. Certainly the financial challenges of sustaining the Church are pressing in the current age, but these of course are reflections of changing demographic patterns in the church—that is, of the aging and numerical decline of the Church. Recent research from Public Religion Research Institute, a Washington, DC, public opinion research firm that explores religion, values, and public life, mark a dramatic growth in the religiously unaffiliated from 1975 and 2016, from 7 percent of the population to 24 percent. As most church folks know, the percentage grows substantially when we look at younger people. Among younger adults, age 18 to 29, the rate of unaffiliation climbs to 38 percent. But unaffiliation is normalizing, according to the PRRI data, with nearly a third of unaffiliated adults being at least 50 years old. The researchers point out that the youngest religious groups in the United States are Muslims, Hindus, and Buddhists, each with majorities of adherents under age 50. Among Evangelical Protestants, Mainline Protestants, and Catholics, the pattern is flipped, each having majorities over age 50. In all three groups, as well, nearly a third are over age 65. This has put obvious strains on congregations and other church organizations.[1]

In addition, as digital culture has changed all sorts of life practices, the means and motivations for sharing God's abundance with world communities has also changed. As we mentioned in chapter 1, digital giving technologies like GoFundMe and Indiegogo have made it much easier for individuals and organizations to develop focused funding campaigns. Likewise, gathering platforms like Meetup, Eventbrite, and Facebook Events make organizing even the most impromptu events a snap. There's lots of good news in that for churches and ministers, but these technologies also contribute to the decentering of churches as places for charitable giving, community engagement, and service. This has significant implications for stewardship.

As we considered the arts of digital ministry in this light, we wanted to focus on those that would tend to avoid the complexities and conflicts about what constitutes lay and ordained ministry "proper." Beyond this, our bias throughout this book has been to focus on ministry practices that enrich and extend face-to-face worship and community rather than advocating for those which, research has shown, tend to compete with face-to-face spiritual relationships and communities. This contributed to the more limited treatment of preaching, and also to our decision not to include worship practices or sacramental ministries, though these are certainly to be found in digital spaces.[2]

The sections that follow describe these arts and offer brief examples of digitally integrated ministers who have effectively included them in their pastoral, congregational, organizing, and other ministry practices. The final sections of the chapter offer three more detailed narratives exploring the practices of digitally integrated ministry by Lutheran pastor Nadia Bolz-Weber, the Reverend Laura Everett, executive director of the Massachusetts Council of Churches and author of *Holy Spokes: The Search for Spirituality on Two Wheels* (Eerdmans, 2017), and Anthony Guillen, missioner for Latino/Hispanic Ministries in The Episcopal Church. We profiled both Nadia and Laura in the first edition because we saw both as being on the leading edge of digitally integrated ministry practice. You'll see in the updated profiles that both have continued to blaze trails in ministry, on- and offline, through the newest social networking platforms and the most old-timey of media.

4.1 Faithful Listening
Widening the Path of Digitally Integrated Ministry

"In the beginning, there was the Word," John's gospel tells us. That has perhaps contributed to Christianity being inherently wordy tradition. We have lots to say, what with proclaiming the Good News, sharing stories of love and hope, advocating to justice and peace, amplifying the voices of those who have been silenced or ignored, and designing top flight liturgies.

But without someone—many someones—to hear, inwardly digest, and act upon all those words, they really are quite meaningless. We came to know the Word among us precisely because, at least some of the time, we were listening. This is, of course, insight into the obvious: for any words to have any meaning, there must be a listener, even if that is an internal listener to the words of the heart and the mind. Yet it is pretty uncontroversial to suggest that listening—attentive listening, deep listening, transformative listening—is increasingly rare. This may be especially true in a 24/7, media-saturated world in which message upon message issues forth from a multitude of sources, including our own social networking feeds, text messaging devices, and sundry other technologies. This is why, we would argue, listening is at the heart of Christian ministry. Indeed, so much do we believe this is the case that we begin our discussion of essential arts of digitally integrated ministry with the practice of listening. Without it, the arts of ministry that follow are hardly ministry at all.

There are elements of classical Christian care of souls (*cura animarum*) that are related to the kind of deep, faithful listening we are thinking about here, including "the ministry of presence, the practice of unconditional positive regard, and the giving of oneself to God for the sake of the care seeker."[3] But, as the Buddhist-Christian pastoral care scholar Duane R. Bidwell points out, these Christian practices can often actually impede a mode of listening unattached to an evangelical, sacramental, or creedal outcome. This is a discipline of listening that depends on setting aside even the most noble of spiritual or personal agendas, resisting the desire to respond to what we hear from the perspective of our own experience, and being open to moments of confusion, doubt, error, mystery, and surprise as the voice, eyes, gestures, and other bodily expressions of another fully engage our own embodied consciousness. That is, we're not listening to discover, in Karl Rahner's phrase, an "anonymous Christianity" hidden within someone's "unchurched" soul. Rather, we're listening to hear another's own voice, to attend to their story with concentration, compassion, and an ability to set aside judgment. In addition, deep listening brings the listener and the speaker into a kind of spiritual alignment when the listener is open to being transformed by the experiences and insights of another in a way that invites a profound honoring of the other—sometimes someone whose story we perhaps do not want to hear at all.

We see this kind of listening, for instance, in the story of Jesus and the Syrophoenician woman in Matthew 15. At first, Jesus would not hear the woman's plea for help for her ailing daughter because an ethnic boundary stood between them. But when Jesus rebuffs the woman with a slur—calling her people "dogs" who do not deserve the "food" he brings to the children of Israel—she hears a more just and compassionate story even in his harsh words. Her deeper listening persuades Jesus not only to effect the healing of her daughter, but also to praise her great faith. This is, ultimately, a faith grounded in a deep listening by one who had heard of Jesus, his teachings, and his miracles, and who was able to have faith in them because of the depth of the truth she had discerned despite Jesus's own questionable behavior in the story.

It is a kind of listening that is central to the ministry of Darleen Pryds. Pryds is a professor of medieval Christian spirituality at the Franciscan School of Theology at the University of San Diego and the author of *Women of the Streets: Early Franciscan Women and Their Mendicant Vocation* (Franciscan Institute, 2010). Professor Pryds's scholarship has focused on the ministries of laypeople in the medieval church, especially women, most of whom were prevented from responding to vocations of teaching, preaching, and presiding. But these are not abstract stories from long ago for Dr. Pryds, as she herself has developed a ministry of care for those at the end of their lives in hospice. For this work, she draws both from Franciscan Catholic resources and from training with the Zen Hospice in San Francisco. In both traditions, deep listening is not merely an element of care, it is a fundamental expression of caring itself.

"Hospice experience," Professor Pryds says, "is a great reminder that people change day-in, day-out, and across the day. So, hopefully, the listening that I bring to people is in each and every visit, because they do change in ways that you can't expect and that you can't anticipate. And that's part of listening deeply—to go in and be willing to be genuinely curious about who you are encountering that day."

Having deep openness to and curiosity about the experiences, perceptions, and feelings of others is not, Pryds suggests, something many of us are prepared for well:

> So many of us, especially in ministry, are trained to be in conversation with people, but often we really have an agenda. We hear a little bit of what someone is saying, but then we interject with a question. That really allows us to steer the conversation in the direction of the person posing the question rather than allowing the person who is speaking to express what is on their heart and on their mind.

It is, we would argue, perhaps a particularly difficult shift in a digitally integrated world that focuses so much on messaging—on sending out ideas, information, even prayers and messages of solidarity and support—rather than being present to and drawing in "what is in the heart and on the mind of another person," says Pryds. "Most people don't ever have the experience of fully expressing themselves," she continues. To be truly deep listeners, we have to "get out of the habit of asking our own questions and allow the path of the conversation to widen."

The good news is that the digitally integrated world has so many more opportunities for this widened reality when we have (digital) eyes to see and ears to hear. A compelling, and perhaps curious, Instagram post might invite us to go beyond liking to say, "I'd love to know more about that!" A Facebook post can be an occasion to hold back on our own thoughts, instead asking the person who posted to tell us more. These seem like simple gestures, but the architecture of social media itself is designed to invite reactive commenting rather than active attentiveness that is akin to deep listening. When we pause and reflect before we comment, when we adjust our response so that, in the helpful metaphor offered by Professor Pryds, we widen the path upon which we can truly travel with others, we are beginning to practice deep listening in a noisy, digitally integrated world. We hope that you will find this by no means simple practice of deep listening as the basis of the arts of ministry we discuss below.

4.2 Offering Hospitality

The Digital Narthex

Where does hospitality begin? For many churches it happens just inside the front door. There, in the narthex or entryway, greeters wait to welcome newcomers to worship. Visitor packets stuffed with information are stacked near the door. Guest books and visitor cards wait to be filled out. Ushers hand out worship materials and help people to their pews. The coffee is on.

These are certainly good practices of welcoming. The problem, of course, is that only the people who show up for church get to experience this hospitality. What's more, even those who come through our church doors can often get the impression that they only exist for us once they fill out a visitor card. Often, our welcome is more of an introduction of us than an embrace of the visitor, whether or not she or he plans to come back again.

> ### Hospitality and Reciprocity
>
> Much of what we and other digital ministers admire has to do with how we open our digital spaces—church and personal Facebook pages, Twitter feeds, etc.—to others. That's certainly important. But it's also important to remember that the world doesn't revolve around our social media presence. Everyone with whom we might want to connect, whom we might want to engage, who might need the ministry we hope to share, isn't going to randomly happen into our digital neighborhood. It's important, then, to get out a bit. Visit other people's personal and group Facebook pages, leaving messages of friendship, encouragement, and support. Leave comments on Instagram photos, and include a link to your Twitter feed or your organization's Facebook page.
>
> Perhaps most importantly, share the digital love by judiciously following people back when they follow you on Twitter, by liking other's Facebook group pages, and by friending people you meet as often as you wait for others to friend you. Nothing says "I only care about you when you're listening to me" like a Twitter user who has a thousand followers, but only follows a couple dozen chosen few. Nothing says "You're only important when you have something for me" like sharing content someone else has posted without giving them credit by name.
>
> Hospitality is not just a matter of opening your digital door, but of being willing to travel across the digital domain on a regular basis. Digital hospitality depends on reciprocity—taking the kinds of walks, even out of our comfort zones, that Jesus called us to as disciples and which the apostles and saints modeled.

Today, digital social media enable congregations to extend hospitality and welcome beyond the front door into digital spaces. Not unimportantly, digital culture demands this. Rather than passively waiting for people to walk through our doors, ministry leaders and congregations must be more active and visibly participative in social media communities—making ourselves available, greeting strangers, finding points of connection, and creating what we might call a digital narthex. But the relational emphasis of social networking sites also presses us to connect in ways that move well beyond the visitor card and brochures about church programs we tend to dole out at the front door.

WHY A WEBSITE WELCOME IS NOT ENOUGH

Websites can certainly provide a measure of hospitality, particularly if they express an attentiveness to the needs of visitors and newcomers, help to tell an engaging story of your ministry, and paint a picture of what someone might expect at worship or other public gatherings. However, websites are simply not enough. Websites, although they increasingly integrate elements of social media, are really primarily about providing information. What is more, websites are not generally social platforms, so people have to already know something about who you are—if not by name, by denomination or by a topic with which you're associated. This means that they have to already be motivated to find you by searching for you on Facebook, Google, or another site.

When people have that motivation, your website can be helpful. But bear in mind that, thanks to the search engine Google, people have more than enough information about most of the basics of your church or organization—and often much deeper detail as well—right at their fingertips. In fact, they often have too much. Some have even said we are suffering from "information fatigue" because there's so much data available about pretty much everything, your ministry and your church included. Information provided on a website is important for people who want to know the who, what, when, and where of your community, but it is no substitute for active and authentic attending and connecting as ministry leaders. People don't need more information. What they want are relationships—with you, with your community, and with others like them who are beginning to explore their faith in a new setting. To the extent that your website can point them to that sort of experience by connecting people to your Facebook community, for instance, highlighting YouTube videos that bring more of your story to life, or inviting folks to your Instagram feed to illuminate the vibrancy of your community, your website is a valuable part of a social media strategy that highlights hospitality. But it's hardly the whole digitally integrated ministry enchilada.

@KLAMACH COMES TO CHURCH

One congregation had a particularly powerful experience of the effect of hospitality in digital spaces on participation in local spaces—a powerful example of the digitally *integrated* nature of life today—when Chris Lawrence, whom Keith had met through Twitter, visited the church Keith was pastoring at

Practicing the Arts of Digital Ministry 159

the time for Sunday services. Lawrence (@klamach) is a spiritual seeker. Part of his search has taken place on Twitter, where he became connected to the church and social media tweetchat (#chsocm) started by Meredith Gould, in which Keith had participated regularly. In a common but often undervalued social media story of unfolding and deepening connection, Chris and Keith became aware of one another, had some casual online engagement, and passed a few questions back and forth—in this case, on Lutheran worship. This all eventually led to Chris's visit to the Lutheran Church of Redeemer.

Chris tweeted about his experience afterward:

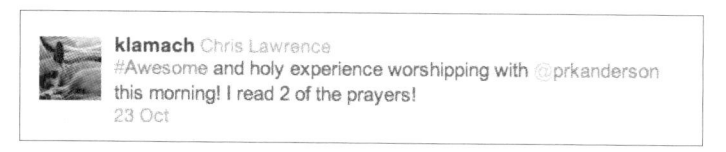

> **klamach** Chris Lawrence
> #Awesome and holy experience worshipping with @prkanderson this morning! I read 2 of the prayers!
> 23 Oct

And, Keith tweeted back his own gratitude for Lawrence's participation:

> **prkanderson** Pr. Keith Anderson
> Thanks for praying! RT @klamach: The Prayers of Intercession I read/lead this morning at Redeemer yfrog.com/odlz4cj
> 23 Oct
>
> **prkanderson** Pr. Keith Anderson
> Awesome to have you! RT @klamach: #Awesome and holy experience worshipping with @prkanderson this morning! I read 2 of the prayers!
> 23 Oct

Chris's blog post added more depth to the experience. "I found myself this morning at a church where, just a mere four months ago," he wrote, "I never would have imagined myself worshipping."

Now, readers might want the end of this story to be that Chris became a member of Redeemer. That didn't happen, and ministry leaders should be cautioned that our presence on social networks is unlikely to fill our churches. After all, there's much more to the increasing emptiness of pews than day-to-day connection to practicing Christians, on- or offline. Still, the experience of hospitality and welcome that played out on Twitter, then still 140 characters at a time, over the course of a few weeks and brought Chris to Redeemer that Sunday is not to be discounted. Even this slight gesture opened a conversation and bridged what was clearly a yawning spiritual gap for Chris. The ongoing

160 CLICK 2 SAVE REBOOT

interaction was *real* ministry—one that integrated digital and local engagement in ways that clearly were meaningful for Chris.

DIGITAL MONASTIC HOSPITALITY: AS IF THEY WERE CHRIST

The monastic Rule of St. Benedict has, for centuries, guided the lives not only of those who join monastic communities, but also of many who seek to live their faith according to a clear and balanced appreciation of the teachings of Christ as they apply to the very practical demands of everyday life.

The Benedictine Rule highlights, in particular, the spiritual significance of hospitality in its instruction with regard to the reception of guests:

> All guests who arrive should be received as if they were Christ, for He himself is going to say: "I came as a stranger, and you received Me"; and let due honor be shown to all, especially those who share our faith and those who are pilgrims.[4]

The monks of the Society of Saint John the Evangelist, an Episcopal monastery in Cambridge, Massachusetts, are greatly influenced by the Benedictine Rule. Their own more contemporary Rule of Life brings the monastic practice of hospitality into digital communities as well as anyone we've seen. Through Facebook, Twitter, Instagram, blogs, and YouTube, these "monks for a new century" open the monastic enclosure to the world, offering the gifts of the monastic tradition, and inviting visitors to engage with the life of the community through pictures, sermons, gems of monastic wisdom, audio and written reflections—all of which make monastic life accessible, visible, and engaging for new generations of seekers. People can feel a part of the community before they walk in the doors, and those who cannot or may not ever have the opportunity to walk through the doors can still find comfort, encouragement, and inspiration.

Digitally updating the ancient monastic practice of desert *ammas* and *abbas* (mothers and fathers) who offered morsels of wisdom along with a bit of food and a place to rest, the community's Instagram feed offers a daily "word" in the form of engaging, highly sharable memes and pictures of the monastery grounds. The brothers take care to be present on Instagram to their more than five hundred followers as well as elsewhere in digital landscape so that their welcome is available to travelers on Facebook, Twitter, and YouTube. This makes invitation, hospitality, welcome, and relationship an ongoing possibility—an act of intention, providence, and grace.

CREATING DIGITAL SACRED SPACE

This practice of digital hospitality has the effect of creating sacred space within the digitally integrated landscape. We do that through a ministry presence which incorporates listening, noticing, accepting, and reaching out in kindness and compassion to the others in our midst. Whenever we receive one another in Christian love, in digital or face-to-face locales, we can suddenly see that we are standing together in spaces made sacred by our very connection. This is no less true in social media locales than in geographic places.

Sacred space in social media can be found in multiple forms. It can be found in designated places like a monastery Facebook page, Instagram feeds with spiritual images and reflections, or a Twitter stream dedicated to prayer and inspiration. Like church sanctuaries, these are places where it is commonly recognized that God is present and the purpose of gathering is to be attentive to that presence. For example, the Abbey of the Arts Facebook page, maintained by writer, spiritual director, and Benedictine oblate Christine Valters Paintner and her husband, John, serves as a quiet place for shared contemplation and reflection within the bustle of the digital world. On it, the Paintners offer inspirational quotes, spiritual commentary, and online "resources for integrating contemplative practice and creative expression."

Since the first edition, the Paintners have emigrated to Galway, Ireland, where they offer retreats and workshops focused on developing various ways of being "monks in the world" through contemplative practice, artistic exploration, and embodied discovery of natural landscapes. Local experiences such as these incarnate the hospitality offered by Abbey of the Arts, and they are illuminated richly in word and image on the Abbey website. But the Facebook page has a dailiness to it that allows it to function as a spiritual resource

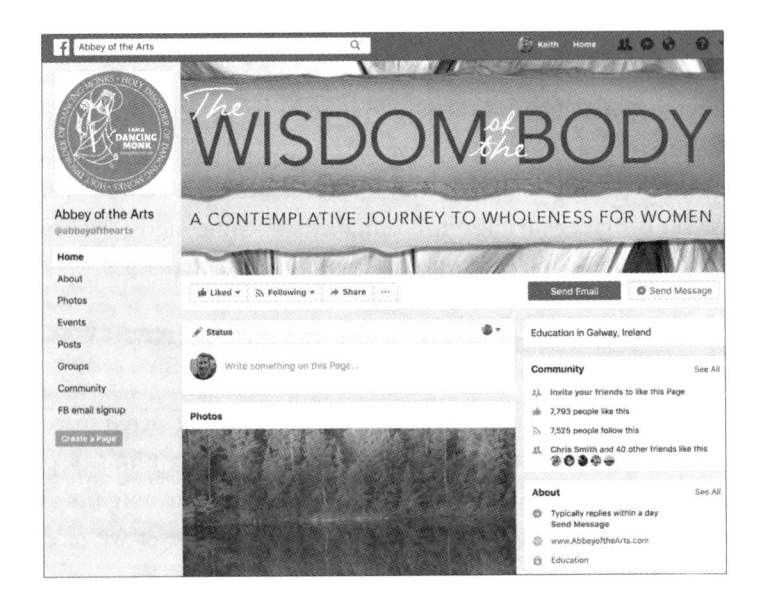

Practicing the Arts of Digital Ministry **163**

as well as a sacred space for people who have connected through workshops or retreats, or who know of the Abbey and those in its extended community only through Christine's writing, visual art, and facilitation of spiritual conversation. Such spaces serve as spiritual oases—reminders that the divine is always in our midst, made known to us through our connectedness to one another and all of creation. And, like the brothers of the Society of Saint John the Evangelist, Christine and John periodically offer a word—literally, one word, in this case—and a stunning image on the Abbey's Instagram feed that shares the ethos of their ministry and invites further engagement with the extended community.

DIGITAL LIMINALITY

Sacred space also becomes apparent to us in less clearly defined, perhaps more random, ways across the social media landscape through the countless sacred moments of deep understanding, the acknowledgement of our common humanity, the sharing of our hopes, and the vulnerability and intimacy we express as we wrestle with our faith and doubt, and seek to heal our brokenness in community. In the welcome and love of others, in reciprocal appreciation, we glimpse our inestimable value to God. These moments pop up all over the digital world, as people connect and engage in ways they might never do in a church or other religious organization.

Sometimes these moments may seem insignificant. A birthday greeting is offered to a Facebook "friend" we may not know at all in person. Someone "likes" a photo you've posted on Instagram of your kid's first day of school. An almost-stranger comments in the perfect way on a tweet. It can seem like nothing sometimes, these small social media gestures. Yet time and again we learn how much they mean to people, how significant they are in the context of daily lives whose challenges and complexity are largely invisible to us. In this way, digital locales often appear to be not unlike the "thin places" of pre-Christian and Celtic tradition, where the line between creation and the divine, the temporal and the eternal, seems less sharply drawn, where we seem able to be more present to God and God to us.

"Liminal spaces," theologians often call these locales and the experience of a spiritual "in-between" that seems possible there. This is, of course, exactly where Jesus asked the apostles and the disciples who followed in their footsteps to go when he called them—and calls us—to share the Good News with "the whole creation" (Mark 16:15). We are called to walk among the people, and in doing so, to progressively trample down the barriers that keep us all from knowing the Kingdom that Jesus promises us is always near. This liminal possibility is richly present in social media communities when we open ourselves to the matrix of networks and relationships available there. In doing so, we claim the digital landscape as sacred space, a locale where the grace of Jesus Christ, the love of God, and the fellowship of the Holy

Spirit (2 Cor. 13:14) is as present as it is in our churches, our homes, our workplaces, our schools, and everywhere else in our physical communities.

4.3 Caring for God's People
Logging In to Digitally Integrated Ministry

It is a paradox of social media that people will share very intimate and sometimes life-and-death matters in social media spaces, even as such sharing immediately becomes both public and permanent. Today, new loves, break-ups, engagements, marriages, divorces, birth and death announcements, health news, and personal locations are all shared online.

Social media can serve as a good "leading indicator" that something is amiss with someone. People share that they've had a hard day, that one of the kids is sick, that dinner was a disaster. They post expressions of grief, news about changes in jobs and relationships. Even updates about lousy weather or political frustrations give us insight into the lives of people in our local and extended communities. When we log in, pay attention, and listen with heart and mind as people share their lives, we often become aware of things we may not have otherwise discovered.

FOR WHOM SHALL WE NOW PRAY?

This kind of open and generous sharing calls us to deep listening and prayer. Indeed, digital ministers recognize that their Facebook, Instagram, and Twitter streams are places of and occasions for prayer.

For Episcopal deacon Diana Wheeler, CDW, who we met in chapter 1, prayer is a vital art in a complex, dynamic practice. A former high school principal who has taken her ministry in a rather different direction in recent years, she defines herself as a "beguine"—a modern-day version of the lay religious community workers who were central to the spiritual revival focused on care of the poor, the sick, and the otherwise marginalized in thirteenth-century northern Europe. Mother Diana is a fixture in San Francisco's LGBTQ community, where she has worked in social ministry for nearly fifteen years. In 2016, she founded Companions of Dorothy the Worker, a dispersed, ecumenical community devoted to ethical ministry with the city's large queer community. Sisters, brothers, and oblates in the community minister at street festivals, in clubs and bars, at protests and vigils, through street services and blessings throughout the liturgical calendar, direct pastoral care as well as a talkline, hotlines during big community events, and text ministries. Among others. Lots of them. "We bring those things that touch people about the Church out into the street," she explains.[5]

Mother Diana describes her work with the Companions of Dorothy as a ministry of presence. "What works in this ministry is that we keep showing up," she says. "Consistently. Every evening on the phone and in the community. Every year with annual events and every weekend for the community's events. I think that is the vocation of religious and working clergy. We are not dependent on the church for our living, so we are able to stay present and not move on to other things. We're able to maintain the relationship."

A big part of Mother Diana's ability to "stay present" unfolds in social media. She remains connected on daily basis through an active Facebook page with a large, diverse community that includes many national and international travelers to San Francisco she's met during major events like the Pride Festival. On that page, on Thursdays, Wheeler turns over her timeline to the prayers of folks in her extensive network. The response of the people to whom she ministers to her weekly prayer request illustrates the digitally integrated practice of ministry that spans boundaries of online and offline spaces. It also shows the ways in which social networking platforms can offer ministries to people who would not be reached by—or, indeed, welcomed into—conventional brick-and-mortar churches. Mother Diana describes the intersection of online and offline spaces in her prayer ministry in this way:

> When I'm in the community, on the streets, I'm not asking anyone to go to church. I'm not trying to push my own agenda . . . anything like that. I'm not trying to get volunteers or people in the pews. And it just exploded in a way that it's hard to do in a church. . . . People have shared their lives with me. Not just on social media, but when we meet in person. Or they might message me.

This deeply relational, incarnational practice translates to the Facebook prayer experience, Wheeler explains:

> Prayer is a very personal thing. And with the people I work with, it can be an uncomfortable thing. They can be embarrassed by it. You know, most

of the people I work with are "unchurched" or they have been rejected by the Church, hurt by the Church. It's hard for them to sometimes be seen as accessing the Church. It's about "I know what's going in your life. This person who represents the Church knows about your life—I share with her. So I feel okay asking for prayer."

She continues, highlighting the advantages of social media for offering spiritual companionship and care to segments of her community who would be unable to access care in a traditional church:

> You don't have to put your body somewhere, right, to get what you need spiritually. You could be at home. You can be across the country. It doesn't matter where you are. You can always connect. And you don't have to go into a place where you might feel unsafe. A lot of folks that I work with have mental health issues . . . anxiety about certain things. They don't want other people to "know their business." So, in a lot of ways, [connecting on social media] is safe. It's safer than going into a building with a lot of strangers that you don't really know and you're not really sure that they want to know you.

As in the case of Diana Wheeler's ministry, embracing social media adds considerable flexibility in caring for the people of God. Depending on the sentiments or needs expressed, digitally integrated ministers can comment, direct message, e-mail, call, or visit in person. Facebook also makes it easy to mark milestones like birthdays and anniversaries, changes in relationship status, new jobs, or a move to a new home. People deeply appreciate these digital expressions of pastoral attentiveness and concern.

This is one area where ministers can sometimes actually save time through social media. Many life updates that have traditionally been received at the sanctuary door after church are now being shared online. Leaving an expression of concern, care, and support can sometimes save a phone call or tracking someone down at church on Sunday. For all the worries we often hear about social media creating another ministry "time suck," it is often a valuable time saver.

More importantly, such digital ministry gestures through the week are more immediate and more closely connected to the news as it has played out in a person's life. When we take a few seconds to check in, we show our attentiveness to members of our community, whether they belong to our church or organization or not.

LIFTING ONE ANOTHER UP

Other ministry leaders orient their social media participation toward encouragement and inspiration. When he served as the Roman Catholic bishop of Indianapolis, Christopher Coyne would regularly post prayers, reflections, information about special observances, as well as a prayer of the day (POD) and quote of the day (QOD):

> **bishopcoyne** Bp Christopher Coyne
> POD: Prayer of Trust - Thomas Merton fb.me/1pMM9EEHN
> 27 Oct
>
> **bishopcoyne** Bp Christopher Coyne
> Still ... QOD: "I know God will not give me anything I can't handle. I just wish He didn't trust me so much." B. Mother Teresa
> 27 Oct

Coyne also shared his own reflections on the readings for the day:

> **bishopcoyne** Bp Christopher Coyne
> Can anything separate you from the love of God? Nothing.
> 27 Oct
>
> **bishopcoyne** Bp Christopher Coyne
> SInce you are in Christ, who can separate you from the love of God? No one.
> 27 Oct
>
> **bishopcoyne** Bp Christopher Coyne
> Romans 8:31-39: Paul ends his argument of chapters 5-8 with a celebration of God's unending commitment to his chosen ones.
> 27 Oct

Importantly, Bishop Coyne did not just tweet and leave it at that. He actively engaged with Twitter followers, discussing the relative merits of the @DivineOffice Twitter feed over the iBreviary application for the iPhone and participating from time to time in the weekly Church and Social Media (#chsocm) tweetchat on Twitter. He answered questions about the faith, translated Latin phrases, explained customs and traditions, and generally helped to make the faith more visible and accessible not only to Catholics, but to a diverse network of followers.

Since 2014, Coyne has served as the Roman Catholic bishop of Vermont and chairman of the Committee on Communication of the United

States Conference of Catholic Bishops (USCCB). He continues to reach out to those within his diocese and the larger church through his now familiar social media presence, oftentimes recording messages as he drives across his diocese. It's not quite Carpool Karaoke, but it works as he invites his flock to be on the road with him. He also hosts a YouTube series on "Everything You Want to Know about the Liturgy," and his own podcast.[6]

Coyne reflects on how his digital presence has helped him connect with the people of his diocese and overcome the distance that his rank and office could create.

> When I go out to parishes and I'm out in public, people come up to me and say, "I follow you on Facebook"; "I follow you on Twitter"; "I feel like I know you"; "You're so human"; "I love your humor." I basically try to follow what St. Augustine said in his treatise on the teaching of Christian doctrine—that a good teacher teaches, pleases and persuades. The pleasing part is not that you say things that people want to hear but that your message is attractive to people and they want to engage it. So I'll put something funny out there, or something personal—like three days ago I had a bad cold and I mentioned it. … Even if it's the first time they've met me, people feel like they know me because they know about my mother and my brothers and sisters, and they know when I'm traveling and what I'm doing.[7]

AFFIRMING THE SACRED IN THE ORDINARY

Beyond critical moments and milestones of people's lives, we can also bear witness to how people are living their ministries in daily life.

One of the common critiques of social networking is that people are just sharing a bunch of mundane stuff. Well, kind of. Yet, this is all part of their holy calling. The Protestant Reformations shifted the seat of vocation from the spiritual elite to everyone—from the priesthood of some to the priesthood of all. It claimed the holy in the midst of all the stuff of everyday life. So, too, the post-Vatican II Roman Catholic Church has affirmed the baptismal call of all believers to minister as disciples of Christ, whether in lay or ordained roles, in the church, the home, the community, and the workplace.

Among the most meaningful things digital ministers can do is name their relationships, their parenting, their work, and their volunteering, with all the associated joys and struggles, as expressions of their faith—as the holy action of disciples. Such quotidian sanctity can be called out in digital communities in ways that are often not possible in face-to-face settings. For instance, one rarely sees someone stand up at a local coffee shop—and we might worry if we did—to announce that she is praying for her ailing aunt or that he just witnessed an amazing act of kindness and generosity between a corporate drone and a homeless person on a busy downtown street.

For the Rev. Mihee Kim-Kort, a Presbyterian pastor, blogger, and author who has ministered to undergraduate students at Indiana University (where she is a doctoral student), acknowledging the "everyday holy" is a digitally integrated spiritual practice that knits together her roles as a pastor, a graduate student, a mother to three kids, a wife. Over the years, she has developed robust, overlapping Twitter, Instagram, and Facebook communities, a popular blog, and an engaging podcast series, *This Everyday Holy*. Her various forays into social media have, she says, grown organically from her digitally integrated life:

> I didn't really have a big plan to, you know, write a blog or do a podcast. It was kind of an extension of ministry for me, but it was also a spiritual

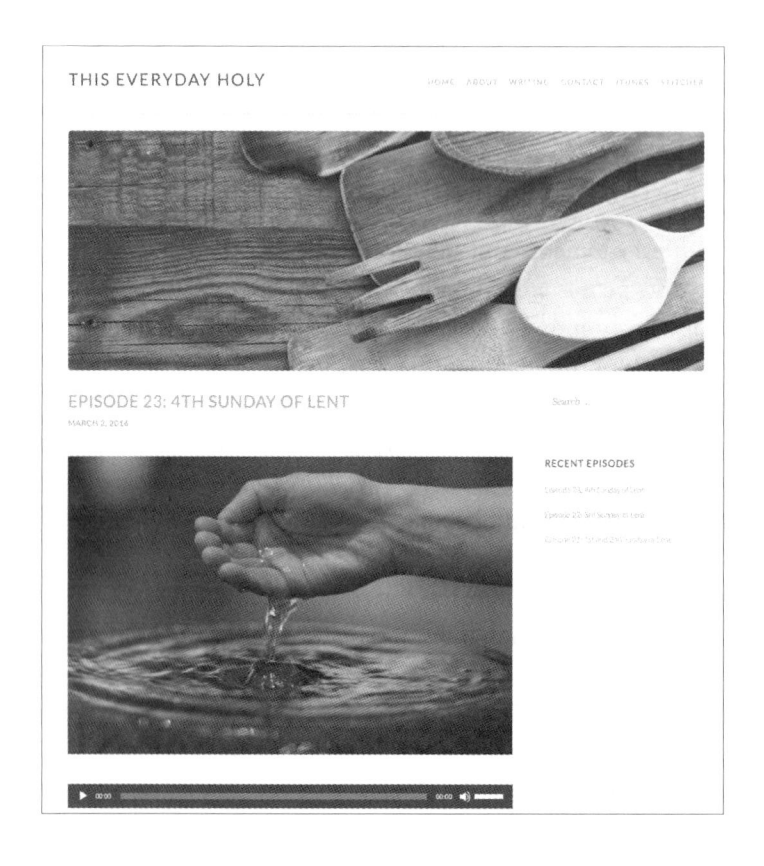

discipline. And it allowed me to be sort of artistic, creative, and to learn something new. So it came really out of the dailiness of my own life and who I am. After a while, because my kids are growing up, and my life is just changing, I've had times when I've just had to take a break and just focus on what's right in front of me. So, I don't have a set formula. I just kind of take it a season at a time, and then you'll see glimpses of that on my Facebook, or Instagram, or Twitter depending on what's going on. But, that really is kind of the point: that we're continuing to share our lives, and that practice is evolving for us. So that's what you see a lot on my social media.

Kim-Kort illustrates an important value of digitally integrated lives as it supports ministry: it allows us to experiment, to evolve, to adapt over time. Nonetheless, even as our social media engagement ebbs and flows, posts on individual and group pages insist on the sacred possibility of all creation—digital and physical—and they witness to a Christian understanding of ordinary holiness that nuances considerably the extreme characterizations of Christians in most broadcast media.

However, the language of affirmation does not have to be overtly religious. Our very presence can communicate God's own presence and care. We can, as Paul wrote to the Romans, "rejoice with those who rejoice, weep with those who weep" (Rom. 12:15) without colonizing it now and forever for Christendom. By our presence, we can point to God's presence in joys and heartache, in the mundane and the sublime. This is far less dramatic than moments of spiritual crisis, but, over the long term, this is how pastoral relationships are built and tended, whether by ordained or lay digital ministers.

It turns out that one of the biggest critiques of social media is actually one of its greatest gifts: the brevity of digital engagement usually offers quite enough space to celebrate small blessings throughout everyday life, to share mustard seeds of faith as we comment, "like," tweet, retweet, and so on with the people of God who wander through the digital landscape during the big and small moments of their lives.

DIGITAL SANCTUARY: SENDING KIRSTIN TO GOD

The sacred potential of caring for God's people is perhaps nowhere more pointed than in the increasing number of Facebook memorial pages that have emerged over the past few years. We may be aware of ones for celebrities like pop icon Michael Jackson or in the case of tragic losses like the suicide of Tyler Clementi, the Rutgers student whose callow roommate leaked a video of him kissing a man. These pages allow for a collective expression of grief and loss and seem to serve as outlets for expressions of the confusion, anger, and anguish that accompany both death and cultural change. And, certainly, it is appropriate for ministry leaders—people trained and experienced in helping others to deal with loss—to participate in such spaces.

But another kind of memorial page has also developed in digital spaces, a kind which connects the personal to the communal and, especially at the end of life, the temporal to the eternal. For instance, through the spring and summer of 2011, a digital sanctuary began to form on the Facebook page of Kirstin Paisley, a lay minister to the homeless, a blogger, a friend to many, and a young woman who was dying of cancer.

Kirstin had been fighting cancer for years, narrating the story of hope and struggle on her blog, *Barefoot and Laughing*, and connecting through this digital ministry to people around the world who were inspired by her honesty, her vulnerability, and her remarkable good humor in the face of so great an ongoing challenge.

When it became clear in the summer that the treatment regimen, which itself had been something of a torment, was not holding the cancer at bay, Kirstin shared the news on her blog and on her Facebook page. She let people know how much they meant to her and how much she wanted them to be with her as she returned to God.

In the weeks after Kirstin's painful, but characteristically hopeful, announcement, her Facebook page became a gathering place for prayer, reflection, gestures of comfort, and love that one would be hard-pressed to call "superficial" in any way. People held vigil with Kirstin on the night she died and prayed around the clock and around the world with those tending to her at home.

"It was remarkable," says the Reverend Andee Zetterbaum, who cared for Kirstin at the end of her life, including helping to maintain her Facebook page and update her blog. "People were so spiritually present on the page, and I know that meant so much to Kirstin. She really felt surrounded by the whole communion of saints as she left this life. It was an unbelievable comfort not just to Kirstin, but maybe even more to those of us who had to let her go."

This "letting go" extended beyond Facebook. Zetterbaum, as she had promised Kirstin, updated the blog as Kirstin became less able to communicate. When Kirstin died on the first day of July, Zetterbaum shared the news on the blog:

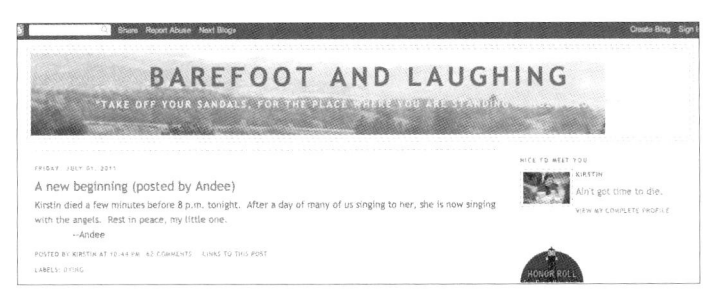

When members of Kirstin's far-flung digital community expressed a desire to be part of the memorial service for Kirstin, Zetterbaum enlisted the help of another friend, Sean McConnell, then the canon for communications in the Episcopal Diocese of California, who videotaped the service and posted it on the video hosting site Vimeo, with links from the blog and Facebook. Social media thus enabled people in a widely distributed community to gather in mourning, love, and hope.

The separation and privatization that characterized modern culture after the printing press and, more so, the Industrial Revolution and the birth of broadcast media, rendered dying, death, and mourning profoundly private, often socially disconnected experiences. Moreover, modernity, with its emphasis on very specific spaces for every life function—birth, education, work, worship, and death—forced an artificial separation between what we came to know as "the sacred" and the "profane," or ordinary spaces in our lives. But Kirstin Paisley insisted that all of the people in her life—those known to her from face-to-face experience, and those known only from digital engagement—mattered in every moment of her life. This allowed them to be active, compassionate participants even in her death, calling forth the sacredness of her life, of their common experience, and of the digital spaces where their relationships often developed.

It is perhaps no small wonder, then, that Kirstin's Facebook page continues to be something of a sanctuary—even seven years later. Friends remember her birthday in September, and stop by from time to time to share memories of their experience with her, prayers for and to her, and, increasingly, to offer welcome to other people dealing with cancer to whom Kirstin's living and dying remain a potent model of faith and hope.

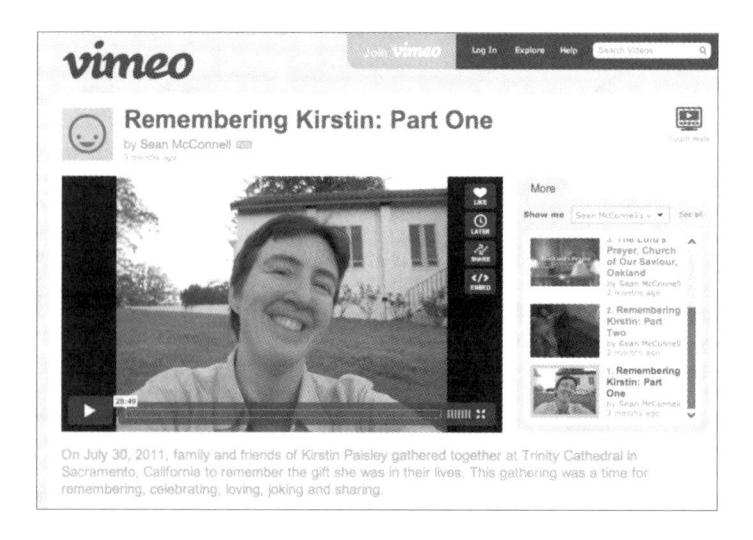

"Kirsten, thank you for helping me find the right words to say to my grandmother who is so very scared to die," writes one recent visitor to the page who was inspired by one of Kirstin's many stories. "I told her the story about you and the cardinal. Even after passing into the next, you and your life still help minister to those in need."

And, recognizing the sanctity of the digital space that held so much meaning in Kirstin's life, Zetterbaum continues to minister to people who visit. "Kirstin created this amazing network," she says. "I don't really know most of these people outside of the Facebook page or the blog, but I know how much they meant to Kirstin and how much they mean to one another now. It's hard to turn away from that as a priest."

Though much has changed in the digital media landscape since we first shared Kristin's story, the practice of tending to the sick and dying, as well as those who care for them, on social networking platforms has only grown in the intervening years. Not long ago, a friend cared for her spouse through a terminal illness negotiated some of the darker hours of that experience by posting on Facebook "Anyone up?" when she couldn't sleep through anxiety-laden nights. People around the world, aided by being in different time zones, reached out to her to offer comfort, compassion, humor, and love.

4.4 Forming Disciples
Learning in Community

Social media is changing the way we learn because it has changed the way we access information and the way we connect with one another. Scott McLeod, a professor of educational leadership at the University of Kentucky, describes it this way: "We no longer live in an information push-out world where we passively receive information that is broadcast out to us by large, centralized entities. Instead, we now live within multidirectional conversation spaces."[8]

The ability people have to find out about almost anything on Google, Wikipedia, or YouTube necessarily changes the role of the ministry leader as educator. Clergy and lay educators no longer function as "resident theologians" by virtue of any special *gnosis* received in seminary or from the shelves of theological books in their offices. They are no longer seen as repositories of information. Rather, in a sea of information, they help others to become theologians themselves, inviting people to reflect critically upon all the information they encounter and to engage that information more deeply through conversation with others. Digital ministers, then, facilitate relationships between people and information rather than imparting information as all-knowing fonts of wisdom. Says Michael Wesch, the Carnegie Foundation's National Teacher of the Year in 2008, "I like to think that we are not teaching subjects but subjectivities: ways of approaching, understanding, and interacting with the world."[9] This relational knowing is as significant for the church as it is for any other part of society today.

Just as websites are not a substitute for hospitality, posting sermons or adult education materials on a blog are not substitutes for formation. A sermon or educational blog is a good service to provide for those unable to attend church on Sunday or those who missed the most recent event with your organization. It can also be a helpful way to learn the practice of blogging. (Indeed, it's how both Keith and Elizabeth got started with social media.) However, it should not be mistaken for a form of engagement. That, says Darleen Pryds, is "a very middle-aged approach to social media." Although she is a medievalist, Pryds is not talking here about media in the Middle Ages, but about a way of seeing social media merely as faster, cheaper tools for broadcasting a message to more people—an approach that tends to characterize those of us "of a certain age" who were not raised with media that facilitated social engagement.

FORMATION ON TAP

Consider, for example, the difference between traditional parish adult education classes and the increasingly popular "theology pubs" offered by churches, seminaries, and other religious organizations. In a traditional adult education class, people gather in the church building to hear a priest, pastor, or lay educator impart information. There may be discussion—some of it in fact quite lively—but the structure of the learning engagement will generally be fairly clearly centered on someone in a "teacher" role who doles out information and questions to the students.

By contrast, at a theology pub, a guest or resident theologian facilitates conversation around the table, and everyone's perspective brings something meaningful to the discussion of, for instance, what incarnation means in the Digital Age, or maybe how grace functions in the lives of postmodern believers. This ranging conversation happens out in the open, in public—the world is not "out there," an abstraction. It is all around. The conversation is open to and engaged with it. This is the same kind of formation that happens in social media: a theological conversation happening in a public place, influenced by life all around it, overheard and overseen, as words like "God," "Jesus," and "shalom" leaven the life around it. The world of faith is not imagined or enacted as something separate from the world of pub-goers and workers and honking car horns. It is all right there.

Two dangers of online formation are that learning can become individualized—between "me and my Bible" or "me and my computer"—and that people can seek out only those who reinforce their ideas, rather than challenge or qualify them. This can happen, of course, in traditional classroom learning settings as well, where students have been trained over time to see learning as an exchange between "me and the teacher" or "me and the book." Like many other practices developed through the modern era, and especially in the Broadcast Age, approaches to learning that highlight the expertise or celebrity of a teacher and amplify the separateness and relative anonymity of learners tend to reinforce many of the most individualistic characteristics of modern culture. It's all about me and what I'm "getting out of" a particular educational session. A further risk is that the group can tend to lean into a sense of false equivalency among varying perspectives—an uncritical "everyone's entitled to their opinion" take that leaves inaccurate or misleading information unchallenged or that doesn't take into account the genuine differences in expertise participants might have. So, having a skilled facilitator—one who can both lift up everyone's insights and gracefully invite respectful critical reflection—is critical. Having clear ground rules to which the group contributes and agrees is also essential to structure both open and meaningful reflection through conversation.

CONVERGENT FORMATION

Ministry leaders have the opportunity through social media to mitigate individualism through what is known as "social convergence"—a fusion of knowledge, perspectives, experience, and insight across social categories like age, class, economic status, race, denomination, and vocation that have traditionally been separated. Clergy are formed this way, over there, in the seminary. Laypeople are formed that way, in the church. By bringing friends, colleagues, parishioners, organizational members, and skeptics together to respond to a post and to one another's comments, social media facilitates reciprocal learning and invites much broader conceptualizations of key issues of concern to people of faith.

One of Keith's favorite things in social media is when pastoral colleagues, parishioners, and nonchurchy friends respond and interact to a social media post. In the wake of the events in Charlottesville in August 2017, Keith posted a video response from San Francisco, standing in front of the Vaillantcourt Fountain at the Port of San Francisco. He first posted it on his church Facebook page, where several of his church members responded, and then shared it on his personal profile, where a range of people, from a Jewish friend, to the organist at his previous church, church members, and church staff at his current church, all responded to him and each other.

Formational convergence can happen on its own when we engage questions of faith and meaning in social networking communities. But it can be amplified with a bit more intentionality, as is the case with the dozens upon dozens of large and small covenant groups that gather on Facebook. Ranging from three to nearly a hundred members, these groups are particularly popular for youth ministry, and most are closed so that would-be participants must be granted access by the group administrators. Although we oppose closing general church pages or groups, we think it's a good idea to limit access to social media groups where teens and young adults participate, where personal information may be shared, or where topics discussed might draw hostile outsiders.

Companionship-based learning and formation can also happen in more traditional educational settings. For instance, Darleen Pryds is an advocate for using social media in seminary education and routinely incorporates it into her classes, creating Facebook groups for each class. She recalls one experience that illustrates the way in which learning integrated with social networking extends formation far beyond the event of a particular class or even a semester's worth of study. Says Pryds:

> The class was small—about ten students. Many of us continued to be in touch through Facebook. I've never had a class continue relationships for so long. So, I see them interacting with each other, they interact with me still, and that wouldn't have happened just through e-mail. It just wouldn't have.

For Pryds's students, then, learning is a part of an ongoing relationship among the students and their professor. It changes over time, through regular or even periodic interaction, with learning developing out of participants' shared expertise and insight. However knowledgeable Pryds may be as a spirituality scholar and a medievalist, her real brilliance in this sort of social learning engagement is her ability to facilitate lifelong knowledgeability among her students.

PREACHING: MAKING PROCLAMATION PARTICIPATORY

Encouraging spiritual knowledgeability—a collaborative critical reflectiveness on questions of faith and meaning—is of course not limited to the youth group, adult education forum, or seminary classroom. Preaching is also a formational practice that can be opened up and enriched by the social, collaborative, relational ethos of social media communities.

Today it has become a common practice for preachers to reach for their iPad rather than the bookshelf to access free and pay digital resources for sermon preparation from sites such as textweek.com and workingpreacher.com, as well as some Facebook groups such as "Sermon Prep from an Open, Inclusive, and Progressive Point of View," which boasts over 1,300 members.[10] Jim Keat, creator of the group, describes it this way: "We've got three simple guidelines: Ask questions to help the sermon you're working on, share ideas and resources (blogs, podcasts, etc.) related to the upcoming lectionary texts, and don't be a jerk." One of the websites Keith returns to again and again is "Dollar Store Children Sermons."[11] Each week, Pastor John Stevens from Zion Lutheran Church in Oregon City, Oregon, posts a short YouTube video with children's sermon ideas that are inspired by items he buys from his local dollar store. A simple search of the hashtag #lectionary on Twitter brings you into a rolling conversation with fellow practitioners and scholars about the upcoming readings from the Revised Common Lectionary.

For digital ministers, sermons can be the work of many. For some of the same reasons that theological conversations have moved to the local pub, preachers are increasingly writing their sermons in coffee shops and other public spaces. Bill Petersen, a Lutheran pastor serving at All Saints Episcopal

Church in Wolfeboro, New Hampshire, "sermonates" at his local Starbucks, and invites his friends on Facebook to stop by:

> Sermonating @ Starbucks Deming Street, stop on by. My favorite barista gave me grief for not being here for a while. . . . she said I must be in need of some good sermon illustrations using the staff (let's hope so).

Here, the sermon is prepared in public and with the public: chatting with the café staff, with people who drop by in person, and with those who link through comments, likes, tweets and retweets in various outposts of the digital community. In this way, preaching, like everything else in social media culture, becomes participatory and collaborative. The sermon is no longer something one person creates and people passively consume. It is something everyone helps to produce. The emphasis shifts from the act of proclamation itself to the conversation leading up to and following it.

This is, of course, entirely consistent with the Latin root of "sermon," *sermo*, which means "discussion." What is transformative here is not the preacher's words, but the conversation, and the way in which it allows a sermon to speak from the experience of all God's people.

THAT'LL PREACH

The *That'll Preach* podcast from Middle Collegiate Church in New York invites its listeners into the room with preachers as they discuss preaching texts and themes for the coming Sunday. The podcast grew out of weekly staff meetings at Middle in which they planned sermons and worship.[12] Jim Keat, who helped launch *That'll Preach*, reflected on the experience:

> I always thought that these were great conversations. We should record these and let the world eavesdrop on them. It would be a great resource for other faith leaders. We tried that. It didn't really work. We just put the mic in the room and it made the conversation awkward and the recording quality was subpar.

They regrouped and *That'll Preach* was born. Keat says that it is "specifically for two audiences, two online communities. One is for people who are coming to Middle, to give a glimpse behind the curtain before you walk in, so you're already primed for what you're going to hear. So we are talking to our congregants. And also to other faith leaders. If you're thinking, I have to preach a sermon, I don't know what to do, you can borrow our ideas. It is really looking at those two worlds."

This conversational open-sourced approach to preaching nicely fits our digitally networked environment, in which people are accustomed to a multitude of voices, not just one. It also lends itself to a culture in which, as *Time* magazine announced, the human attention span is now officially shorter than that of a goldfish.[13]

Indeed, many preachers will tell you that the most successful sermons are the ones inspired by conversation. Whereas a preacher might have only had a few face-to-face conversations during the week that would influence a sermon, the regular "sermonating" practices of digital ministers illustrate that, through social media, preachers can be connected to hundreds of conversations, each filled with new ideas and perspectives that allow the Word to live in a much richer, more relational form. And these are conversations not just with parishioners, but also with colleagues and friends around the world—people who share our faith and those who don't. At times, ministry leaders may initiate the conversation by inviting others to participate with them by posting an idea, an image that's inspired them, or a sentence they've written for an upcoming sermon. They also might post the lectionary readings for the week or pose a question—all with the purpose of eliciting conversation engagement. Thus, the sermon is a collaborative project, not just the musings of a religious "expert."

What's important here is not so much that a better sermon emerges from this networked, relational process—though surely this is the case. What matters is that the process of developing sermons in this collaborative, other-centered way is profoundly formational, engaging a wide array of people in shared reflection on scripture, the life of the church, and its place in the world today. The common practice of spiritual-reflection-in-context that digital ministers like Petersen, Keat, and Kim-Kort encourage goes well beyond the sharing of any biblical factoid, however illuminating. It reaches beyond even loving Christian encouragement and inspiration, important though that is. It also models a way of learning that takes its cue not so much from the seminary as from the sanctuary and, more particularly, the communion table, where we all gather to feast on the Word as we prepare to join together as one body.

4.5 Building Community
A Digital Global Parish

As we've seen, digital social media offer powerful ways to build community. They facilitate increased awareness of each other's lives, providing more occasions for connection and conversation, as well as for the discovery of common interests and passions. The initial social media connection may begin with a designated ministry leader, but the strength of any faith community rests not on relationship to a lay or ordained leader, but on people's relationships to one another and the growth of that trust to develop over time.

At a minimum, ministry leaders and organizations ought to serve as conduits, helping to build community by making digital introductions: tagging people, linking to their work, making friend suggestions, retweeting, and mentioning. This helps members, friends, and colleagues to become aware of one another and sets the stage for friending and following.

Emily Scott, the founder of St. Lydia's Dinner Church in Brooklyn, New York, told us about how these connections developed on Facebook with people from St. Lydia's:

> I'm always really delighted when I come across a conversation on someone else's Facebook page that's among congregants. . . . [I] think, "This is so amazing. These people didn't know each other before they were coming to this church. And these relationships are forming." So, in that way, it's easy for someone to come to the church, meet a few people, go home and friend them on Facebook and get engaged in that way. . . . It comes before that phase where you're hanging out with each other or it encourages actually hanging out with each other because it's easy to find one another on Facebook.

Many people worry that digital relationships will eclipse face-to-face engagement. However, studies show that people active in social networks are more likely to be engaged in face-to-face volunteerism and faith communities.[14] This is because people who long for community seek it out in many forms, and people who connect in meaningful ways enjoy opportunities to extend that connection in both online and offline settings. Thus, one of the important roles of ministers in social network sites is to cultivate a sense of community that moves between both online and offline locales.

CONNECTING WITH THE LOCAL COMMUNITY

A key ingredient to building a strong community is social capital. Social capital is a term popularized by Robert Putnam in his best-selling book *Bowling Alone: The Collapse and Revival of American Community*, which tracks the alarming weakening of community in America—a trend, it should be noted, that rose primarily out of the separation fostered by broadcast media and which has begun to abate as social media have developed.[15] Social capital can be defined as "the collective value of all 'social networks' [who people know] and the inclinations that arise from these networks to do things for each other."[16]

David Crowley is working to strengthen social capital in eight Massachusetts communities, including his hometown of Woburn, through the nonprofit organization he founded, Social Capital, Inc. The organization has programs that promote youth leadership, volunteerism, and civic engagement. Crowley himself is an avid user of social media and sees a role for it to play in the work of building community:

> At the end of the day, our goal is to get people more engaged and connected, and we have to think about where people are. [C]larifying the role that technology plays for us—that it's a means to an end—actually pushed us to say it's not just about our website, it's about using whatever means are out there that make sense to achieve our goals.

Crowley (@DC_Woburn) models this in his own social media practice. He personally checks in around his home community on Facebook, highlighting local institutions and activities like the children's library program and the farmers' market. He identifies local people on Facebook and Twitter and interacts with them regularly. He is deliberate, purposeful, and consistent, using digital and face-to-face connections to reinforce one another and strengthen community connections.

Crowley particularly likes Twitter for its ability to create entirely new connections and build relationships within a local community:

> The openness of the platform was pretty exciting and consistent with our mission. . . . Part of our approach is to have the community be a welcoming place for anybody, whether you've been here for three generations or three days. . . . But the reality is that it doesn't often happen that way. I think [Twitter] does have this way of opening up and inviting. . . . You can engage even if you don't have an existing relationship with me.

He continues, highlighting the way in which Twitter conversations create opportunities for face-to-face connection:

> What I like about using social media in a local setting is that we might start chatting on Twitter about eating local foods, but then there's a potential, if there is real shared interest there, to go and do something offline, create a more substantial relationship.

BRIDGING AND BONDING SOCIAL CAPITAL

It is worth noting, too, that Crowley makes sure to model the kind of mutually engaging community his organization promotes by practicing reciprocity within his local Twitter community, following back everyone who follows him. This creates a clear message that he's about genuine, balanced community rather than about blasting out messages that highlight his perspectives over the insights of others. This develops social—and spiritual—capital in two particular ways—bridging and bonding.[17] *Bridging capital* creates connections between people who don't already know one another, helping people discover common points of intersection, creating new relationships and links. *Bonding capital* strengthens the ties between people with existing relationships. Twitter is particularly good for building bridging social capital, while Facebook is good for building bonding social capital. Developing either, however, depends on exercising reciprocity in how you engage with others.

A HOLY NETWORK

For Luther Seminary's Adam Copeland, social media is central to creating and sustaining community, and he sees different relationships developing on different platforms and in different ways. Copeland, a Presbyterian minister, did a stint as a mission developer for a Lutheran young adult ministry in the university town of Fargo, North Dakota. Copeland's challenge from the Evangelical Lutheran Church in America (the largest body of Lutherans in America) was to create community among the forty-five thousand young adults in the Fargo-Moorhead area who are not connected to a church. "Obviously," says Copeland, "what we're doing in the church just isn't connecting for young adults," which motivated the ELCA's leaders to take more of a community organizing approach to engage.

The resulting mission, "Project F-M" (Fargo-Moorhead), focused on engaging eighteen- to twenty-five-year-olds by listening to their stories and attending to how questions of faith and meaning play out in their lives. Copeland initiated a number of innovative occasions for connecting—theology pubs, a "WTF" (Where's the Faith?) study group, and "Holy City" worship events at parks, train depots, and other locations around the city—but these connections depend heavily on social media.

"Social media is the primary way I connect with young adults," said Copeland. During the project, he shared information on upcoming events with the more than three hundred members of the group page, but he went well beyond using the page simply as a digital bulletin board. "I write messages to anyone who's come to an event who's on Facebook," Copeland explained. "I want people to know we saw they were there, we know their name. And then I let them know about what might be coming up, and give them a link to a Google map to the event."

Copeland endeavored to encourage day-to-day interactivity among participants on the page by, for instance, posting short notes about what people talked about at the most recent theology pub and asking follow-up questions. "I want to invite people to reflect," he told us, and that invitation might result in people sharing links to more information on the topic, comments, or, in one case, a Robert Louis Stevenson poem from one of the folks who attended a theology pub on how God speaks to us today.

All of this digital engagement reinforces the face-to-face engagement and, not unimportantly, extends it across the networks of all the participants. Said Copeland of how this supports his ministry and how different social media platforms come into play in his ministry:

> Because I am as active as I am in social media, I have a pretty wide view of the community, and I know a lot of what's going that I really wouldn't otherwise know. . . . I use Facebook to be a friendly figure from the church, to be connected to different communities, and to share resources. . . .
>
> I use Twitter to make connections more, most often locally. And I ask questions on Twitter or share short comments that don't really rise to a Facebook post.

> The blog is really my filter. . . . it's where I'm thinking through things, and mostly that engages colleagues in ministry. It's a way for me to reflect, to explore different ideas, and it functions as a kind of check within a community. It keeps me aware that I'm not in ministry alone.

This integrated, multiplatform social media participation gives digital ministers like Copeland the opportunity to develop and nurture a variety of communities among those he serves. Such practices are especially important for connecting with people who, for whatever reason, have not felt invited into our communities or who feel alienated from them. Says another young adult minister, Alicia Saunders, a campus minister at a Roman Catholic high school in California's Central Valley, "If I weren't on Facebook, my students would hardly know I existed. I'd just be 'that chick who makes everyone go to chapel.' It's ironic, maybe, but by being who I am on Facebook—just really myself, not all Ms. Religion—I'm more real to the teenagers I serve."

A HUMBLE WALK

Pastor Jodi Bjornstad Houge is building community and making faith connections in the West End neighborhood of St. Paul, Minnesota, where she founded Humble Walk Lutheran Church, a mission start of the ELCA. It began with a vision of a Christian congregation deeply embedded in the life and rhythm of the West End neighborhood. Bjornstad Houge explains:

> We recognized that most people don't come looking for a church, in our demographic. And so, we thought from the beginning, "We know this. The church is sinking." The facts are on the table for the mainline denominations. So, we're not going to do these big glossy things that try and draw people to our cool, fancy, hip church. We're going to be where people already are and try to be the church where they are.

Humble Walk's first worship services were held in a coffee shop, and since then they have worshipped in a storefront, a public park, an art gallery, and a retirement home. Humble Walk intentionally has all of its gatherings in public spaces within the West End in order to worship, learn, and serve "where people are."

    This is parish ministry in its broadest sense, where the borders and walls between insiders and outsiders, church and community, are blurred and even erased. One of those public places is Facebook, where Humble Walk hosts an active group page.

    The Facebook group is Humble Walk's central meeting place as well as its main form of communication. In addition to weekly "enouncements" and updates, there are also moments of random fun and inspiration, and expressions of care and gratitude. Facebook keeps the congregation connected and helps them connect to the community. Indeed, Facebook helps Humble

Walk to fulfill its mission of embedded, decentralized ministry because it serves as the congregation's central hub.

Humble Walk's social media participation has everything to do with nurturing local community and face-to-face relationship, developing the social capital that will carry the faith to successive generations and to people who have often been excluded from mainline churches. When we recall, as we discussed in chapter 1, that Facebook and Twitter are particularly active sites of engagement for people under age thirty and, especially on Twitter, for people of color, we see the significance of extending our ministries into digital communities by way of strengthening, rather than competing with or replacing, local communities.

4.6 Making Public Witness

At the heart of building community—and every art of ministry, digital or otherwise—is the love of neighbor. Making public witness is about making that love visible in online and off-line environments. This may include food and clothing collection for needy neighbors, helping to build a home with Habitat for Humanity, advocating on particular issues, or standing with neighbors in challenging times. Today it also includes using social media platforms to raise awareness, rally people to a cause, and call them to action.

Social media have vastly expanded the ability to communicate, publicize, coordinate, and share this work. In *Here Comes Everybody: The Power of Organizing Without Organizing*, Clay Shirky writes, "The current change, in one sentence, is this: most of the barriers to group action have collapsed, and without those barriers, we are free to explore new ways of gathering together and getting things done."[18] We have seen this in powerful ways in the 2011 Arab Spring and Occupy Wall Street, which Douglas Rushkoff called, "America's first true internet-era movement."[19] It has continued through the Black Lives Matter movement and other social justice networks whose actions are coordinated, documented, and illuminated largely through social media. Church leaders and organizations are just beginning to leverage the power of social media for advocating and acting for social justice.

LIFTING UP EVERY VOICE

Jamye Wooten is among those at the forefront of using social media for social justice. The founder of KineticsLive.com, "an information ministry that integrates theological reflection and practice, and uses dialogue as a catalyst for social change," Wooten has leveraged a range of online platforms to make visible, challenge, and engage the social and spiritual needs of the greater Baltimore area.[20] Wooten sees social media as a critical conduit for information within and beyond his community—information, he argues, that would largely be ignored without greater, more consistent amplification.

For instance, Wooten has used Twitter hashtags to develop extended learning campaigns such as #BlackChurchSyllabus and organizing efforts such as #MLK2Baker. Wooten launched #BlackChurchSyllabus in 2015 to cultivate resources from black scholars, religious leaders, and activists. "Whether we're talking about police violence or systemic injustice and violence in the African American community, we need to think theologically about what's happening in these times and the role of the church," Wooten explained. The campaign drew suggestions from a wide range of Twitter users such as Professor Candice Marie Benbow of Rutgers University, Professor Valerie Bridgeman of Methodist Theological School, the Rev. Dr. Alton B. Pollard of Howard University School of Divinity, Rahiel Tesfamariam of *Urban Cusp Magazine*, the Rev. Dr. Ralph C. Watkins of Columbia Seminary, and author and Claflin University professor Johnny Bernard Hill. Their collaborative efforts produced an extensive list of books, articles, and multimedia materials that was shared widely across social media platforms. Contributors created memes with syllabus titles, quotes, and images of important thinkers at the intersection of African American studies and religion. In addition, it called upon the diverse community of Twitter and, as the campaign spilled into other platforms, Instagram and Facebook users into new conversations. People met not only the authors referenced in the syllabus, but also the contributors to the syllabus, all important voices in African American religious scholarship, church leadership, communications, and social justice practice. Fans of the hashtag also called out to prominent black thinkers, pastors, and activists to add to the list, and national publications such as the *Huffington Post* wrote about the hashtag project.[21]

The work of Wooten on the #BlackChurchSyllabus project is instructive for ministry leaders and congregations beyond what we might see as an emphasis more on formation than social action per se. However, because Wooten developed the syllabus collaboratively through social media engagement, the interaction of contributors and admirers of the syllabus, action born out of established and new relationships—all of these things mark what creative potential of social networking to extend the work of the Church more broadly. As Shirky writes, "Our social tools are turning love into a renewable building material. When people care enough, they can come together and accomplish things of a scope and longevity that were previously impossible; they can do big things for love."[22]

Wooten's 2016 #MLK2BAKER hashtag project extended this momentum further. Here, Wooten harnessed social media again to challenge activists in the black community to "move #BeyondReActivism, beyond the tweeting and protest of #blackdeath to a sustained movement #OrganizingForPower, or holistic community development where the end goal is not reform or rights, but power."[23] Using a broad range of media platforms—from memes on Instagram, Pinterest and Twitter, to blog posts, community presentations through the grassroots Baltimore United for Change coalition, and a line of t-shirts highlighting key social justice themes and exemplars, Wooten actively engaged the Baltimore activist and church communities to consider the theological foundations of organizing for justice, taking collective action, and using media resources to advance peace, justice, and empowerment in African American communities. All of this contributed to rich, dynamic engagement in the Baltimore activist community, cultivating conversations and connections that support common work for justice and illustrate the incarnational center of digitally integrated ministry. Further, because Wooten's work played out across digital and local space, it makes a nominally local experience of witness a national, even global one. Certainly, if our churches can't grasp the significance of this kind of engagement, we give up any hope of having relevance or engaging meaningfully in the lives of people today and in the generations to come.

4.7 Stewarding God-Given Resources

One of the most common questions we have fielded over the years since the first edition is around whether and how the practice of digital ministry translates into members and money for the church's mission. In short, will it pay the bills? In the first edition we wrote that "The ROI of digital ministry is hearts set free in the Gospel," and we continue to believe that to be true. We see it as the fundamental reason for digital engagement. Our more nuanced response now, however, is that the church economy, like larger local, regional, and national economies, is shifting dramatically as a result of the internet and new digital technologies. Self-driving vehicles, to name just one example of a technological change that promises to dramatically change the lives of millions of people, will change not merely the way we travel, but the nature of mechanized transportation, the work that has up to now required human vehicle operators, and all of the economic structures implicated in the transportation market and the diversity of commercial industries and social practices that depend on transportation.

Analysts predict that self-driving cars will reduce healthcare costs as accidents are reduced. They'll reduce labor costs for transporting goods and staffing transportation services like taxis and busses. They'll free up acres and acres of parking and highway space and will lower reliance on fossil fuels, improve the environment. As well, they'll create more discretionary time for watching movies, enjoying nature, and maybe even participating in a church community.[24] That all seems much to the good. But if you were involved in the ground transportation industry as a truck driver, a taxi driver, a transportation logistic manager, a driver's ed teacher, a parcel delivery person, and so on, the extra time you'll have available won't seem so much like a "luxury." You've got about fifteen years to begin retooling or building up your retirement nest egg.

Stewardship in the Digital Age has taken a little longer for the church to sort out compared to the other arts of ministry in this chapter. Still, we are beginning to see the outlines of stewardship practices that leverage social media, enabling faith communities and organizations to communicate our missions and invite people to participate in achieving them through common worship, formation, social justice action, etc., but also encouraging them to support it financially in ways that are more convenient and more thoroughly embedded in their digitally integrated lives. It's impossible to say exactly where stewardship is going, but from our perspective we see a trend toward a hybrid approach to stewardship, which includes traditional pledging but also invites special giving, grants, revenue streams, and crowdfunding—all of this supported by more and more sophisticated and user-friendly digital technologies.

CROWDFUNDING PLATFORMS

A cadre of crowdfunding platforms, notably Kickstarter (2009), GoFundMe (2010), and Indegogo (2008), have grown in popularity over the last several years. They enable people to contribute and share causes they support with friends. In 2015, people gave an estimated $34 billion globally, half of that in U.S., through crowdfunding sites.[25] In 2016, Pew Research reported that 22 percent of Americans had donated through one of these crowdfunding sites, mostly giving to a handful of causes with contributions under $50. Further, their research shows that the most common reason for participating in a crowdfunding campaign is to help someone in need.[26]

It's always important to know the terms of use for each site before you create a campaign. For Kickstarter, which is typically used to launch new projects, the giving goal must be reached for the creator to receive any of the money. Sites like GoFundMe have no such requirement. Whatever is raised goes to the cause or recipient with categories of campaigns like medical, volunteer, emergencies, education, animals, charity, faith, community, and more. (It is also important to note that all of these sites have fees associated with them.)

What makes for effective crowdfunding practice? Adam Copeland, director for the Center for Stewardship Leaders at Luther Seminary and editor of *Beyond the Offering Plate: A Holistic Approach to Stewardship,*[27] told us that stewardship, whether traditional or digitally integrated, is grounded, above all, in relationship:

> Giving is based on a relationship. To the extent that social media and other digital tools help establish and continue to connect folks in life-giving relationships, that absolutely supports connections of financial gifts. Similarly, using social media tools can help continue that relationship, to report back and be transparent about what the gifts are doing and change this gift from an abstract, "I give to this organization," to something more personal through telling stories through social media, to understanding my gift to the organization helps support this particular story that I see on their Facebook page.
>
> For example, if my friend asks me to give to his 5k fundraiser, I give because of my relationship with my friend, and I'm very happy to do so,

but it's not ultimately that I care about the particular cause because it magically came across my Facebook feed; I care about my friend. It's something my friend cares about, which is beautiful. It's mirroring, it's responding to the real cares and concerns of people's lives and to the extent that we use social media to invite folks into those cares and concerns so that we might invite them into the joy of giving, then that is a wonderful use of the tool. In some ways it's so enormous but it's beautiful and small.

The relationship, then, is mediated through this technology, but then I have the opportunity to invite others into it and then inviting them to give is taking a step on the relationship journey. It's saying: "I already have these connections with these organizations or nonprofits or things that I care about and I'm asking you to participate with me in them and help us create something new. There's this thing we want to exist in the world. Do you want to see it to? If so, let's create it together. We need you to be part of this project and because of your gift it will become a more fulfilling and better end goal as a result." Congregations don't do that well. Everything is already established. The cherry is already on top of the budget. But we invite people to support the mission rather than inviting them to help develop a process.

If, as Copeland says, giving today is grounded in relationship more than ever before, it comes as no surprise to us that some of the ministries we have chronicled since the first edition, which have learned to use digital social media and invested in face-to-face and digitally networked relationships, are the very ones leading the way toward this new hybrid practice stewardship. Crucially, you can't just create a GoFundMe campaign and expect people to fund it. You have to do the groundwork of building relationships first and your need and vision have to be specific and compelling. While older members of our congregations are propelled by a sense of duty, younger generations want to know and see how their gifts make a difference in the world.

ST. LYDIA'S DINNER CHURCH

For example, in 2013 when St. Lydia's Dinner Church in Brooklyn wanted to open up a new storefront space, it not only raised funds from within the congregation but launched an Indegogo campaign that raised an additional

$33,000 from 263 funders.[28] Former pastor Emily Scott observed, "Everyone felt like they had a role to play, and the energy and excitement of the campaign was contagious. . . . A campaign like this builds community in a serious way," she said. "A few days into the campaign, I realized that I wasn't the only one refreshing my browser every few minutes to see when the donations were coming. . . . It was an exciting thing that the community could participate in, and it built a lot of ownership."[29] Further, the storefront, as they planned it, was not only designed for their unique dinner church worship format, it also functions as a coworking space during the week, which means that people can pay to use St. Lydia's during the week as a shared office space.

STORM HOME

Humble Walk Lutheran Church raised $9,000 in 32 days on a Kickstarter campaign to create an album of new original music used in their worship services.[30] Pastor Jodi Hogue reflected, "Artists got to write songs. Our studio people got to do what they are created to do. We get to give it all away. And we got to invite others along in the process."[31]

Both St. Lydia's and Humble Walk had laid the groundwork for success by investing in relationships over time, which meant being generous with their insights and learning, sharing their stories, ideas, practices, and experiences through social media (including being willing to share their stories with us), so that by the time they were ready to launch their campaigns, they had a network of people that were already interested and invested in, and had benefitted from their ministries. Potential givers already felt a personal, relational connection to these communities so that when they asked for support, people were motivated to support them.

TRINITY PLACE SHELTER

When the boilers at Trinity Lutheran Church of Manhattan/Iglesia Luterana Trinidad in Manhattan died on the coldest day in New York City in twenty-five years, the congregation turned to the crowdfunding site CrowdRise for help.[32] Trinity Lutheran has been home to Trinity Place Shelter, a transitional shelter for LGBTQ youth for over ten years. It was not just a matter of how they were going to keep the building warm once a week for worship but providing warmth each and every night for their guests. This approach helped them connect with a wider range of supporters beyond the congregation. The socially networked nature of the crowdfunding site allowed the passionate supporters of Trinity Place Shelter to share the need with their friends and to raise funds themselves through the site to help Trinity meet its goal. In the end, they raised over $41,000—well beyond their goal—and replaced the boilers.

CHANGED LIVES CHANGE THE WORLD

Now, you might be thinking, as Keith did: "These are unique churches, and remarkable ones at that. They are supposed to think out of the box and they have more flexibility than most traditional congregations. How do traditional congregations begin to live into this emerging practice of stewardship?"

Inspired by the stories and insights from Copeland and these faith communities, Keith's church introduced a stewardship campaign called "Changed Lives Change the World," which highlighted and sought to strengthen those crucial relationships within the congregation by sharing stories about how his church has changed people's lives and how they are inspired to go out and change the world.

At the heart of the campaign was a video series, a combination of professionally produced and homespun videos taken with smartphones, in which people shared their first-person stories about how the mission and ministry of the congregation had profoundly influenced them and how they participated in that mission within and beyond the church. The videos were created for an internal audience to inspire them to financially support the congregation's ministry for the coming year, but they were also shared across the church's social media platforms to share with a broader audience the individual stories that make up their larger congregational story. This approach emphasized relationships between parishioners as the motivation for giving to support the church's mission rather than simply giving to meet a budget number.

4.8 Extended Profile

Rev. Nadia Bolz-Weber, founding pastor of House for All Sinners and Saints in Denver and New York Times best-selling author of Pastrix and Accidental Saints

When we first profiled Nadia Bolz-Weber, she was already a rock star in our eyes. Since then, millions more people have joined the club and come to appreciate Nadia's perspective, ministry, and unique, powerful voice. When we interviewed Nadia for the first edition, we found her to be refreshingly honest and original. She clearly had an instinct for how digital social media could shape and extend the faith community she founded and the larger church. Those early investments in digital networking have lifted Nadia and HFASS as inspirations for many. We are happy to say that we knew her when.

Nadia Bolz-Weber is the founding pastor of House for All Sinners and Saints (HFASS), an emerging church Lutheran mission start in Denver, Colorado. Bolz-Weber is recognized among her peers as one of the most unmistakable voices in the church. She is active on Twitter and Facebook, and maintains a popular sermon blog and personal website.

Bolz-Weber's entry into social media began with blogging when she was a student at Pacific Lutheran Theological Seminary in Berkeley, California. "I just needed an outlet. Some people encouraged me to do it. They said, 'You should have a blog. You're always spouting off at the mouth. So, you should really do it that way.' . . . I was encouraged by others. I had an external call to blogging."

"With Facebook, it was personal and then eventually it became a way to get the word out there. I didn't intend to be a public figure on Facebook, it's just the more speaking I did, the more people were friending me who I didn't know. Once again, there was a sort of external call. People would say, 'Thanks for posting that,' or, 'We're going use that,' or, 'I appreciated your sermon.'"

"It all happened without it being a contrivance, without it being a technique or plan or strategy of any kind," Bolz-Weber explains. "Also, people in my environment, in my cultural context, are pretty tech savvy. They're native to this stuff, so it's just natural."

One of the reasons Bolz-Weber is so effective is that she has a clear and consistent voice—the same voice you hear whether you talk to her in person, text her, or tweet back and forth. It is also well defined. You can find it on her Twitter handle and blog title, "Sarcastic Lutheran"—a name she can't remember how she came up with, but which seems appropriate to everyone who encounters her. She is, indeed, "sarcastic" in a way that both loves and critiques the church. She runs from anything that reeks of an overwrought theology or which has the taint of church marketing. For instance, Bolz-Weber may invite people to worship by quipping, "It doesn't suck."

Describing her voice, Bolz-Weber says:

Honest to God, I'm just me. I just am lucky enough to have work in which I can totally be who I am. I'm just lucky to have a job where I can have a consistent voice, and that voice is actually mine. I have a lot of colleagues for whom that's not true. They have to really manage their own personalities to a large extent in their work, and I don't. Since I don't, I think that's really inviting to other people. They get it when they're around me or read something I write. They know that it's just a real person, a whole person, who is flawed and faithful at the same time and who's inviting for them in a way that more manicured personalities aren't going to be as inviting. I try to keep it real as much as I can, and sometimes that gets me in trouble, but sometimes it's a really transformative thing for myself and others.

While Bolz-Weber doesn't claim a neatly coordinated digital ministry strategy, she does follow what we might call digital spiritual practices that invite engagement in her local and distributed communities, provide inspiration and encouragement, and connect digital disciples to those in the House for All Sinners and Saints community:

Before morning prayer I'll often throw up a tweet that says, 'Text or Facebook or tweet your [prayer] requests,' and people do. We, literally, on Wednesday mornings, are praying for a bunch of people we don't even know. But it's like this promise we are sending out: We promise that if you send us something—it doesn't matter who you are, or what connection you have or don't have to the community—we'll pray for you. And that connects us to all kinds of people.

Like other particularly effective digital ministers, Bolz-Weber uses social media to make sermon preparation a communal practice with both formational value and sacramental echoes. For instance, when preparing a sermon, she asked her Facebook friends what came to mind when they heard "John 3:16"—"For God so loved the world that he gave his only Son, that everyone who believes in him may not perish but have eternal life." She received a remarkable forty-seven responses, and what the majority of people pictured was Rollen Stewart, a born-again Christian fixture at sporting events who wears a rainbow wig and holds up signs that say "John 3:16," with a matching t-shirt (or a coordinating one that reads "Jesus Saves" on the front and "Repent" on the back) to help bring the point home. Stewart's whacky rainbow wig and stadium proselytizing was the launch point for Bolz-Weber's sermon.[33]

Unlike other preachers we admire who use social networking to develop sermons collaboratively, Bolz-Weber's focus here was more about the basics of social media participation that we discussed at the beginning of the chapter: listening, attending, connecting, and engaging. We certainly recommend that you surf over to the full sermon, but we won't rehearse it all here. What we highlight as a best practice in digital ministry, though, is the sustained attentiveness that Bolz-Weber paid to what Rollen Stewart (and what many of us see as manipulative or even abusive uses of John 3:16) meant to members of her community. Her sermon spoke to their frustration and to the offense that misguided uses of scripture cause to those truly intent on sharing God's love with all people—sinners and saints alike. Bolz-Weber preached specifically to the concerns of her community, echoing what she heard as their concern that "the best way to exclude someone else is to make the entire God-loving-the-world thing not about God's extravagant Love, but about our belief." This is the fruit of deep, prophetic listening, as is the reassurance she offers at the end of the sermon:

> God has swept you up into God's redemptive love for the whole world and there is nothing for you to add: no amount of belief, no giving up of sweets during Lent, no good works. Nothing.

Now, clearly, Bolz-Weber is a gifted theological thinker and an inspiring writer. We need not doubt that she would have come up with an awesome sermon without such engagement. But it would have been *her* sermon, *her* insights, *her* reflections. And while surely those, too, would have been lovely and encouraging, what her Facebook conversation permitted was the crafting of a sermon that spoke from and for and to the people she serves. Such prophetic homiletics doesn't require social media, but social media does open the pastor's study to lots more voices.

And to that, the people generally say, "Amen."

4.9 Extended Profile
Massachusetts Council of Churches

Since we first met Laura Everett, then the newly appointed executive director of the Massachusetts Council of Churches, Everett and the Council have become recognized locally and nationally for their ecumenical work and their use of digital social media. Everett herself has chronicled how her networked approach to life, ministry, and bicycling in her book Holy Spokes: The Search for Urban Spirituality on Two Wheels.

Our original extended profile revealed the seeds of institutional self-understanding and digital practice that have led to a flourishing of Everett as a public leader in Massachusetts and beyond, and the Mass Council as one of the more forward-looking ecumenical bodies in the country.

The Massachusetts Council of Churches, an ecumenical organization whose mission is to help churches to work together to "express Christian unity as fully and visibly as possible," faced the same sort of challenges all churches see in a time of incredible cultural change—only multiplied by 1,700.

The 1,700 or so member churches supported by the council depend in particular on executive director Laura Everett and her small staff for access to information about what's going on in the statewide faith community that they wouldn't get through denominational channels. And, because the mission of the organization highlights expressing unity "through joint planning, mutual counsel, and common programming," it's important that they have that information in a timely manner and in a form that highlights how neighboring churches can participate in key initiatives and events.

"Historically we've thought about the Mass Council of Churches as being a kind of hub and the denominations are spokes," says Everett, "so information comes in and goes back out and it was up to the staff and the board to be a conduit for that information." In a way, the organization was a preinternet information aggregator, passing along news from the Presbyterian church in Lowell to the Methodist church in Tewksbury, if it seemed like there might be a common interest.

Through a strategic planning process that highlighted communications, Everett explains, the council "clearly acknowledged that the communications networks that we were previously using just weren't viable. . . . In the time that I've been there, most of [the member denominations] have stopped printing paper newsletters. In the last seven years, it's become clear that the lag time was increasing with every year."

But new ways of communicating and the need for faster information sharing was not the whole of the problem. Through the early 2000s, says Everett, "the nature of a council of churches was changing. . . . As denominational structures have changed, that is not necessarily the only place in which we want to think about ecumenism happening, or our only partners. Our communication strategy needed to match what our organization was."

As with many churches, individual ministry leaders, and other religious organizations, the council considers Facebook to be central to a more networked communication approach. "That's where most of our people are right now," says Everett, so the sharing of information moved from e-mails and faxes to posts on the group's Facebook wall. Here, the significance of communicating within a network, rather than as the hub broadcasting to isolated spokes, immediately became clear. Says Everett, "It turned out it hasn't been that big a shift because I was always forwarding those e-mails anyway. But the ripple effect is bigger now that I can take that e-mail I would have sent . . . and put it up online and tag you in it."

This connects the story on the council's Facebook page to the networks of everyone who has liked the page, vastly expanding the organization's reach, but, more than that, expanding the diversity of people whom they are engaging. This more widely networked engagement depends, of course, on developing relationships in meaningful ways. Everett and the council staff approach nurturing in two ways—the first having to do with content, the second with reciprocity.

Because members are already networked themselves, passing around news that everyone is getting through denominational channels, and increasingly across them, is hardly a value-added service. So, Everett focuses on enriching the content she shares. "I try to make sure to have a little something you wouldn't know from the *Globe* article I linked to—something I know about the people that are in play or the relationships we've built," she explains. "I always want to be communicating beyond a posed photo."

Everett describes the work they do on behalf of members as being like "a curator" of information and connections. She asks questions about the information she comes across as she considers what it means for members. Everett explains her editorial approach to sharing information of interest to member churches:

> If I come across stories on human trafficking, gambling, immigration, the environment, poverty, I'm always asking, "What does this tell about my organization? What am I supposed to glean from this relative to your organization? How can I link things together that haven't been put together to add value to the content, to tell a larger story." . . . I have a goal for myself of getting something up three to five times a day, during the work day. I wanted it to be related to Massachusetts, related to ecumenism, or to one of the denominations, to one of our member churches that others might not hear about.

Getting out even enriched content to a more diverse matrix of networks isn't the whole of the social media strategy used by the Massachusetts Council of Churches. Building relationships is critical, and that requires close listening and attentiveness to what members are doing and sharing in their social media spaces. Everett takes particular care to share the accomplishments of member churches and to acknowledge the contributions of others, an act of digital graciousness that goes a long way toward deepening connections:

> I go to the Facebook news feed and 'like' a ton of stuff and thank people—especially when I use something from a denomination or one of our local churches, even to share it. I make sure to give credit and praise people for good ministry. One of the best things about my job is that I get to see some really great ministry in a ton of places. It used to be that, as the hub, we were the only ones who had access to that privileged information.

These relationships have helped the council to make connections within congregations that would not have been possible in the Broadcast Age. "When I started all this I was thinking about how we get our message out," says Everett. "But what it's allowed me to do more of is see what I need to respond to. One of the things social media has been really good for is helping us connect with individual congregations and individual people that are passionate about ecumenism."

This networked, relational digital ministry requires, according to Everett, "integrity across platforms" and a balancing of voices that she navigates across the organizational page and her own Facebook page and Twitter feed.

Her sensitivity to the role of a leader within an organization with a longer ministry horizon is particularly instructive. Everett makes sure to post first on the council Facebook page and then to share on her own wall. She explains:

> Sometimes it seems like people like the personal voice better, but it's the Mass Council of Churches. It's not the Council of Laura. I don't ever want to be in a position where nobody else can do the work afterward because I've so become aligned with the organization that there's no other imaginative possibility.

In the end, Everett is convinced that engaging in social media communities is critical for shaping a positive, productive conversation about Christian unity:

> If we're not there, we're conceding space. Somebody else will take it. And if I'm not helping to craft a conversation, an intelligent conversation, about Christian unity, it will happen somewhere else, but it will happen without me. I can't presume the authority, but media can cultivate it by creating a good space and having good content and asking thoughtful questions and giving thanks for the good ways that people do manifest that unity.

When we asked Everett six years later to reflect back at how that early work has paid dividends, she told us:

> The Massachusetts Council of Churches continues to use our social media presence to amplify the creative ministry and work for reconciliation we see among our constituency. Often now, we gather up what we see on social media and share it, through social media and through our newsletter. We also use Facebook and increasingly Twitter to help source stories for more traditional media outlets. For example, when a reporter asks me what local churches are doing to address white supremacy in their congregations, I'll pose the question to our Facebook followers. We post less often than when we began. Now as a staff of three, we always sign our posts so that our community knows who is behind it, for example writing "~Rev. Laura." We try to spend more time listening and then amplifying, not just promoting our own events or initiatives. We always try to take a photo and tell a story of a community when we visit in person. Through our in-person visits to local congregations and our online connecting, we've built up credibility internally with our consistency of

individuals, congregations, and denominations and externally with media outlets and the wider community. Our credibility is dependent on being timely, well-connected, and spiritually wise.

This continued investment in the networked and relational approach to digital ministry enabled the Council to quickly and poignantly respond when tragedy struck Boston.

> Our pastoral and prophetic role in convening and curating became most clear to me in the days after the Boston Marathon Bombing. I was away on vacation on Monday, April 15, 2013, when the bombing occurred. Almost immediately, we began working with our interfaith colleagues to formulate a collective response. Much was unclear at the time. As I traveled back to Boston, I noticed churches across Massachusetts posting that they were opening their buildings for prayer that night. From the Massachusetts Council of Churches Facebook page, I posted a request: "Church, if you're open for prayer or services tonight, please post here."
>
> By the time I finally got back to Boston on Monday night and the wireless networks were moving again, I looked on the public website for the Boston Globe, boston.com. A headline read "Church Services in Boston." I clicked the headline, and was directly transported to our own Facebook post. Throughout the day, people shared their plans for ecumenical and interfaith prayer vigils based on our earlier post. Because of our preexisting relationships and asking the right question, people had shared their plans with us. Because of our preexisting relationships with the local media, they turned to us as a curator and convener of information they couldn't access on their own. I never created a press release, and yet, we were the trusted source in a confusing time. Again and again, in times of local crisis and national struggle, we've used this strategy to ask what our community is thinking and doing. At other times, when the news isn't covering us, we become the media, telling stories of experimentation and vitality to our constituency.

Everett points out that even the most intentional practitioners of digital ministry must continue to learn and evolve.

> We are learning to be quick and flexible. We are learning a curious combination of digital ministry and incarnate experiences, not one replacing the other but working together so that our digital ministry supports our in-person ministry and our in-person ministry supports our digital connections.

4.10 Extended Profile

The Rev. Canon Anthony Guillen, missioner for Latino/Hispanic Ministries in The Episcopal Church

Anthony Guillen's (@misionerolatino) enthusiasm, well, for just about everything, but especially using social media for ministry, is contagious. Guillen is the missioner for Latino/Hispanic Ministries of The Episcopal Church and a self-described social media evangelist for the church at large. He travels around the United States and Latin America providing training, tools, and support to help, as he says, "raise digital disciples" in the church.

Guillen's passion for digital ministry was fueled by its ability to share the gospel and the story of the church, and in particular the heavy use of social media and digital devices among the Latina/o community. He told us:

> One day I saw a report how much Latinos were connected and I did some research and found that my perception of Latinos and social media usage and smartphone usage was way beyond what I would have ever imagined. The numbers were staggering, and not just in the US but all of Latin America. I would say today that 85 percent of Latin America is connected to social media, and mostly Facebook.
>
> According to the data, Latinos own more smartphones than anybody else in this country, more iPads than anybody else in this country, and Latinas, women, have more social profiles than anybody else in this country. That's what the data says so unless your congregation is really extraordinary and there's nobody connected there, I would go back and check.

Guillen says that Latina/o culture, with the high value it places on family and friendships is a natural fit for social media, as it allows people to keep connected and nurture those important relationships in their lives. He holds workshops all over the United States and Latin America teaching ministry leaders how to leverage the power of social media to evangelize and build community. As Kyle Oliver, frequent collaborator with Guillen, says, "Anthony has always taken the opportunity to learn from marketers and other experts about how to reach recent immigrants, Latinos who have been in the U.S. a long time, and people living near Episcopal churches in Latin America. The result is tight-knit community of Christians learning from and supporting each other across two languages and even more cultures. And

Anthony's network has served as an example for all Episcopalians seeking to better use and understand technology in their contexts."

You can see this work play out mostly on Facebook, as he shares links, Facebook live videos of worship, and training sessions. He skips past the explanations and just puts everything that he's doing out there for people to connect with and learn from. This is in part because pictures and videos fit his natural personal style. He told us, "Pictures for me are very easy because I'm not a writer. I'm a people person. So I can take pictures and I can post them and try to get people engaged in that way. That's my way of communicating."

This penchant for the visual content, on which he may comment in both English and Spanish, lends itself to Guillen's on-point selfie game. While selfies are frequently derided as simply narcissistic, Guillen uses selfies and his winning and welcoming smile to introduce his friends to emerging leaders from around the church, vouching for them, and, no small thing, lifting up ministry leaders of color. These selfies are not contrived but authentically Guillen. In his digital ministry practice, Guillen is able to draw on the gifts of his Latino culture and combine it with the power of connection through social media to enrich the entire church. As Guillen reminds us, "We're in the church. We're in the relationship business. And we forget or we haven't figured out that social media is about relationship, just like church is."

DIGITAL MINISTRY STRATEGY: THE ARTS OF DIGITAL MINISTRY

The following questions are designed to help you reflect on how you are practicing the arts of digital ministry. Reflect on them for you personally and, either on your own or with a group, in the context of your ministry community.

1. Using the LACE framework for Digital Ministry, reflect on the ways you currently—or may in the future—listen, attend, connect, and engage in social networking.

Listening—taking time to get to know people in social networks rather than shouting your message

---

Attending—being present to the experiences and interest of others

---

Connecting—reaching out to others in diverse communities in order to deepen and extend networks

_____
_____
_____

Engaging—building relationships by sharing content, collaborating, connecting people to others

_____
_____
_____

2. Using the categories we described for the arts of digital ministry, note where you see yourself as most comfortable now and what might be a growth area for you. How might you develop in your growth areas? You might want to complete this assessment for both yourself and for your church or organization.

	Comfort Zone?	Growth Area?	How?
Faithful Listening	☐	☐	
Offering Hospitality	☐	☐	
Caring for God's People	☐	☐	
Forming Disciples	☐	☐	
Building Community	☐	☐	
Making Public Witness	☐	☐	
Stewarding Divine Resources	☐	☐	

NOTES

1. Robert P. Jones and Daniel Cox, "America's Changing Religious Identity: Findings of the 2016 American Values Atlas" (Washington, DC: Public Religion Research Institute, September 6, 2017).

2. See, for example, the Darkwood Brew online ministry lead by Eric Elnes, which holds online worship services each Sunday at http://www.onfaithonline.tv/darkwoodbrew/. Likewise, members of church communities in the virtual reality site Second Life have explored the idea of offering a virtual Eucharist. On this, see Bosco Peters, "Virtual Eucharist: Can Sacraments Work in the Virtual World?," Liturgy (Blog), June 28, 2009, http://www.liturgy.co.nz/blog/virtual-eucharist/1078. Elizabeth explored the challenges of such ministries to face-to-face worship in *Tweet If You ♥ Jesus: Practicing Church in the Digital Reformation* (Harrisburg, PA: Morehouse, 2011), 61–64.

3. Duane R. Bidwell, "Deep Listening and Virtuous Friendship: Spiritual Care in the Context of Religious Multiplicity," *Buddhist-Christian Studies* 35 (2015): 4.

4. Timothy Fry, OSB, *The Rule of St. Benedict in Latin and English with Notes* (Collegeville, MN: Liturgical Press, 1981), ch. 53:1–3.

5. See: www.companionsofdorothy.org and www.facebook.com/companionsofdorothytheworker/.

6. Learn more at http://bishopcoyne.org.

7. Zoe Romanowsky, "A Bishop Who Tweets, Podcasts and Talks to the Flock from His Car," Aleteia, February 1, 2015, https://aleteia.org/2016/02/01/a-bishop-who-tweets-podcasts-and-talks-to-the-flock-from-his-car/.

8. Scott McLeod, "Are We Irrelevant to the Digital Global World in Which We Now Live?" *UCEA Review* 52 (Summer 2011): 1–5. Available online at http://www.ucea.org/storage/review/Summer2011Review_lowres.pdf.

9. Michael Wesch, "From Knowledgeable to Knowledge-able: Learning in New Media Environments," *Academic Commons*, January 7, 2009, http://www.academiccommons.org/2014/09/09/from-knowledgable-to-knowledge-able-learning-in-new-media-environments/.

10. See https://www.facebook.com/groups/SundaysComing/.

11. See https://dskidsermons.com/.

12. See http://www.middlechurch.org/about/blogs/thatll-preach.

13. Kevin McSpadden, "You Now Have a Shorter Attention Span Than a Goldfish," *Time*, May 14, 2015, http://time.com/3858309/attention-spans-goldfish/.

14. Lee Rainie, Kristen Purcell, and Aaron Smith, "The Social Side of the Internet," Pew Research Center, January 18, 2011, http://www.pewinternet.org/Reports/2011/The-Social-Side-of-the-Internet.aspx.

15. On this see, Janna Quitney Anderson and Lee Raine, "The Future of Social Relations," Pew Internet & American Life Project, July 2, 2010, http://pewinternet.org/~/media//Files/Reports/2010/PIP_Future_of_Internet_%202010_social_relations.pdf.

16. "Social Capital Primer," accessed November 11, 2011, http://bowlingalone.com/?page_id=13.

17. Robert Putnam, *Bowling Alone: The Collapse and Revival of American Community* (New York: Simon and Schuster, 2001), 23.

18. Clay Shirky, *Here Comes Everybody: The Power of Organizing without Organizing* (New York: Penguin, 2008), 22.

19. Douglas Rushkoff, "Think Occupy Wall Street Is a Phase? You Don't Get It," CNN.com, October 5, 2011, http://www.cnn.com/2011/10/05/opinion/rushkoff-occupy-wall-street/index.html.

20. See Kineticslive.com/about-us.

21. Antonia Blumberg, "40 Essential Books for any #BlackChurchSyllabus, January 3, 2017, https://www.huffingtonpost.com/entry/these-books-need-to-be-on-your-blackchurchsyllabus_us_55d65fbae4b020c386de2b19.

22. Shirky, *Here Comes Everybody,* 142.

23. Jamye Wooten, "Is the Hashtag Leading Us to an Ella Baker Style Movement?" .Base, May 5, 2016, https://btpbase.org/is-the-hashtag-leading-us-to-an-ella-baker-style-movement/.

24. Ben Schiller, "How Self-Driving Cars Will Change The Economy And Society," Fast Company, March 18, 2015, https://www.fastcompany.com/3043305/how-self-driving-cars-will-change-the-economy-and-society.

25. Ben Paynter, "How Will the Rise of Crowdfunding Reshape How We Give to Charity?" Fast Company, March 3, 2017, https://www.fastcompany.com/3068534/how-will-the-rise-of-crowdfunding-reshape-how-we-give-to-charity-2.

26. Aaron Smith, "4. Collaborative: Crowdfunding Platforms," Pew Research Center, May 19, 2016, http://www.pewinternet.org/2016/05/19/collaborative-crowd-funding-platforms/.

27. Adam Copeland, ed., *Beyond the Offering Plate: A Holistic Approach to Stewardship* (Louisville, KY: John Knox Press, 2017).

28. Emily Scott, "St. Lydia's Dinner Church," Indiegogo, accessed December 23, 2017, https://www.indiegogo.com/projects/st-lydia-s-dinner-church#/

29. Adam J. Copeland, "A Broader Appeal: How Crowdfunding Inspires Creative Ministry," *Christian Century*, May 2015, https://www.christiancentury.org/article/2015-05/broader-appeal.

30. See https://www.kickstarter.com/projects/1824965938/humble-walk-artist-compilation.

31. Ibid.

32. See https://www.crowdrise.com/trinityplaceboilerfundhelpreplacetheheaterfortrinitychurchandtrinityplaceshelter1.

33. Nadia Bolz-Weber, "Sermon on John 3:16 : 'Weirdos [Sic] and Violence,'" *Sojourners,* March 28, 2011, https://sojo.net/articles/how-did-john-316-become-about-weirdos-and-violence.

CONCLUSION
Digital Incarnation

> In most relationships that begin in digital locales, the reality of relationship—if it develops out of expressed and felt personal authenticity, if it opens people to each other's stories and functions as a source of mutual enrichment—invites connection face-to-face. This desire for incarnation, as we churchy types might call it, is the real beauty and power of digital ministry.

WE FINISHED WRITING AND EDITING the bulk of the first edition of *Click 2 Save* just as the snow was starting to fly in Boston, Keith's hometown at the time, and winter rains began to fall in San Jose, where Elizabeth lives. But when we met face-to-face for the first time, it was nothing like that. For a few days in the late fall, Keith left behind what turned out to be the first snow of the season to wing his way into a gloriously beautiful Northern California weekend. Our Facebook walls blossomed with photos of the Monterey coast drenched with sun, the Carmel Lone Cypress just before sunset, San Francisco's Grace Cathedral reaching up to a deep blue, cloudless sky on the warm Sunday when we had the opportunity to hear our editor, Stephanie Spellers,[1] preach about how the church can change—must change—if we have any intention of continuing to do God's work in a world in which "the way we've always done it" simply doesn't resonate with most people.

According to researchers at the Pew Forum on Religion & Public Life, about 30 percent of people who were raised as Roman Catholics will leave the church as adults, half of those affiliating with another religious tradition, half with none at all. Bleak though that may sound, for mainline Protestants, the picture is even bleaker. More than 50 percent of people raised in Methodist, Lutheran, Presbyterian, Episcopalian, and Congregationalist churches will leave as adults, about a third of those claiming no identification with institutional churches.[2] And, as most of us involved in churches probably know from our own observation and experience, the drain among the fifty-and-under crowd is significantly greater—which kind of makes both of us churchy, spiritual freaks.

Clearly, we have to do something different if we're going to continue to connect with believers and seekers and engage them in the very real work of creating God's kingdom on earth. And, yet, at the end of the day, it is just as clear that we cannot simply "click to save"—to save the church, to save souls (whatever that might mean in these postmodern, post-Christian times), to save the world. Though this may mean that we've led you down something of a digital primrose path, it's clear to us that participation in social networking communities is not the answer.

That is, at least not on its own. Not as a tool, or a gimmick. Not as an add-on to "real" ministry practice.

DIGITAL MINISTRY IS NOT DIGITAL MARKETING

Throughout this book, we've echoed, quite deliberately, two key themes that bear repeating one more time as we come to the end of this particular part of our pilgrimage together. The first is that digital ministry is not the same as digital marketing. Very much at the center of the challenges facing the church is the challenge of communicating what the Gospel means—how it invites us to live in the light of God's grace in relation to one another and creation—with new generations of seekers and believers. But communicating is sharing language, ideas, stories, images, and so on with others, in community, in service of the common good. That is, in relationships of mutual respect and caring. In communion.

Marketing, on the other hand, is about relating transactionally to others—not *being in relationship with*, but *relating to* others—by way, according to the folks at Merriam-Webster, "of promoting and selling products and services." For whatever marketing might do in the service of another, it wants something back. Marketing wants you to buy, join, pledge, pay.

That doesn't mean that all marketing is inherently evil or even just plain bad. We have lots of respect for people who tell the stories of their products and services with integrity and creativity. And we admire those who understand the importance of respectful, long-term relationships with customers. Still, we have assumed throughout *Click 2 Save* that marketing is not the way of Christ, and it's not the purpose of digital ministry. As Elizabeth insisted in *Tweet If You ♥ Jesus*, "It's not that 'church marketing sucks,' as much as it is that marketing the church sucks."[3] It's just not how we think ministry is meant to play out in the Christian tradition.

DIGITAL MINISTRY IS RELATIONAL AND NETWORKED

This assumption leads directly to the second theme that we've nailed to the doorposts throughout the book: digital ministry is relational and networked, and these relational networks reach far beyond the local church.

Now, as it happens, we think this is true of all ministry. We take our cue on this from Jesus's instructions to his most immediate disciples, who were called not to establish churches per se, but to journey throughout the nations (Matt. 10:1–19; Matt. 28:16–20), to share God's healing love among God's people (e.g., Matt. 8:14–17, 9:18–32; Mark 2:1–12, 9:14–29; John 5:1–9, and to proclaim God's kingdom (Luke 9:1–3) not as some futuristic fantasy, but as real and present in the love and compassion of one human being in relation to another. "They departed and went through the villages, bringing the good news and curing diseases everywhere," Luke's gospel tells us (Luke 9:6). Christianity, it turns out, is a road trip, not a building. It is relational and networked. And, certainly, it is mobile.

DIGITAL MINISTRY IS INCARNATIONAL

All of which bring us to perhaps the most important theme, one which came into sharp relief for us on that autumn weekend when we first met face-to-face, we two writers and our editor, along with the artist who created most of the images in the first edition of the book. We had gathered to weave together the final threads of the story we offer in *Click 2 Save*—a story about how relational, networked ministry in digital spaces and in local churches and religious organizations is the best hope for making the church relevant and engaged in everyday life again.

Fully two-thirds of American adults are active in social networking communities. Nearly 100 percent of teens are actively online and 80 percent regularly use social networking sites. The bulk of both teens and adults use their digital participation as a vital and vibrant part of their relationships with friends and families.[4] Digital engagement is now the reality of human experience in America and in most of the world.

What's more, the available data tell us over and over again that digital media are profoundly incarnational. They do what broadcast media could never do: connect us more deeply to those we know already, and extend real and meaningful relationship to those we may know only indirectly—only as links in the helixed DNA of the Body of Christ. But for the two of us, as our digital relationship developed while Elizabeth was researching and writing *Tweet If You ♥ Jesus* and blossomed into a genuine friendship through the writing of this book, the data we mined as we worked on *Click 2 Save* was mere confirmation of what we knew in our actual, physical bones: digital media had connected us spiritually, and the truth of that connection had a deep incarnational pull. Our weekly video hangouts made us want to hang out in person, to break bread, and to tramp common ground together.

So it was that our time together that late October weekend played out as the incarnate end of a digitally integrated pilgrimage, the penultimate stop of which was on the ground where the technology that allowed us to connect was, in some fashion at least, created: the Apple headquarters in Cupertino,

Keith on pilgrimage in Cupertino, California.

California. There, not long after the death of Apple founder Steve Jobs, people from around the world had come to walk the Apple campus, to make real in their bodies the space from which a remarkable spirit of creativity, collaboration, and beauty had contributed so much to individuals, relationships, and communities. We paid homage with the rest.

But that, of course, was not the whole of it. Our time together was populated with other friends and other conversations, our network expanding in relational depth even as we completed the last phases of the book.

Perhaps not surprisingly, this part of our pilgrimage closed in worship, our friendship tied to a faith that is at the core of our commitment to practices of ministry centered on listening to others, attending to the needs of the world the church serves, connecting across diverse and widely distributed networks, and engaging believers and seekers wherever they may be. This, notwithstanding our periodic frustrations with what can seem like the church's intractable inability to engage the world as it is *now* and our eagerness to contribute to new ways of being the Body of Christ in the world. Our worship, then, was something of a prayer of gratitude for the opportunity to work together on this project and a petition for a more widely networked community of ministry leaders who are eager to try new approaches to church, new ways of animating the Body of Christ in the digitally integrated world.

We pray that you are among those leaders. We hope you will join us in this pilgrimage, connecting your digital ministry to those of others who see Facebook, Twitter, YouTube, and other social networking communities as real and significant sites for practices of mission and ministry that are as transformative as they are incarnational. We hope you will invite disenchanted and disengaged believers and seekers into relationships that move easily from digital spaces to local ones, and back again. We know our friendship and faith have benefited from the journey, and we know your participation on the road ahead will only bring more of the blessings we have shared to more people and communities across the world. We hope that together we can all click—and connect and invite and engage and tell our stories of faith and its implications far and wide—and thus help revitalize the church we love. The church that has saved us both.

NOTES

1. Stephanie Spellers, Sermon at Grace Cathedral, San Francisco, California, October 30, 2011.

2. Pew Forum on Religion & Public Life, "U.S. Religious Landscape Survey: Religious Affiliation: Diverse and Dynamic," February 2008, 21–38. Mainline Protestant affiliation change average calculated from "Retention of Childhood Members of Protestant Religious Groups," 31.

3. Elizabeth Drescher, *Tweet If You ♥ Jesus: Practicing Church in the Digital Reformation* (Harrisburg: Morehouse, 2011), 127.

4. Anna Lenhart, et al, "Teens, Kindness and Cruelty on Social Networking Sites: How American Teens Navigate the New World of 'Digital Citizenship,'" Pew Internet & American Life Project, November 9, 2011, http://www.pewinternet.org/~/media//Files/Reports/2011/PIP_Teens_Kindness_Cruelty_SNS_Report_Nov_2011_FINAL_110711.pdf. See also Aaron Smith, "Why Americans Use Social Media," Pew Research Center, November 15, 2011, http://www.pewinternet.org/Reports/2011/Why-Americans-Use-Social-Media.aspx?src=prc-headline.

ADDITIONAL RESOURCES FOR DIGITALLY INTEGRATED MINISTRY

The expanded second edition of *Click 2 Save* can hardly hope to cover the range of resources that can help us to understand the cultural, theological, and spiritual effects of new media. The resources that follow are some of our go-tos for understanding as best we can the dynamic new reality in which ministry unfolds.

BOOKS

Campbell, Heidi. *Digital Religion: Understanding Religious Practice in New Media Worlds.* Grand Rapids, MI: Baker Academic, 2016.

———., *Networked Theology: Negotiating Faith in Digital Culture.* New York: Routledge, 2010.

Hoover, Steward. *Religion in the Media Age.* New York: Routledge, 2006.

Horsfield, Peter. *From Jesus to the Internet: A History of Christianity and Media.* West Sussex, England: Wiley, 2015.

Hutchings, Tim. *Creating Church Online: Ritual, Community and New Media.* New York: Routledge, 2017.

Jenkins, Henry. *Convergence Culture: Where Old and New Media Collide* New York: NYU Press, 2006.

Mahan, Jeffrey H. *Media, Religion and Culture: An Introduction.* New York: Routledge, 2014.

McLuhan, Marshall, Quentin Fiore, and Jerome Agel. *The Medium Is the Massage: An Inventory of Effects.* San Francisco: Hardwired, 1996.
Siker, Jeffrey S. *Liquid Scripture: The Bible in a Digital World.* Minneapolis, MN: Fortress Press, 2017.
Wagner, Rachel. *Godwired: Religion, Ritual and Virtual Reality.* New York: Routledge, 2012.

ARTICLES

Anderson, Keith. "Re-Mediation in the D-I-Y Church." *Bearings,* October 6, 2017. http://www.thebtscenter.org/re-mediation-in-the-diy-church/.
Bobkowski, Piotr S., and Lisa D. Pearce. "Baring Their Souls in Online Profiles or Not? Religious Self-Disclosure in Social Media." *Journal for the Scientific Study of Religion* 50, no. 4 (2011): 744–62.
boyd, danah. "Why Youth Heart Social Network Sites." In *Youth, Identity, And Digital Media,* edited by David Buckingham, 119–42. Cambridge, MA: MIT Press, 2007.
Drescher, Elizabeth. "Five Social Media Trends That Are Reshaping Religion." *Religion Dispatches,* December 28, 2011, http://religiondispatches.org/five-social-media-trends-that-are-reshaping-religion/.
———. "The Internet Is Not Killing Religion, Religion is Killing Religion." *Religion Dispatches,* April 22, 2014, http://religiondispatches.org/the-internet-is-not-killing-religion-religion-is-killing-religion/.
Hedt, Nathan. "Missional Spirituality Among Digital Natives: Technology, Spirituality, and Mission in an Age of Social Media." *Lutheran Theological Journal* (December 2, 2013): 187–202.
Keat, Jim. "Hashtagging the Good News of Social Media." *Bearings,* October 12, 2017, http://www.thebtscenter.org/hashtagging-the-good-news-of-social-media/.
Louis, Paul T. "Digital Awakening: Religions Communication in a Virtual World." *Journal of Dharma* (January–March 2015): 131–44.
Smith, James K. A. "Alternative Liturgy: Social Media as Ritual." *Christian Century* (March 6, 2013): 30–31, 33.
Wiseman, Karyn. "A Virtual Space for Grace: Are There Boundaries for Worship in a Digital Age?" *Liturgy* 30, no. 2 (2015): 52–60.

BLOGS, ONLINE MAGAZINES, AND PODCASTS

Adam J. Copeland (blog), adamjcopeland.com/blog.
The BTS Center, *Bearings,* thebtscenter.org/bearingsblog.
Duke Divinity School, *Faith and Leadership* (blog), faithandleadership.com.
Jamye Wooten, *Kinetics Live,* kineticslive.com.
"The Liturgists" (podcast), theliturgists.com/podcast.
Reid Hoffman, *Masters of Scale* (podcast), mastersofscale.com.
Membership Vision (blog), membershipvision.com/latest-posts.
Christian Theological Seminary, *New Media Project* (blog), cpx.cts.edu/newmedia/blog.
"Popping Collars" (podcast), poppingcollarspodcast.com
Princeton Seminary, *Princeton Institute for Youth Ministry* (blog), iym.ptsem.edu/resources/the-iym-blog.
Seth Godin (blog), sethgodin.typepad.com.

WEBSITES

Harvard University, *Berkman Klein Center for Internet and Society,* cyber.harvard.edu.
Virginia Theological Seminary, *e-Formation,* eformationvts.org.
Fuller Seminary, *Fuller Studio,* fullerstudio.fuller.edu.
Heidi Campbell, *Network for New Media, Religion and Digital Culture Studies,* digitalreligion.tamu.edu
Pew Research Center, *Internet & Technology,* pewinternet.org.
Salt Project, *Salt,* saltproject.org.
Mary Hess, and Lynn Schofield Clark, *Storying Faith,* storyingfaith.org.